Additional Praise for

KILL SWITCH

"With a grasp of history combined with his insider experience and knowledge, Adam Jentleson has written a clear, concise, and compelling book on the history and evolution of the filibuster, and the rise of its abuse and misuse by Mitch McConnell and Senate Republicans. Our system cannot operate without a functional Senate. Jentleson gives us the reasons why and a path forward."

—Norman Ornstein, coauthor of
It's Even Worse Than It Looks and *One Nation After Trump*

"The Senate is now profoundly rigged, with rules that make it easy to pass tax cuts for the rich and to pack the courts for the powerful but allow the minority party to block bills to assist ordinary families. The Senate is now the graveyard for bills to improve health care, housing, education, worker rights, or to tackle issues like criminal justice, immigration, gun safety, or climate chaos. The biggest culprit of this corrupted, paralyzed Senate is the filibuster, which was born out of the determination of white, wealthy, privileged interests to block civil rights for minority Americans. If you want to understand the Senate's descent, its potential path back to relevance, and how vital that path is to restoring a government 'of, by, and for the people,' then this book is essential reading."

—U.S. Senator Jeff Merkley

"The Senate is the epicenter of American political dysfunction: the place where ideas with broad support are sent to die while those backed by plutocrats and extremists are set into law. In this analytically rich yet highly readable insider account, Adam Jentleson shows why today's undemocratic Senate is an affront to the Framers' vision—and how we can fix it."

—Jacob Hacker, best-selling coauthor of
Let Them Eat Tweets and *Winner-Take-All Politics*

KILL SWITCH

THE RISE OF THE MODERN SENATE AND THE CRIPPLING OF AMERICAN DEMOCRACY

ADAM JENTLESON

LIVERIGHT PUBLISHING CORPORATION

A Division of W. W. Norton & Company

Independent Publishers Since 1923

For information about permission to reproduce selections from this book,
write to Permissions, Liveright Publishing Corporation, a division of
W. W. Norton & Company, Inc., 500 Fifth Avenue, New York, NY 10110

For information about special discounts for bulk purchases, please contact
W. W. Norton Special Sales at specialsales@wwnorton.com or 800-233-4830

Manufacturing by Lake Book Manufacturing
Production manager: Lauren Abbate

Library of Congress Cataloging-in-Publication Data

Names: Jentleson, Adam, author.
Title: Kill switch : the rise of the modern Senate and the crippling of
American democracy / Adam Jentleson.
Description: First edition. | New York : Liveright Publishing Corporation,
2021. | Includes bibliographical references and index.
Identifiers: LCCN 2020042077 | ISBN 9781631497773 (hardcover) |
ISBN 9781631497780 (epub)
Subjects: LCSH: United States. Congress. Senate. | Representative government
and representation—United States. | Proportional representation—United
States. | Democracy—United States. | Filibusters (Political science)—
United States. | United States—Politics and government—1945–1989. |
United States—Politics and government—1989–
Classification: LCC JK1161 .J46 2021 | DDC 328.73/071—dc23
LC record available at https://lccn.loc.gov/2020042077

Liveright Publishing Corporation, 500 Fifth Avenue, New York, N.Y. 10110
www.wwnorton.com

W. W. Norton & Company Ltd., 15 Carlisle Street, London W1D 3BS

1 2 3 4 5 6 7 8 9 0

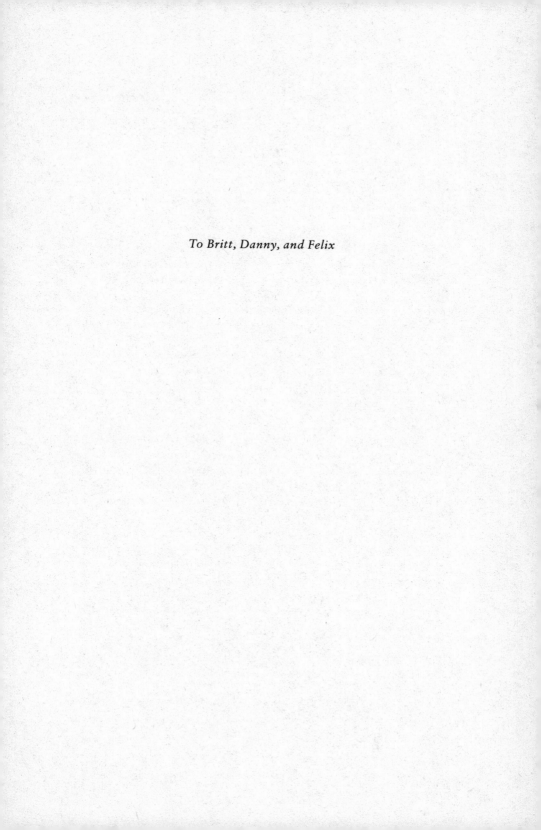

To Britt, Danny, and Felix

To establish a positive and permanent rule giving such a power, to such a minority, over such a majority, would overturn the first principle of free government.

—JAMES MADISON, letter to Edward Everett, August 28, 1830

All that can save you now is your confrontation with your own history—which is not your past, but your present.

—JAMES BALDWIN, "How to Cool It," Esquire, July 1968

CONTENTS

INTRODUCTION

The Little Harm Thesis

THE FIRST TIME I SET FOOT IN the Senate Democratic cloakroom, I was a nervous, twenty-nine-year-old staffer, thrilled to be entering the Senate's inner sanctum. I had a mental image of the fabled room from Robert Caro's magisterial account of Lyndon Johnson's Senate years, *Master of the Senate*, which my former colleagues had given me as a farewell present after I accepted a job working for Senate majority leader Harry Reid. Caro describes the room as crackling with power and possibility, packed with senators of competing factions eyeing one another warily in anticipation of a momentous vote. More than any other space in the Capitol, the cloakroom is senators' private domain. There, they are unbothered by reporters, out of view of the public, surrounded mostly by other senators, and insulated by the unspoken codes of senatorial life. The few staffers in the room are meant to be seen and not heard, to speak only if asked a question. I had been warned about the strict codes of behavior. No phones, no loud conversations—better not to talk at all. Like all staffers, I was expected to stand over to the side, out of the way of the senators passing through the cramped L-shaped space.

The cloakroom is the shabby sibling of the illustrious Senate chamber. Preoccupied with the more glamorous of the two—with the chamber's sweeping curve, its shiny mahogany desks arrayed in rows, and the viewing galleries ringing it like grandstands—you

could walk past the cloakroom countless times without really notic-
ing it. Windowless, carpeted, and low-ceilinged, with a few brown
leather couches and matching, worn armchairs, it looks like the
coat-check area of a restaurant that used to be popular forty years
ago but now caters to early birds. There is a minifridge. On top
of it sit a cheap coffeepot, paper cups, creamers, and sugar pack-
ets. The smell of stale coffee lingers. Only a row of antique phone
booths evokes past glories. Lyndon Johnson used to stand in the
aisle between two booths, clutching a phone from each, stretching
the cords so he could talk into one, then turn and shout into the
other. Now, senators take their cell phones into the booths to make
calls. Walking by, you might catch a glimpse of a septuagenarian
senator huddled in one, cell phone to their ear, a binder-clutching
staffer stationed just outside, ready to tell them whom to call next,
and what to say.

The reason the cloakroom of legend feels like a nondescript hallway today is that what used to be a place where deals were struck is
now a place where orders are handed down, the Senate's power more
like that of a soul-crushing bureaucracy than of a great deliberative
body. From the era of civil rights and the Great Society to ours, the
Senate has been in a state of steady decline, as the decentralized,
open, and relatively obstruction-free institution that the Framers created was transformed into something altogether unrecog-
nizable. Always known for its plodding pace, today's Senate has
become utterly calcified. Not all the changes that have shaped the
modern Senate occurred within the institution itself. In the 1950s,
party affiliation was not always tied to ideology, and bipartisanship thrived amid the endless cross-party combinations that were
possible on any given issue. Many conservatives were Democrats
and many liberals were Republicans; indeed, the most conservative
members of the Senate at the time were Democrats, and some of the
most liberal were members of the GOP. With senators casting their
votes according to crosscutting regional and ideological alliances
more than party loyalty, the most significant issues of the day were

commonly decided by bipartisan votes. Today, the nation is largely sorted by party, by ideology, by geography, and more.

But in large part, the Senate's decline was set in motion by senators themselves, who found that suffocating the institution with genteel gridlock served their interests. Motivated by their all-consuming desire to protect Jim Crow and building on the work of obstructionists who had come before them, southern senators of the early twentieth century honed a procedural tool to empower, for the first time in American history, a minority of senators to systematically block bills favored by the majority. The Senate sits at the heart of American government, and every bill that becomes a law must pass through it. The Senate also controls the confirmation of every federal judge, from the district courts up to the Supreme Court, along with the confirmations of thousands of positions in the executive branch. By imposing their will on the Senate, the nerve center of American government, a minority of senators found they could impose their will on the entire nation.

In the Jim Crow era, southern senators were driven to create new means of obstruction by one overriding goal: preserving white supremacy. They faced a Congress and a public that wanted to take at least rudimentary steps toward basic protections for black Americans decades before the first post-Reconstruction civil rights bill finally passed in 1957. From the 1920s through the 1940s, legislation to end poll taxes, combat lynching, and roll back employment discrimination possessed everything bills had previously needed to become law. They were passed by majorities in the House of Representatives, supported by majorities in the Senate, and backed by presidents of both parties. The support these measures enjoyed in Congress was consistent with public opinion at the time. In 1937, Gallup conducted its first poll of federal anti-lynching laws and found support at 72 percent nationally, with majorities favoring them in every region— including the South, where support was at 57 percent.[1] Gallup first canvassed the public on poll taxes in 1941 and found that 63 percent of Americans supported ending them.[2] Protecting black Americans from extrajudicial killings and improving their access to the ballot were woefully insufficient steps at best, merely enforcing the rights already guaranteed by the Fourteenth and Fifteenth Amendments, and would have still left them facing widespread oppression and deeply ingrained racism in every region of the country. Even so, some of the civil rights measures that enjoyed majority support during this period were comparable to those that would appear in the 1957 bill that cracked open the door to meaningful progress. But for decades before that bill passed, in the face of majority support, southern senators' obstructionist innovations succeeded in blocking every civil rights bill that came before the nation.

By the time I arrived in the Senate, the tool developed by southern senators to block civil rights bills in the Jim Crow era had come to be applied to all Senate business. Today, it is the norm for pragmatic solutions to urgent problems of all kinds, backed by broad majorities in Congress and the public, to fail in the face of obstruction by a minority of senators. The grind of relentless gridlock has rendered the once-dynamic cloakroom lifeless and has broken the institution itself. This expansion of obstruction was not inevitable. Since the early days, leading voices within the Senate called on it to take different paths. The story of how the Senate ignored them while marching steadily toward decline is, in large part, the story of the modern Senate.

THE TOOL THAT white supremacist senators honed in the Jim Crow era to defy the majority is the filibuster, as we know it today. The focus of much of this book, the filibuster has become the Senate's most famous feature, due in part to its portrayal in the movie *Mr. Smith Goes to Washington*, which helped make Jimmy Stewart a star. Despite being synonymous with the Senate, the filibuster was nowhere in the Framers' vision for the institution, and indeed is antithetical to it. The filibuster first appeared in the middle of the nineteenth century, after all the Framers had died and as the need to maintain slavery led southerners to search for new ways of defying the majority. For decades, one generation after another of obstructionists honed and strengthened the filibuster, but it was the southerners of the early twentieth century who made the crucial change. They figured out how to use the filibuster to raise the threshold for passing bills in the Senate from a simple majority, as the Framers had intended, to the supermajority that has become standard in the modern Senate. (For the purposes of this book, any threshold higher than a simple majority will be referred to as a supermajority; today, the threshold to override a filibuster in the Senate is three-fifths of the body, or sixty votes out of one hundred senators.) Before that crucial turn, the filibuster was a delaying tactic, and was rarely successful in the end against a determined majority. But after the supermajority requirement was introduced, the filibuster could reliably stop bills, and it began being used to do just that.

The filibuster has never been the exclusive property of southern reactionaries; as we will see, it has sometimes been deployed by liberals and progressives, and occasionally to historic effect. But from its inception to today, the filibuster has mainly served to empower a minority of predominantly white conservatives to override our democratic system when they found themselves outnumbered, blocking progress that threatened their power, their way of life, and the priorities of their wealthy benefactors, from the slaveholders of the nineteenth century to the conservative billionaires of today. From John Calhoun, the antebellum father of nullification who argued, on the Senate floor, that slavery was a "positive good," to Richard Russell, the post–World War II puppet master of the Senate who swore that "any southern white man worth a pinch of salt would give his all to maintain white supremacy," to Mitch McConnell in our own time, who declared that "the single most important thing we want to achieve is for President Obama to be a one-term president," southern senators invented the filibuster, strengthened it, and developed alternative histories to justify it.[3] Over two centuries, they were able to shape the Senate and thereby the nation, retrofitting the Framers' vision to give themselves, a factional minority, veto power over every law the nation passes. Speaking in grave, stentorian tones, and making frequent reference to a tendentious account of the Framers and Senate history, they convinced us that this was the way it was meant to be.

But it was not. The Framers would have abhorred the filibuster. Their vision for the Senate was of a chamber that was thoughtful and deliberative, but where the majority ruled. For half a century after the founding of the nation, the Senate operated according to their plan. Typically, senators would debate a bill for as long as they felt it was valuable and productive to do so, and when debate had run its course, the bill would come up for a simple-majority vote. Senators prided themselves on self-policing against obstruction. But if obstruction got out of hand, they had recourse to procedures that would end debate and bring the bill in question to a vote. The Framers created rules for ending debate because, while they never met the filibuster itself, they anticipated that obstructionists would try to invent something like it. The Framers were realists who wrote the Constitution in the shadow of the Articles of Confederation, the disastrously ineffective system of government that allowed a minority of members of Congress to block the majority from acting. They had seen firsthand that allowing a minority to block the majority did not promote deliberation. Instead, they warned that it would create an irresistible temptation for a "pertinacious minority" to sabotage the majority, leading to "contemptible compromises of the public good" and eroding majority rule, which they widely regarded as the "first principle" of the democracy they created.[4]

Far from embodying Senate tradition, the way the filibuster is deployed today—routinely and silently, yet instantly raising the threshold for passage from a majority to a supermajority—is a recent development, one that sets the modern Senate apart from two centuries of history. Conceived as a delaying tactic in the mid-nineteenth century and endowed with the power to impose a supermajority threshold in the early twentieth, the only issue it was deployed against with any consistency was civil rights, through the 1960s. But in our own era, senators began using the filibuster to impose a supermajority threshold on every bill's path to becoming a law, stopping the many that cannot clear it in their tracks and bringing the Senate itself to a grinding halt.

To see the modern Senate in action—or, rather, inaction—turn on C-SPAN2 any day the Senate is in session. Tuesday and Wednesday are your best bet, since even when the Senate is in session it usually takes half of Monday and Thursday off, and all of Friday. If you happen to catch the Senate when the floor is open, there's a good chance you won't hear anyone speak, because the chamber will probably be in a "quorum call," a state of suspended animation that blocks all action while the leaders of the two parties negotiate a path forward on a bill that, in all likelihood, is facing a filibuster. But that filibuster will be nothing like the *Mr. Smith* version, because today, the filibuster can be deployed with none of the effort or drama it used to entail. Even after southern senators strengthened the filibuster in the Jim Crow era, it still demanded tremendous energy and coordination to deploy, like an early computer that needed a team to operate. Since then, the filibuster has become streamlined to the point that it can be launched by lifting a finger, as easily as opening an app. In addition to becoming more user-friendly, the new filibuster also shields the user from accountability. In the modern Senate, the filibustering senator never has to set foot on the floor, or explain their reasons for blocking the bill at hand. But as the filibuster became easier to use, it lost none of its potency. Today, the filibuster is not just a powerful tool giving the minority a veto over every bill that comes before the nation—it's a convenient one, too.

Over the past half century, the filibuster has also become entwined with structures of top-down, partisan control that have transformed the Senate from a free and open body to one where every step is negotiated by the two party leaders, while the other ninety-eight senators await their marching orders. On C-SPAN2, you may be lucky enough to catch a speech on the Senate floor. The senator giving it will probably be reading prepared remarks, which they'll be seeing for the first time as they read them aloud. The chamber they're speaking to will probably be mostly empty; if other senators are present, they won't be paying attention to the speaker. More staff than senators will be in the chamber, hanging back along the wall or sitting on the benches in the corner, penned in by a wooden railing. As soon as the senator who's speaking finishes, that senator will leave the floor, staff in tow, to return to their office or head off to an event. Senators spend the vast majority of their time fundraising, and their brief sojourns on the floor are afterthoughts, if they register at all. Whatever the senator's speech was about, it almost certainly will have no impact on the bill notionally under discussion, and will change no minds. The negotiations between the leaders about how the Senate will proceed take place behind closed doors, far from public view. In an ironic twist, the senators stealthily filibustering the bill will inevitably be doing so in the name of unlimited debate, invoking grand principle to justify naked obstruction, despite the fact that nothing bearing even a passing resemblance to debate will be taking place. Watch for an hour or two, or just a few minutes, and you'll see this scene play out on a constant loop, as public servants mill about a legislative wasteland while the business of the nation quietly fails.

OBSERVING THIS SAD, subdued scene, it would be impossible to conclude that the modern Senate is a deliberative body—let alone the "world's greatest," as the tagline goes—in any credible sense of the word. The cliché that's most often invoked to justify the current state of the institution is the idea of the Senate as a "cooling saucer," an apocryphal coinage most often attributed to George Washington. "According to legend," McConnell once explained, when Washington "was presiding over the constitutional convention, someone asked him, what is it [the Senate] going to look like?

He said, like the saucer under the teacup. The tea is going to slosh out of the saucer and cool off. Nothing happens quickly in the Senate."[5] Senators use this anecdote frequently, but there is no historical record of the conversation ever occurring. The simile seems to have originated in the 1870s, and to have entered widespread circulation after appearing in *Harper's Monthly* in 1884, more than a century after the nation's founding. Washington, of course, could not have been using the saucer to justify the filibuster because the filibuster didn't exist in his time. Even in the *Harper's* piece, the saucer was not invoked to explain the filibuster but the existence of a bicameral Congress, since, as the article states, there had been at the Constitutional Convention "a variety of opinions as to a Legislature of one or two Houses."[6] Rather than inherited wisdom, the saucer as it is used today is pure artifice. The modern Senate is not a place where legislation goes to be "cooled." As America faces enormous challenges, the Senate has become a kill switch that cuts off broad-based solutions and shuts down our democratic process.

Minority rule is a defining feature of our era. The first two decades of the twentieth century have witnessed the revival, intentional and not, of previously dormant anti-democratic features of our system. From 1888 to 2000, no president won the White House while losing the popular vote, but two of the four presidents elected this century came to power that way. In states like Wisconsin, North Carolina, and Michigan, gerrymandered districts have endowed Republicans with power in Congress and state legislatures that far exceeds their share of the vote. That power allows them to block bills that would bring their power more into line with their vote share, such as a series of bills recently blocked by Michigan Republicans that would have made it easier to register to vote and harder for Republican officials to pick and choose who gets to vote.[7]

But it is the Senate that sits at the heart of our era of minority rule. Designed to guarantee the minority a voice but not veto power within a system of majority rule, the Senate's minority protections have been inflated into tools of minority domination. The most important of those protections was the decision at the Constitutional Convention to give every state equal representation in the Senate, regardless of population size. At the time, the issue was highly contentious and nearly scuttled the entire convention. Today, the mismatch between the largest and smallest states has grown orders of magnitude greater than it was at the nation's start. The Framers warned that even the comparatively smaller discrepancies that existed in their time would prove a dangerous source of injustice. That injustice is exponentially greater today than anything they imagined in their time.

As polarization pushed rural areas into Republicans' column and urban areas toward Democrats, Republicans' strength in low-population states created a widening discrepancy between the number of seats they hold in the Senate and the share of the population they represent. At no point in the twenty-first century have Senate Republicans represented a majority of the American population, even at their high-water mark of fifty-five seats from 2005 to 2006.[8] Nevertheless, they helped the two Republican presidents in our century (each of whom lost the popular vote at least once) to pass major legislation and reshape the federal judiciary. In 2016, Senate Republicans representing a minority of the national population controlled the Senate. They used their power to block President Obama from filling the Supreme Court seat vacated by the death of Justice Antonin Scalia, leaving the seat open for Donald Trump to fill in 2017, securing a conservative majority on the nation's highest court. In 2009, at its ebb over the last twenty years, the share of the population represented by Senate Republicans sank as low as 35 percent. But even that was enough to block much of President Obama's agenda.

For their part, Senate Democrats have represented a majority of the American population at every moment in the twenty-first century so far, regardless of whether they controlled a majority of the seats in the Senate, with the share of the population they represented rising as high as 65 percent in 2009—the same year, of course, as

Republicans' low point. While control of the Senate will continue to pass back and forth between the parties, the bloc of votes Republicans need to wield veto power is virtually impervious to electoral results. The forty-one seats required to block anything the majority wants to pass can be assembled entirely with seats from the deepest-red states in the nation, those Trump won by an average of 24 points in 2016. Regardless of which party is in power, the modern Senate guarantees a minority of predominantly white conservatives the ability to impose their will.

As someone who has spent his career working for Democratic causes, my own politics are obvious enough. But I have written this book in the sincere belief that our democracy is healthiest when both parties compete to win the support of a majority of the nation. Empowering one of the two major parties to impose its will not through persuasion, but through the use of opaque parliamentary tactics, creates a deeply unhealthy and perhaps unsustainable dynamic in our democracy. It's also probably detrimental to Republicans, allowing them to keep their heads in the sand as the world changes around them, appealing to an ever-narrowing slice of the population whose demographic and actuarial trends are all headed in the wrong direction.

Americans seem to have a gut sense that our country was not supposed to run this way. But for many, the Senate's Byzantine rules and traditions, combined with the self-assuredness of its defenders, make it hard to pin down why. This book aims to fix that. For seven years, my job was to understand everything about how the Senate works, down to the most minute procedural detail, and explain it in clear terms to reporters and the public. As a senior aide to the Democratic leader, I was in the room to witness many of the major events of the Obama administration and came to understand the innermost workings of the Senate during a time of rapid decline.

This book tells the story of that decline in two parts. The first narrates the struggle to bring the filibuster into existence in the nineteenth century, as part of white supremacists' mission to preserve slavery, and then their efforts to strengthen it during the early twentieth century to maintain Jim Crow. The second part shows how the modern, post–civil rights Senate began applying the filibuster to a broadening range of bills and issues, and married the old vision of minority rule with new, rigid leadership structures. Under McConnell, this marriage allowed the GOP base of wealthy, white, anti-choice conservatives—a reactionary superminority I call the WWACs—to impose its will on the majority as never before. Throughout, I show how the tectonic shifts that have shaped American politics recently— from demographic changes to the rise of powerful trends like polarization and negative partisanship—have intersected with the story of the modern Senate. A great deal of valuable work by scholars and journalists has explained these developments, and this book relies on much of it. But I believe the Senate is the critical juncture in our democracy and national life, the point where the broad trends meet the mechanics of wielding power in America.

This is not a particularly uplifting history. But unlike many of the structural features that determine the politics of our era, the Senate is relatively easy to reform. Changing or getting rid of the electoral college, for example, would likely require a constitutional amendment or face long court battles that would, in all likelihood, end at a Supreme Court controlled by conservative justices installed by the minority. Other necessary steps, like reforming the judiciary, expanding voting rights, or extending statehood to the District of Columbia, require legislation that must pass through the Senate and would almost certainly be blocked by the filibuster if the Senate is not reformed. Fixing the Senate, though, requires only fifty-one votes and a reasonable plan. As this book will show, reforming the Senate is not just possible in theory but has been a regular occurrence throughout its history. The Senate is not frozen in amber, as the defenders of minority rule often suggest. Rather, it has been transformed every few decades, and some of the most radical changes came from the very forces preaching continuity and tradition. Others were made by reformers seeking to restore the Framers' vision. The Senate is an ever-evolving institution, and change is not only possible but traditional. This book is unsparing about the problems facing the Senate and, by extension, the nation. But it ends with a plan for change that is aimed at restoring a reasonable level of responsiveness to the popular will—and that can, all importantly, be achieved immediately by a willing majority.

THE DEFENDERS OF the Senate's status quo have never had a talent for self-awareness. A popular defense of the filibuster, still circulating today, is what's known as the "little harm thesis." According to it, the filibuster has done little harm. Those who might beg to differ include the millions of black Americans who endured systematic violence and oppression during the nearly one hundred years during which the filibuster blocked civil rights bills from passing. Yet the harm wrought by the filibuster is not an artifact of a bygone era. Today, it stops us from addressing a range of pressing problems that do not lack for pragmatic solutions. On climate change, filibuster-induced paralysis has pushed us to the brink of missing our last chance to act before warming trends become irreversible. Income inequality and the racial wealth gap persist at unsustainable levels as the filibuster blocks remedies. After the Supreme Court gutted the Voting Rights Act of 1965, the crown jewel of civil rights–era legislation, efforts to restore it have been quashed by the threat of filibusters.

The little harm thesis and the self-congratulatory school of thought it represents are elaborate attempts to avoid reckoning with the reality that the Senate is broken, the consequences of its failure are vast, and those responsible are the senators themselves. The fog surrounding the institution has helped it evade a true accounting for too long. If we are to create a more equitable democracy, we have to shine a light on—and fix—the dysfunctional institution at its center: the United States Senate.

Part I

RISE OF
THE FILIBUSTER

Chapter One

BIRTH OF A NOTION

WHEN I THINK ABOUT my time in the Senate, I see a broken man. I was standing a few dozen steps from the Senate floor, in the inner office of the Senate majority leader, Harry Reid. It was an April day, and gray light streamed in through the high, west-facing windows of the Capitol building. Two high-backed, engraved wooden chairs with crimson cushions sat facing each other in front of a dark green marble fireplace, below a gilded Rococo mirror. A grand suite first commandeered for the leader's use by Lyndon Johnson and nick-named the Taj Mahal, it had brass chandeliers hanging from fifteen-foot vaulted ceilings, which were emblazoned with the state seal of Nevada, Reid's home state. "Battle Born" was the state motto, and it was an apt description of Reid, a former boxer raised in a house made of railway ties in the tiny mining town of Searchlight, Nevada, who had fought his way to becoming one of the most powerful leaders in Washington, DC. But that day, he and the dozen or so members of his staff who stood around the chairs were defeated, and his grand office felt small.

Reid, my boss, sat in one of the high-backed chairs. In the other sat a middle-aged man with broad shoulders and a kind, open face. His name was Neil Heslin. He was there because four months earlier, on December 14, 2012, his six-year-old son, Jesse, had been shot dead in his first-grade classroom. The Christmas tree he and Jesse had planned to decorate still stood bare in his living room, back home in Newtown, Connecticut. It would be four years before Neil would take it down.[1] A registered Republican, Neil had come to Washington with other parents of children who had been murdered that day to try to persuade senators to vote for the most rudimentary restrictions on guns.

In a functioning system, they would have succeeded. They convinced fifty-five senators from every region of the country to support a bill to enact universal background checks on gun purchases, a policy supported by nine in ten Americans, according to a Quinnipiac poll at the time.[2] The bill was written and introduced by two senators who could not have been more different, but had found agreement on this issue: Joe Manchin, a rough-edged, populist Democrat from West Virginia, and Pat Toomey, a preppy, country-club Republican from Pennsylvania. Their bill had secured the support of left-leaning gun control groups like the Brady Campaign, and of right-leaning gun rights groups like the Citizens Committee for the Right to Keep and Bear Arms.[3]

But the support of a broad, bipartisan majority of senators, of advocacy groups from across the political spectrum, and of an overwhelming share of the American public was not enough. Opponents of the background-checks bill invoked a twentieth-century rule that, ironically, was invented to curtail obstruction by ending the kind of marathon filibusters that many people picture when they think of the Senate. But over the years innovative obstructionists had repurposed the rule into a new kind of filibuster that was quieter, and far more lethal, than the old kind. Using this repurposed rule, the threshold for the background-checks bill to pass had been quietly raised from a simple majority to sixty votes, without a single senator having to say a word. And there was nothing the bill's supporters could do about it. There was no great debate, no one standing on the floor for hours, just quiet failure in an empty chamber. Fifty-five senators supported the bill, forty-five opposed it, and the bill was defeated. The forty-five senators who defeated the bill represented just 38 percent of the American people.[4]

When the vote was called, it had not mattered that the opponents of the bill lost the debate in the court of public opinion by a landslide, because at no point in the supposedly democratic process had it been necessary for the bill's opponents to persuade the American people of the merits of their position. All they needed to do was hold together a minority of senators, most of whom would not face voters at the polls for several years, long after the sitting president and many of their colleagues in the House of Representatives had come and gone, and by which point this bill would be a distant memory. There was very little pressure on the opponents of the bill to cross party lines because they were accountable almost exclusively to people who looked and thought like they did: white conservatives. As recently as a few years prior, it had been common for Republican senators to represent states Democratic presidents won, and vice versa, creating pressure on them to cross the aisle on key issues. But now, for the first time in American history, the Senate, like the rest of the country, had been almost completely sorted, so that most Republican senators represented red states and Democratic senators blue states. Moreover, the bill's opponents were protected by the National Rifle Association, which launched a major lobbying campaign against the bill, fueled by anonymous donations whose origins the American people and campaign finance watchdogs can only guess at.[5]

In this system that rewarded party discipline and loyalty, insulated by millions of dollars in support from special-interest groups, senators were unlikely to pay any political price for opposing a bill supported by 90 percent of Americans. Sure, the conversations with tearful parents begging senators to think of their slain children may have been difficult to endure. But all a senator had to do was make it through the fifteen minutes or so they reserved on their schedule for them. When the time was up, an aide would interrupt to tell the parents that they were sorry, but the senator really had to go, and it was off to fundraisers and pep rallies with like-minded people who would lavish them with praise and campaign contributions for standing firm against common sense and basic human decency.

The vote deciding the bill's fate had taken place shortly before we found ourselves in Reid's office, standing around in silence. As reporters filed their stories in the press gallery one floor above, we waited for Neil to speak. "Well . . . ," he said, to break the silence. He bowed his head and trailed off. His broad shoulders shrugged, and it seemed like he was struggling to hold back tears. He didn't need to say anything, because there was nothing more to say. His only son was dead and his government had failed to give a damn.

The shootings continued. On June 12, 2016, a shooting at the Pulse Nightclub in Orlando, Florida, would briefly become the deadliest mass shooting in America, as a gunman shot forty-nine people dead. On October 1, 2017, a gunman fired into a crowd at a music festival in Las Vegas, killing fifty-eight concertgoers. On February 14, 2018, a gunman walked into Marjory Stoneman Douglas High School in Parkland, Florida, and killed seventeen students and staff. Overall, between the Newtown massacre and July 2020, more than twenty-six hundred people would be killed in mass shootings in America.[6] Many of the massacres would be carried out with the same AR-15 assault rifle that had been used in the Newtown shooting. Many of the shootings took place in schools, and many of the victims would be children.

Neil's government didn't just fail him and the other Newtown parents, and it didn't just fail the children who would be gunned down in the years to come. As it had with increasing frequency in the years before Newtown, the United States government failed the millions of Americans who made up a large, bipartisan majority that supported a reasonable solution to an urgent national problem. In the wake of a massacre of first-graders, the American people had asked their government to pass specific, moderate policies to make future massacres less likely. But because the Senate lies at the heart of our legislative process, a minority of senators, who represented an even smaller minority of the population, were able to impose their will not just on the Senate itself, but on the entire country, and block those commonsense solutions. As young people continue to be killed in mass shootings, the official stance of the entire United States government is indifference because a minority in one chamber of one of the three branches believes that easy access to assault rifles is a higher priority than protecting children's lives.

Neil and the other parents wanted to know how this could happen. We explained Senate procedure and political realities, but their eyes asked deeper questions: How did it get to be this way? How was this possible in a democracy? How could the government so callously disregard such a reasonable call to action? The answers lie in the transformation from the Senate envisioned by the Framers to the modern Senate we know today.

MINORITY RULE HAS BECOME such a pervasive and often unquestioned part of American political life that it's worth pointing out that yes, America is a democracy. To be sure, it's a flawed one that often fails to live up to its grand claims to be a nation of, by, and for all people. But the most fundamental characteristic of democracy—the idea that majority rule is the fairest way to decide the outcome of elections and determine which bills become law—is baked into our founding ideas and texts.

Yet the emphasis we now place on the rights of minority factions has become so exaggerated that it's not unusual to hear prominent voices make claims such as, "We live in a republic, which means 51 percent of the population doesn't get to boss around the other 49 percent."[7] That comment came from a United States congressman, Dan Crenshaw of Texas, a Republican who entered because he won his 2018 election by a vote of 53 to 46 percent.[8] But if the vote had been 51 to 49, or even if Crenshaw had received a single, solitary vote more than his opponent out of the thousands of ballots cast, he still would have won. In a democracy, that's not one side bossing the other around, it's just how the system works.

The "republic, not a democracy" trope popular with people like Crenshaw on the right relies on a semantic twist. When the Framers wrote the Constitution, the word "democracy" meant *direct* democracy—the kind practiced in ancient Greece, where citizens voted directly on the laws themselves, without elected officials as intermediaries. If the Framers had called the United States a democracy in their time, they would have been arguing that every law the government passed should be, in effect, a ballot initiative. To the Framers, a "republic" meant what we today call a democracy: a system where the people elect their representatives, who then write and vote on laws.

The defining feature of a republic, the Framers stated time and again, was majority rule. James Madison called majority rule "the republican principle."[9] James Wilson, the leading legal theorist among the Framers and one of the original six members of the Supreme Court, said that "the majority of the people wherever found ought in all questions to govern the minority."[10] Benjamin Franklin wrote that a system where "the minority overpowers the majority" would be "contrary to the Common Practice of Assemblies in all Countries and Ages."[11] Majority rule was a foundational principle. The British philosopher John Locke, the single greatest influence on the Framers, explained in his *Second Treatise on Government* that majority rule was endowed by nature as the will of the people: "The act of the majority passes for the act of the whole, and of course determines, as having by the law of nature and reason the power of the whole."[12] Thomas Jefferson, who believed that majority rule was "founded in common law as well as common right" and "is the natural law of every assembly of men," was in Paris when the Constitution was being drafted.[13] But in a letter to Madison, who acted as the informal secretary of the convention, he advised, "It is my principle that the will of the majority should always prevail."[14]

There was a reason the Framers were so focused on the issue of majority rule. The Constitution was the second draft of American government. The first draft, the Articles of Confederation, had been a complete disaster. And there was broad agreement that the main failing of the Articles was its requirement that in order for a piece of military, tax, or spending legislation to pass, two-thirds of the states had to vote for it.[15] Since those categories encompassed most major legislation, especially during wartime, the Articles effectively required supermajority support for the federal government to act on all of the most significant challenges it faced. The result was frequent gridlock, which the Framers wanted to avoid. Roger Sherman of Connecticut was the only delegate to the Constitutional Convention to sign all four of America's founding documents. Reflecting on the weakness of the Articles during the convention, Sherman said that "to require more than a majority to decide a question was always embarrassing." For his part, Wilson agreed that "great inconveniences" had "been experienced in Congress from the article of confederation requiring nine votes [out of thirteen] in certain cases."[16] Requiring a supermajority threshold for federal action under the Articles had been a mistake, the delegates agreed, and they were determined not to make it twice.

The Framers were well acquainted with arguments in favor of supermajorities, such as the theory that they promote consensus. But they had seen firsthand that such theories did not match reality. As Alexander Hamilton wrote in Federalist 22, requiring a supermajority "is one of those refinements which, in practice, has an effect the reverse of what is expected from it in theory." The idea of supermajorities was "founded upon a supposition that it would contribute to security," he continued. But instead, he explained as someone who had seen the effects firsthand, "its real operation is to embarrass the administration, to destroy the energy of the government, and to substitute the pleasure, caprice, or artifices of an insignificant, turbulent, or corrupt junto, to the regular deliberations and decisions of a respectable majority."[17]

No one gave the balance between majority rule and minority protections more thoughtful consideration than James Madison, the steady hand guiding the Constitutional Convention. A shy, slight man, Madison was frequently sick and unable to handle the physical demands of the military. So he turned his patriotic fervor to public service, and poured himself into studying political philosophy. Free of Adams's vanity and Jefferson's pomposity, unburdened by Washington's iconic status and blessed with an incisive, nimble mind, Madison was able to synthesize competing ideas more effectively than any of his contemporaries. Madison tends to be conservatives' favorite source to quote in defense of minority rights in the Senate, because he took the need to prevent the majority from running roughshod over the minority seriously. In his writings and correspondence, he often cites the dangers of untrammeled majority rule. But the minority protections he devised to guard against majority tyranny were far more modest than defenders of the Senate today make them out to be. Madison stopped well short of advocating for supermajority thresholds or giving the minority any sort of veto power over the will of the majority. Like the other Framers, Madison favored a system of majority rule at every point where a decision was to be made, aside from the handful of exceptions enumerated in the Constitution for extraordinary cases like impeachment and constitutional amendments.

Invoking Madison in defense of minority rule often involves a fair amount of cherry-picking, which is invited by Madison's tendency to credit a wide range of perspectives. A typical Madisonian construction lays out the arguments on both sides before revealing his own views. A few lines after some of his most famous expressions of concern for the rights of minorities, he goes on to state that while majority rule may not be perfect, it is the best available system. Throughout his half-century career—as the philosopher behind the drafting of the Constitution, as the salesman of the final product, and as secretary of state and later president—Madison was strikingly consistent, always coming down firmly on the side of majority rule.

Madison's view of minority protections was limited enough that he firmly opposed the Constitution's single biggest protection for minority rights. At the Constitutional Convention, small states demanded the same number of representatives in Congress as big states. Madison opposed them, demanding that representation be awarded proportionally, giving big states more power. This became the single most contentious issue of the convention. The smaller states feared being overrun by the big states, and the convention almost ran aground over the disagreement. According to one estimate provided to the delegates, if senators were allocated by population, Virginia would have had ten and Delaware one. For their part, the big states contended that they contributed far more to the federal government in terms of tax revenue and other resources, and that it was simple fairness for them to have a larger say in the use of those resources.[18]

As the debate raged during the sweltering summer of 1787, the convention remained deadlocked over the question of representation. In a last-ditch effort to break through, on July 3, the delegates selected a committee to make a report on the issue, and then recessed to celebrate Independence Day. When they reconvened on the fifth, the committee delivered its recommendation: a bicameral legislature in which the number of representatives would be decided by population in one chamber, and in the other, all states would have an equal number.[19] Madison rejected this settlement, and with some vehemence. The small states were being obstinate, he believed. The delegates had exhausted the issue, and now it was time, in his view, for the big states to join together and implement the will of the majority.[20]

Rising to address his fellow delegates, Madison delivered a passionate treatise on the fairness of majority rule. He declared that the convention had been reduced to the choice of "either departing from justice in order to conciliate the smaller states, and the minority of the people," or "justly gratifying the larger States and the majority of the people." Given this choice, he "could not himself hesitate" as to which he would make. By siding with the big states, he explained, "the Convention with justice and the majority of the people on their side, had nothing to fear." But woe betide the incipient nation if they sided with the small states, he warned. If they did, "with injustice and the minority on their side, they had everything to fear." After weeks of debate, the delegates had exhausted all options for compromise, he argued, and it was time to make a decision. Conceding to the small states would only kick the problems down the road: it "was in vain to purchase concord in the Convention on terms which would perpetuate discord," Madison said. This supposed champion of minority rights gave the delegates a dose of realpolitik, arguing that the majority should exert its will and the small states would come around because they simply had no other choice. With a hint of threat, he said he "could not suspect that Delaware would brave the consequences of seeking her fortunes apart from the other States." Turning to another troublemaker, New Jersey, Madison said he could not imagine that they "would choose rather to stand on their own legs, and bid defiance to events, than to acquiesce under an establishment founded on principles the justice of which they could not dispute."[21]

Voicing a theme to which he would return time and again, Madison acknowledged that in a perfect world, the delegates would reach a consensus. But since that did not appear possible, the majority should rule. "Harmony in the Convention was no doubt much to be desired," he said. But they had been discussing the proposal for weeks, and now it was time to act. What should happen, he concluded, was that "the principal states comprehending a majority of the people of the United States should concur in a just and judicious plan," and pass it over the objections of the small states. Once they did, he had "the firmest hopes" that the smaller states would "by degrees accede to it."[22]

In the face of Madison's challenge, the small states invoked their own version of majority rule to argue the justice of their cause. Oliver Ellsworth, a delegate from Connecticut and later chief justice of the Supreme Court, argued that under the Articles "no salutary measure has been lost for want of a majority of the states." The problem with the Articles, he contended, had been the need for a supermajority, not the equal voting power of the states. Ellsworth backed the idea of a bicameral legislature, one where representation would be awarded proportionally to population in one chamber, and equally in the other, with every state getting two senators. With a palpable fear that the convention would fail if the small states did not get what they wanted, in a concession that "oozed with unease," according to one scholar, the compromise plan was accepted, and the Senate was created.[23]

The decision to create a Senate where every state was afforded two senators regardless of size while states enjoyed proportional representation in the House of Representatives became known as the Great Compromise and is widely regarded as the deal that saved the Constitutional Convention. When it came up for the decisive vote, it passed by the barest majority, on a vote of 5 to 4.[24] Majority rule created the Senate and salvaged a compromise—and perhaps the Constitution itself.

WHENEVER PROPOSALS FOR supermajority thresholds were raised at the convention they were summarily dismissed. Their leading advocates were the slave states, who anticipated that changes to navigation and commerce laws would threaten slavery since the South's economy was almost entirely reliant on exports. To protect it, they pushed for a provision requiring a supermajority to pass all legislation governing interstate commerce and the navigation of waterways—a broad category in those days. They were firmly rejected.[25] At another point, a delegate raised the idea of requiring supermajorities for common legislation; he was met with silence, and the convention quickly moved on.[26] In the end, the convention made clear that supermajority thresholds should be reserved for the matters of greatest consequence, such as impeachment, treaties with foreign nations, and amendments to the Constitution. On all other matters, the delegates were clear that the Senate was to be a strictly majority-rule institution.[27]

When it was time to sell the Constitution to the American people, the Framers made majority rule central to their argument, especially in the Federalist Papers, which were authored by Madison, Hamilton, and John Jay. In Federalist 22, Hamilton takes on the advocates of supermajority rule, explaining that "what at first sight may seem a remedy, is, in reality, a poison." It would be wrong "to subject the sense of the greater number to that of the lesser," because if "a pertinacious minority can control the opinion of a majority," the result would be "tedious delays; continual negotiation and intrigue; contemptible compromises of the public good." Decision-makers would sometimes fail to find consensus, he acknowledged, since there are times when issues "will not admit of accommodation." But in such instances, if the minority was allowed to block the majority, the government's "situation must always savor of weakness, sometimes border upon anarchy," Hamilton wrote. When consensus failed, Hamilton argued, the "public business" must "go forward." Allowing a minority faction to stop the majority invited all kinds of mischief and interference, he warned, explaining that such a system "gives greater scope to foreign corruption, as well as to domestic faction, than that which permits the sense of the majority to decide."[28]

Madison took a turn advocating for majority rule in Federalist 58. Characteristically, he goes out of his way to acknowledge those with whom he disagrees, and to recognize the legitimacy of their point of view: "That some advantages might have resulted from such a precaution [of supermajority rule], cannot be denied," he writes. "It might have been an additional shield to some particular interests, and another obstacle generally to hasty and partial measures." But then Madison proceeds to explain why "these considerations are outweighed by the inconveniences in the opposite scale." If a minority was allowed to block a majority, he writes, then "in all cases where justice or the general good might require new laws to be passed, or active measures to be pursued, the fundamental principle of free government would be reversed. It would be no longer the majority that would rule; the power would be transferred to the minority."[29]

In Federalist 10, Madison again lays out the importance of minority protections, before siding with majority rule. This is his most eloquent rendition of the potential for majority tyranny, and conservatives quote it frequently. But taken as whole, it is not a jeremiad against majority rule, but rather an explanation for why the overall system he helped design strikes the best balance between minority protections and majority rule. Madison explains that the combination of elected representatives (as opposed to direct democracy) and the large size of the country protects against majority tyranny. He acknowledges concerns "that measures are too often decided, not according to the rules of justice and the rights of the minor party, but by the superior force of an interested and overbearing majority," and that such complaints "are in some degree true." There was, he concedes, danger that a majority would "sacrifice to its ruling passion or interest both the public good and the rights of other citizens." But from there, he goes on to explain how the American system mitigates this threat. First, he establishes "the republican principle" of majority rule: "If a faction consists of less than a majority, relief is supplied by the republican principle, which enables the majority to defeat its sinister views by regular vote." Then he explains two additional factors that provide protection against tyranny of the majority. The first is "the delegation of the government . . . to a small number of citizens elected by the rest." The second is the size of the country: "the greater number of citizens, and greater sphere of country," means that forming a majority requires uniting a broad array of factions—a good thing, Madison explains, because it guarantees that any majority will represent a broad range of interests. "It is this circumstance principally which renders factious combinations less to be dreaded," he writes. "Extend the sphere, and you take in a greater variety of parties and interests; you make it less probable that a majority of the whole will have a common motive to invade the rights of other citizens." The beauty of these two factors working in tandem—a representative government and a big country populated by a diverse array of people—is that in them "we behold a republican remedy for the diseases most incident to republican government."[30] In America, Madison argued, majority rule would not trample minority rights because any majority in a country as big and diverse as ours would by definition represent a wide-ranging cross-section of interests.

To be sure, Madison and the other Framers structured the Senate to offer protections for minority interests and to guarantee a thoughtful, deliberative process. First and foremost, the Senate gave all states equal representation, despite Madison's reluctance. On top of that, the Framers layered provisions to guarantee that senators would be older (and, presumably, wiser), more insulated from political winds, and more accountable to a broader and less whimsical population. They required senators to be a minimum age of thirty, compared to twenty-five in the House. They assigned senators terms of six years, as opposed to two years in the House and four for the president. And they made senators accountable to the interests of an entire state, not just a district as in the House. Today, to win election, House members need to secure a majority in districts that average about seven hundred thousand people, while senators need to appeal to entire states, whose median population is over four million. Finally, to promote stability, the Framers staggered Senate elections so that only one-third of senators are up for reelection at any given time; in the House, by contrast, all 435 members face election every two years. Together, these were the features designed to make the Senate a deliberative body, and to protect against the whims of majority mobs. Notably absent is any mention of supermajority thresholds, the filibuster, or even the principle of "unlimited debate" its defenders today claim it upholds.

A consistent theme is the focus on the whole system. Throughout the Federalist Papers, Madison emphasizes that it is the system itself, not any individual feature, that provides the minority with protections. In essence, he argues, the many checks and balances built into the system will make it challenging for a majority to pass new legislation. For a bill to become a law, it must secure majorities in two chambers of very different composition, where members are accountable to different audiences of voters; in the Senate, the bill is guaranteed to endure extended (albeit not unlimited) debate. If the bill passes Congress, it must then be signed by the president, who is accountable to a national audience of voters. And then the law can be challenged in the courts, whose members are accountable to no voters, and serve for life. Madison was right to present this as a daunting series of hurdles. To this day, the United States has more "veto players," as political scientists dub them, in its system of government than any other democracy.[31]

The beauty of Madison's system, the interlocking nature of the pieces, is also what makes it vulnerable to being derailed by obstruction. To alter the system, you don't have to change the whole thing, just one part. With its built-in minority protections like equal representation for states, the Senate is the part of the system most vulnerable to manipulation by a minority. Gumming up the works can be done by a minority of states—or even by a single person, such as a southern senator with a sophisticated understanding of power and a deep-seated drive to defy the majority.

JOHN CALDWELL CALHOUN did not come to Washington from South Carolina to divide the nation. He came to unify it, behind himself, as president.

A tall, wiry man with deep-set eyes and a square jaw, his coarse gray hair swept up and, in his later years, down to his collar, Calhoun struck those who knew him as deeply intelligent and eloquent, if doctrinaire and guarded. He had an explosive temper. There was a ghostlike quality to him; acquaintances' descriptions of him depict him as aloof and even a bit immortal seeming, his mind always elsewhere and his form not entirely temporal. He was a capable conversationalist but had trouble forming lasting friendships, and reliably fell out with allies. In the 1830s Calhoun became a favorite of the British writer Harriet Martineau, albeit "a favourite of whom she seems rather ashamed," according to a contemporary of hers writing in the *Edinburgh Review*. Martineau's description of Calhoun cannot be improved upon: she dubbed him "the cast-iron man, who looks as if he never had been born, and never could be extinguished."[32]

In the period surrounding the War of 1812, Calhoun was a union-ist, a leading war hawk, and an ardent advocate of federal power. John Quincy Adams, the son of the second president, described Cal-houn as someone who was "above all sectional and factional prej-udices more than any other statesman of this Union with whom I have ever acted."[33] At this early stage of his career, as a member of the House of Representatives, Calhoun dismissed discussions of states' rights as trivial. "I am no advocate for refined arguments on the Constitution," he said in an 1817 speech. The Constitution "was not intended as a thesis for the logician to exercise his ingenuity on. It ought to be construed with plain, good sense," he contended.[34] To a young Calhoun, "good sense" meant the firm exercise of federal power. A passionate supporter of Hamilton's vision of a strong fed-eral government wielding centralized power, Calhoun said he had a "clear conviction" that Hamilton's system was "the only true policy for this country."[35] Indeed, Calhoun thought the future of the South lay in being closely tied to the federal government, and sought to steer federal investments, especially military bases, to states like his home, South Carolina.

Having gained a national profile, he ran for president in 1824. While he did not win, he did get the most votes for vice-president at a time when the two offices were elected separately. The presiden-tial election that year ended without a clear winner. Neither of the two leading candidates, John Quincy Adams and Andrew Jackson, secured a majority in the electoral college, so the election went to the House to break the tie, according to the process laid out in the Con-stitution. Henry Clay, then Speaker of the House, had also run for president that year. He lost, but he was able to play kingmaker in the chamber he controlled. In return for Adams's promise to appoint

him secretary of state, Clay gave his bloc of votes in the House—
and the presidency—to Adams. The deal sparked outrage, quickly
becoming known as the "corrupt bargain," and it embittered Calhoun toward both Adams and Clay. As Adams's vice-president,
Calhoun simmered in his discontent, fuming that Clay "made the
President against the voice of his constituents," and calling the deal
"the most dangerous stab, which the liberty of this country has
ever received."[36]

Calhoun's bitterness would alter the course of the Senate and
the nation. Before the end of Adams's first and only term, Calhoun
found an outlet for his outrage and a way to hedge his bets if his
plan to become president as a unionist did not work out. By 1828,
the South was roiling with anger at a tariff imposed by Adams,
which southerners decried as the "Tariff of Abominations." Britain was selling manufactured goods to America at cut-rate prices,
which made it harder for the American manufacturing industry,
concentrated in the North, to compete. The 1828 tariff slapped a
38 percent tax on imported goods, which reduced Britain's purchas-
ing power and made it less inclined to buy southern cotton. Even
as he remained a unionist in public, Calhoun made his first, secret
foray into sectionalism. Anonymously, he penned a pair of mani-
festos called "Exposition" and "Protest," where, for the first time,
he developed the theory that would become known as "nullification." His arguments were fierce but his thinking convoluted: his
theory was that states could call individual conventions to examine
the constitutionality of specific federal laws. If the state convention
decided a given law was unconstitutional, the state could nullify it.
Despite the impracticality of having states call individual conventions to decide whether to follow individual laws, the basic idea that
states should be able to pick and choose which federal laws they
obey would prove enduring.[37]

Calhoun had kept his authorship a secret because it would have
been untenable for him to publicly rally South Carolina behind nullification while serving as Adams's vice-president. But in the 1828

election, Calhoun threw his support behind Andrew Jackson, who was elected in a landslide. For a while, Jackson and Calhoun were close allies, and the South Carolinian was seen as a potential successor to Jackson as the leader of the new, dominant political machine called the Democratic Party. "John C. Calhoun, an honest man, the noblest work of God," Jackson toasted him at a banquet.[38] But soon Calhoun found himself on the outs with Jackson. In a major scandal, Calhoun's wife refused to meet with the wife of another cabinet member, who was rumored to have loose morals, and the cabinet erupted into what became known as the "petticoat affair." Jackson sided against Calhoun, calling a meeting of his cabinet to defend the honor of the accused woman: "She is as chaste as snow!" Jackson cried to his cabinet.[39] Ridiculous as it may sound, the petticoat affair split Jackson's cabinet into warring factions, and pushed Calhoun outside Jackson's inner circle.[40] Around the same time, Jackson found out that when Calhoun had been war secretary in 1818, he had advocated for Jackson to be court-martialed after he, as a general in the army, had unilaterally decided to invade Spanish territory during the Seminole War. When Jackson found out about it a decade later, he wrote Calhoun demanding to know if it was true. Calhoun tried to explain himself but admitted that it was. Jackson had probably deserved to be court-martialed, but it didn't matter. Jackson informed Calhoun that their friendship was "forever at an end."[41]

As Calhoun's power in the Jackson administration waned, he brooded and looked for another path. Casting his eyes home to South Carolina, he saw a faction in need of a champion. Calhoun had already broken with his unionist past with his "Exposition," albeit surreptitiously. Now, the South was running hot. Slavery had begun forcing a series of legitimacy crises that would eventually erupt into the Civil War. The Framers had written a twenty-year ban on abolition into the Constitution and enshrined enslaved peoples' dehumanization by treating them as three-fifths of a person, punting the problem to future generations. For a while, it looked like slavery was bound to remain contained. In 1787, the Northwest

Ordinance passed unanimously, banning slavery in the Midwest; southerners supported it for several reasons, but mainly they were focused on protecting slavery within the South, not expanding it. But in 1794 the cotton gin was invented, making cotton farming massively profitable. In 1815 the Napoleonic wars ended, reopening trade routes with Europe. By the 1830s, the South had a massively profitable cash crop and an enormous market in which to sell it. But it lacked a national leader. And the threats were coming from all sides: the global abolitionist movement drove Britain to ban slavery in its colonies in 1833, freeing more than eight hundred thousand enslaved people. The abolitionist movement was taking hold in America as well. In 1831 William Lloyd Garrison published the first edition of his abolitionist newspaper, *The Liberator.*

The South needed a leader. For Calhoun, sectional power was not the presidency, but it would do. And he never stopped hoping that it would one day take him to the White House.

IN THE 1830S, unionism ceased to be a viable path for Calhoun's ambitions and he completed his transition into an open nullifier. Nullification would define his career but be rejected on a national scale—eventually, at grave cost in human life. But in the decades leading up to the Civil War, Calhoun would find ways to nurture the underlying concept—the idea of a minority veto over the will of the majority—first from the vice presidency, then from his new perch in the Senate, and the institution would never be the same.

During this period, Calhoun's doctrine of nullification met its most talented opponent in Senator Daniel Webster of Massachusetts. "God-like Daniel" was a "raven-haired fellow, with an eye as black as death" and a voice that moved audiences to tears, as one observer remembered.[42] Another contemporary, the young Harvard scholar George Ticknor, recounted that watching Webster speak, "three or four times I thought my temples would burst with the gush of blood."[43]

In 1830, Webster turned a floor debate over the sale of western lands into an attack on nullification. The vice-president is the president of the Senate, and at the time would preside over the chamber most days. On this day, Calhoun was sitting in the presider's chair when Webster launched his attack. Since he could not attack Calhoun directly, Webster attacked his protégé, Senator Robert Hayne of South Carolina. Webster decried the nullifiers' stance that the union was "to be preserved while it suits local and temporary purposes" but "sundered whenever it shall be found to thwart such purposes."[44] Hayne rose to respond. As Calhoun passed him notes from the rostrum, he decried unionists like Webster "who are in favor of consolidation" and "adding strength to the federal government."[45] With the galleries rapt, Hayne unsheathed a threat: "If the gentleman provokes war," he said ominously, "he shall have war."[46]

Initially, observers thought Hayne—and by extension Calhoun—had won the day.[47] "Congratulations from every quarter were showered upon the speaker," Charles March, a friend of Webster's, wrote about Hayne.[48] That night, another friend, Edward Everett, called on Webster, who was contemplating a reply. He asked Webster if he'd taken notes on Hayne's speech. Webster "took from his vest-pocket a piece of paper about as big as the palm of his hand," Everett recalled, and replied, "I have it all."[49] Webster didn't need detailed notes because he had identified the southerners' weak spot. As he confided to Everett that night, Hayne and Calhoun had articulated "a system of politics" which "went far to change the form of government from that which was established by the Constitution, into that (if it could be called a government) which existed under the Confederation."[50]

The next day, Webster delivered what is widely regarded as the greatest speech in Senate history. An aggressive defense of the right of the federal government to act in the national interest, "Webster's Second Reply to Hayne" is still memorized by schoolchildren for its famous line, "Liberty and Union, now and forever, one and inseparable!" The response from the packed galleries in the Senate was ecstatic. "The exulting rush of feeling with which he went through the peroration threw a glow over his countenance," March recalled, writing that Webster "seemed touched, as with a celestial fire." When Webster was done, the audience "gazed as at something more than human. So Moses might have appeared to the awe-struck Israelites."[51] Webster wrote to Madison, enclosing "a copy of the speech delivered by me on a recent occasion," humbly noting that he did "not feel that I have the slightest right to call on you for any expression of opinion."[52] He did not need to worry. Madison replied that several people had sent him the speech already, and he liked it.[53]

Soon the debate over whether a minority had a right to block the federal government would drive the country into what became known as the nullification crisis. South Carolina, putting Calhoun's "Exposition" into action, refused to pay what it owed the federal government under the Tariff of Abominations. Clay forged a compromise, but not before Jackson sent troops to South Carolina. The South backed down, but the irresolvable and now very public tensions between Calhoun and Jackson led the vice-president to resign in 1832. He was appointed to an open Senate seat in South Carolina, and easily won reelection on his own terms.

By leaving the vice-presidency for the Senate, Calhoun traded his shaky national power for more solid sectional power. When he stepped down from the vice-presidency, medals were minted in South Carolina declaring him the "First President of the Southern Confederacy."[54] The former unionist was now irrevocably committed to finding new ways for the South to resist the North. Exactly as Webster had confided to his friend the night before his reply to Hayne, Calhoun was determined to pull the United States back toward a form of government like the one "which existed under the Confederation"— one where a minority could impose its will on the majority.

LIKE FUTURE GENERATIONS of conservatives, Calhoun had invoked Madison in defense of his ideas during the nullification crisis. But unlike today's conservatives, Calhoun had to contend with the fact that Madison was still around to respond. The longest-lived of the major Framers, Madison fielded numerous inquiries about his views on nullification and responded in detail. Asked to respond to Calhoun, he complied.

Calhoun's main claim to Madison's ideas was rooted in the fact that back in 1798 Madison had authored a resolution passed by the Virginia legislature declaring the Alien and Sedition Acts unconstitutional. But as Madison explained, Calhoun was distorting his ideas to inflate the limited protections for factional minorities he had designed into larger powers that went beyond anything Madison intended. Madison believed the system he had created offered an aggrieved minority all the tools they could reasonably demand— protections that were designed to allow a minority not to block or nullify but to persuade. They guaranteed the minority a prominent platform, the Senate floor, from which to make their case to the public, ensuring that they would never be silenced and would always have ample opportunity to get their message across. If they were successful, they could change minds and win the debate at hand. If not, they could try to increase their power at the ballot box in the next election and put themselves in the majority.

In keeping with this view, Madison's Virginia resolution did not claim that Virginia could nullify laws it regarded as unjust. The resolution was indeed an aggressive statement that the Alien and Sedition Acts were unconstitutional. But instead of declaring the laws void, Madison sought to rally other states to join Virginia and work to repeal them. As the resolutions were being debated in 1798, Madison wrote to Jefferson, who favored a stronger assertion of states' rights, and outlined why he favored a softer version. Madison explained that he preferred "using general expressions that would leave to other States a choice of all the modes possible of concurring in the substance, and would shield the Genl. Assembly agst. the charge of Usurpation in the very act of protesting agst the usurpations of Congress."[55] Madison's commitment to working within the system proved successful, as most of the provisions of the offending Acts were repealed within two years of their passage. In 1830, looking back, Madison explained that the Virginia resolution was an effort "to produce a conviction every where, that the Constitution had been violated by the obnoxious Acts and to procure a concurrence and co-operation of the other States in effectuating a repeal of the Acts."[56]

Far from providing intellectual succor to Calhoun, Madison firmly rejected the idea of nullification. "It follows from no view of the subject," he wrote in one note, "that a nullification of a law of the U.S. can as is now contended, belong rightfully to a single State."[57] In another, he explained that "the nullification expressed by S.C. in which a single state initiates a process which is to give in its result an authority of 7 over 17 States, will be in all sober minds, be [sic] unanimously pronounced to be equally unconstitutional, preposterous, and anti-republican."[58] Maintaining remarkable consistency with the Federalist Papers, published more than forty years earlier, Madison once again explained that the dangers of giving veto power to a minority outweighed the potential benefits. That "the seven might, in particular instances be right, and the seventeen wrong, is more than possible. But to establish a positive and permanent rule giving such a power, to such a minority, over such a majority, would overturn the first principle of free government, and in practice necessarily overturn the government itself."[59]

Decades after the founding, Madison felt justified in instructing minorities to work through the process to address their grievances, and to accept the will of the majority if their efforts at persuasion failed, because in his view, the system had proved that it worked. "Experience seems to have shewn," he wrote in 1830, that "there is, as yet a sufficient control, in the popular will, over the Executive and Legislative Departments of the Government." He returned to the Alien and Sedition Acts, pointing out that when they "were passed in contravention of the opinions and feelings of the community, the first elections that ensued, put an end to them." The way to prevent majority tyranny was not minority domination, he explained, but to trust the interlocking checks built into the overall system. "Against an undue preponderance of the powers granted to the Government," he noted, ". . . the Constitution has relied on 1. the responsibility of the Senators and Representatives in the Legislature of the United States to the Legislatures and people of the States. 2. the responsibility of the President to the people of the United States; and 3. the liability of the Executive and judiciary functionaries of the United States to impeachment."[60] To dissatisfied minority factions, Madison's message boiled down to "Trust the system."

By Madison's final years, he had seen the government from all sides, inside and out. As his career wound down, he seemed satisfied with his work. Toward the end of his life, in a vintage construction, he wrote, "In Republics, where the people govern themselves, and where, of course, the majority govern, a danger to the minority arises from opportunities tempting a sacrifice of their rights to the interest, real or supposed, of a majority." But then came the inevitable turn: "No form of government, therefore, can be a perfect guard against the abuse of power. The recommendation of the republican form is, that the danger of abuse is less than any other."[61] A system based on majority rule may not be perfect, Madison allowed. But in the course of human history, it was the best anyone had come up with.

In 1834, less than two years before he passed away at his home in Montpelier, Virginia, Madison engaged the topic once more, writing, "We must recur to the monitory reflection that no Government of human device, and human administration can be perfect; that that which is the least imperfect is therefore the best." The "abuses of all other governments have led to the preference of Republican Government," as "the best of all governments because the least imperfect." Madison concluded, *The vital principle of Republican Government is the lex majoris partis, the will of the majority.*"[62]

IN HIS TIME, Madison's vision seemed to win out. But Calhoun, and his vision of minority rule, would outlive Madison. Calhoun would make headway in the years to come, but he would continue to struggle with a stubborn challenge posed by Madison's system: despite its minority protections, the Senate was still a majority-rule body. The tactics necessary for a minority to stop a bill would take a century to develop and even longer to be wielded with any frequency. Indeed, the idea that one day a minority in the Senate could block anything it wanted might have been too much for even Calhoun to hope for. But once he arrived in the Senate, he got to work forging the tools that would one day give his successors that power.

Chapter Two

"VICTORIOUS IN THE MIDST OF UNBROKEN DEFEATS"

IF YOU HAD ASKED James Madison what he thought of the filibuster, his answer would have been, "What's a filibuster?" The filibuster did not exist, in practice or in name, until after all the Framers passed from the earth. It was not a part of the Senate they created and the evidence suggests they would have opposed it, just as they balked at the southern delegates to the Constitutional Convention who proposed a supermajority threshold for regular legislation. The idea of majority rule and, as we will see, of extended but *limited* debate, was so fundamental that a tactic like the filibuster could not come in through the front door; it needed a back way in. In the middle of the nineteenth century, that way would begin to appear through an idea that today is held up as a pillar of the Senate, but which would have probably befuddled the Framers: the idea that a Senate minority is entitled to *unlimited* debate, which they are free to define in any way they please.

In the nineteenth century, the idea of unlimited debate at least bore some connection to reality: on the rare occasions that antebellum senators invoked this new idea, they stood on the floor and debated. Today, the idea of unlimited debate is invoked constantly, but it has been divorced of all meaning. To witness the Orwellian use of the phrase today, take a look at the "debate" that led to the defeat of the background-checks bill in 2013. Before the Senate

even opened its debate on how to respond to the Newtown massacre, a bipartisan commission of experts spent months examining possible policy responses. When the Senate debate began in the
spring, many of the bills that came before the chamber, including
the background-checks bill itself, were based on the recommendations of that panel. As debate opened, the senators who opposed the
background-checks bill were invited to have their say, with nothing that could be reasonably construed as restrictions on how long
they could take to make their case. So far, this was the process the
Framers intended: a methodical approach to a difficult issue where
senators worked across party lines, with a wide-open floor debate
where the minority was free to try to persuade the American people
of the merits of their case.

But this is where the process veered into absurdity, as it does on
virtually every bill in the modern Senate. For the most part, the
senators who opposed the bill declined to debate it. During the
week the bill was on the floor, the leader of the opposition, Senate minority leader Mitch McConnell, mostly avoided commenting
on it while whipping votes against it in private. He did find time
to discuss his reverence for former British prime minister Margaret
Thatcher, delivering a Senate floor address celebrating her life and
legacy.[1] He also found time to introduce a resolution celebrating the
recent March Madness triumph of the University of Louisville men's
basketball team (he's a big fan).[2] But on the leading proposal for
the federal government's policy response to the massacre of twenty
first-graders, the leader of the opposition contributed a grand total
of two minutes of floor debate.[3]

McConnell's performance was the rule, not the exception, as
most members of the minority followed his lead. In a debate that
stretched over a week, the forty-five senators who opposed the
background-checks bill spoke for a grand total of two hours and
twenty-four minutes.[4] All but a few minutes' worth of this "debate"
came in the form of prepared speeches, read to a mostly empty
chamber. The longest speech by a member of the opposition was

seventeen minutes long; most were ten minutes or less. When Joe Manchin and Pat Toomey took to the floor and offered to engage in an open discussion with anyone who had concerns about their bill, the opposition declined to take them up on it. The chamber remained mostly empty as the two senators, one Republican and one Democrat, gamely tried making their case to colleagues who refused to listen.[5]

And here is where the process descends from farce into dangerous dysfunction: even though the members of the minority were on the wrong side of 90 percent of the American people, and even though they declined to engage in any real debate on the Senate floor, they were able to impose their will by invoking the principle of *unlimited* debate. It did not matter that the members of the minority were not debating or holding the floor in anything resembling the popular image of a filibuster. By claiming their supposed right to unlimited debate, the minority was able to force the majority to resort to an onerous procedure that today, for reasons we will examine, requires clearing a supermajority threshold of sixty votes to "end" this non-existent "debate" and proceed with the bill. If the proponents of a bill can't get those sixty votes, the bill fails and the minority wins, without ever having to actually debate the issue.

This claim to unlimited debate is what defeated the background-checks bill, along with countless other commonsense, bipartisan solutions in the modern Senate. It is the central claim underlying the filibuster as we know it today. And it is a claim that traces its lineage not to James Madison and the Framers, but to John Calhoun.

MADISON AND THE FRAMERS took a commonsense approach to debate in the Senate. They believed debate should be thoughtful, topical, and respectful, and that as long as it remained so, it should go on for as long as senators wanted. When it became clear to senators that the debate had run its course, the Framers believed it should be brought to a close, and the issue at hand should come up for a majority vote. But in the single most important example of a minority protection in the Senate being inflated beyond recognition, the Framers' clear support for extended productive debate has been turned into a justification for unlimited obstructive debate.

The Framers saw debate as a critical protection for the minority because it guaranteed them a chance to make their voices heard. Madison's Federalist 62 (titled "The Senate") explains that the Senate should be a place that guards against "the propensity . . . to yield to the impulse of sudden and violent passions."[6] But he explains that the Senate should perform this cooling function through its structure: by having fewer members than the House, with longer tenures, a higher minimum age, and a statewide constituency.[7] Federalist 62 is Madison's main essay laying out his comprehensive view of the Senate, and it does not contain a single word about unlimited debate.

Consistent with Madison's vision, the original Senate established boundaries that encouraged extensive, thoughtful debate, but provided senators with tools to rein it in if the debate became obstructive. Five of the nineteen original rules the Senate adopted in 1789 placed limits on debate. When Thomas Jefferson was vice-president (and as such, president of the Senate), he wrote a manual on congressional procedure that includes a number of restrictions on debate. In the section titled "Order in Debate," Jefferson writes, "No one is to speak impertinently or beside the question, superfluously or tediously." He also explains that if senators decide one of their colleagues has become tedious, and "by conversation or any other noise they endeavor to drown his voice," then the tedious senator should defer to his colleagues and "sit down." Jefferson's manual was printed and handed out to senators, and it functioned as a code of conduct in the Senate's early decades. Not only did the senators follow Jefferson's guidance, they prided themselves on it. Avoiding unnecessary delay and being respectful of each other's time were points of senatorial pride.[8] As Martin B. Gold, author of one of the foremost texts on Senate procedure and former counsel to Republican Senate majority leader Howard Baker, puts it, "The possibility that a minority of Senators could hold unlimited debate on a topic against the majority's will was unknown to the first Senate."[9]

The most consequential of the Senate's early rules governing debate was called the "previous question" rule. The legislative equivalent of giving your kids a five-minute warning to turn off the television, it is a vote to wrap up debate and move to the final vote that will decide the fate of the bill at hand. It is a common rule: it is used by most state legislatures in America and national legislatures across the globe.[10] When it was included in the original Senate rules, it was not at all controversial.

But in one of the most significant copy edits in American history, the Senate got rid of the previous question motion while it was cleaning up its rule books at the turn of the nineteenth century. In 1806 the Senate edited its rules at the suggestion of Vice-President Aaron Burr. After being indicted for killing Alexander Hamilton, Burr was making an unexpected star turn in the Senate, where he had just overseen the impeachment trial of Supreme Court Justice Samuel Chase, an episode fraught with danger for the Senate and the nation. It was the Senate's third impeachment trial, but by far the most complicated. The first was of a senator persuasively charged with treason who had already been expelled from the Senate, and the second was of a judge accused of drunkenness and insanity. By contrast, Chase was essentially accused of being too partisan, a trickier charge to navigate at a time when partisanship was a grave but not necessarily impeachable sin. A staunch Federalist who was relentlessly critical of Jeffersonian Republicans, Chase was impeached by Jefferson's allies in the House, forcing the Senate into difficult decisions about what crimes merited removal from office. The Senate made the right call and voted against removing Chase from office. The trial was a significant moment for the institution. Still in its infancy, it had shown itself capable of conducting a fair process on one of the most fraught issues a government can face. Burr was praised for overseeing the trial "with the dignity and impartiality of an angel, but with the rigor of a devil," and his conduct was considered crucial to its success.[11]

When Burr bade farewell to the Senate, everyone knew it was likely the last time, given his indictment. With emotions running high, Burr delivered a speech celebrating the Senate as "a sanctuary; a citadel of law, of order, and of liberty."[12] His speech about the greatness of the Senate was well received by his audience of senators, some of whom regarded it as "the most sublime, dignified and impressive ever uttered," according to a report in the *Washington Federalist*—an organ of Hamilton's Federalist party, not inclined to sympathy for Burr. The *Federalist* report continued, "The whole Senate were in tears, and so unmanned that it was half an hour before they could recover themselves sufficiently to come to order."[13] Burr paired his speech with recommendations for cleaning up the Senate's rule book, which he had used during the trial. At a time when senators prided themselves on adhering to the firmly established norms against superfluous debate, one of the edits Burr suggested was eliminating the previous question rule, since it appeared to be unnecessary. Within a few decades, leading lights of the Senate would come to believe the change had been a grievous error and try to restore the previous question rule. But in the moment, senators barely noticed. As Brookings Institution congressional scholar Sarah Binder testified at a 2010 Senate hearing on rules reform, the Senate got rid of the previous question rule "not because senators in 1806 sought to protect minority rights and extended debate. They got rid of the rule by mistake."[14]

The loophole this change created went unnoticed for years, as the Senate continued to adhere to the prevailing norms against superfluous debate.[15] As loopholes often do, it lay dormant until the right person came along to exploit it. In the 1830s, driven from the Jackson administration and looking to reestablish his power, John

Calhoun arrived in the Senate, where this loophole opening the door to a new principle of unlimited debate lay waiting.

BY THE TIME Calhoun became a senator himself, he already had practice eroding the norms guarding against obstructionism in the Senate. In the early decades of the Senate, a senator behaving tediously could be stopped by the presiding officer, who would call the offending senator to order. But that was before Calhoun held the job of presiding officer. Under the Constitution, the vice-president is the president of the Senate, a role that gives them the power to preside over the Senate and cast a vote in the event of a tie. Today, vice-presidents preside only on major occasions, but in the early decades they presided most days. As Adams's vice-president, Calhoun presided over the Senate for years before becoming a senator (as when he presided over the Webster-Hayne debate). In 1826, bitter at Adams over his "corrupt bargain" with Clay, Calhoun's ears seemed to perk up when Senator John Randolph of Virginia rose and launched into a highly personal tirade against Adams, giving voice to the views Calhoun shared.[16] Normally, a screed like Randolph's would have prompted the vice-president, as presiding officer, to intervene and call the vituperative member to order. But to the shock of the senators in the chamber, Calhoun let Randolph go on. "As the other senators listened in horror, Randolph rose to new heights of maliciousness," said Senator Robert Byrd of West Virginia, a scholar of the Senate who delivered a series of lectures on the history of the institution. Randolph stunned his audience by comparing Adams and Clay to "Blifil and Black George," the well-known villains of the novel *Tom Jones*. Calhoun sat on his hands, remaining "oblivious to the many appeals to call Randolph to order," as Byrd recounted.[17] But when senators rose to defend Adams and Clay, Calhoun quickly cut them off.[18]

The incident caused an uproar and led to the deterioration of the presiding officer's power to call obstructionist senators to order. The pro-Adams newspaper *National Journal* published an attack on Calhoun by someone using the pseudonym "Patrick Henry," who was widely suspected of being Adams himself. Clay challenged Randolph to a duel, before which Randolph, the better dueler, resolved to miss Clay even if it meant his own death. "I will never make a widow and orphans," Randolph later said. He shot around Clay a few times as Clay missed his own shots, before the two men shook hands and made up.[19] For his part, Calhoun neatly wrapped his personal bitterness in lofty principle. He "masked his enjoyment" at Randolph's attack, Byrd explains, and "gravely insisted that, since he was not a member of the Senate but merely its presiding officer, he had no wish to usurp its power and interfere with debate."[20] This was, to use a term of art, bullshit. When a senator moved to appoint a committee to help the Senate clarify the role of the presiding officer, Calhoun—suddenly happy to intervene—ruled him out of order.[21]

The debate over Calhoun's conduct raged for years. Aware of the damage that had been done to the norms governing debate, senators tried to undo it. In 1828, the Senate sought to eliminate the ambiguity Calhoun had used as an excuse to decline to call Randolph to order, and formally revised the relevant rule "to authorize the presiding officer, or any senator, to call a member to order."[22] However, the Senate is governed not just by its formal rules, but by a combination of norms and precedents as well.[23] Calhoun had set a new norm, and that bell could not be unrung. Over time, the power of the presiding officer to call senators to order faded. The previous question rule was already gone; now, at Calhoun's hand, one of the adjacent norms senators had used to prevent dilatory debate had been eliminated, too.

All of this happened before Calhoun joined the Senate. But when he arrived as a member himself, he was in urgent need of new methods for blocking the majority. It was the middle of the nullification crisis, and his opponents—Jackson and Clay—were seeking to push through a bill authorizing federal troops to collect the tariffs South

Carolina owed. On the Senate floor, Calhoun and his allies railed against what became known as the "Force Bill." But they were powerless to do anything more than talk, and walked out in protest as the bill passed.[24] If Calhoun was going to defy Jackson and the North on behalf of the South and slavery, he was going to need a stronger procedural weapon.

IN 1841, the Whig senators who were working together to block a Senate printing contract probably did not think they were changing the course of Senate history.[25] A half century after the founding, organized obstruction was still rare. But the printing contract was one of the biggest patronage prizes the Senate had to offer, and as the Whigs creatively coordinated to block it (and steer it to their favored printer instead), their colleagues watched with interest.[26]

A few months later, Calhoun deployed their tactics on a much grander scale against his old nemesis, Henry Clay. Combining the Whigs' tactics with his own righteous defense of minority rights, Calhoun waged what was one of the first filibusters in Senate history. Arguably, it was the first true antecedent of the filibuster we know today. While historians have identified a few instances in the five decades between the founding and 1841 where senators spoke at length to delay a measure they opposed, it is the fusion of speechifying with the principle of minority rights that came to define the filibuster and give it its enduring power. That fusion was Calhoun's innovation. At the time, no one called his performance a filibuster. The practice was still so rare that it did not seem to need a name, and it would be another decade before the term entered the Senate lexicon. But a filibuster it was.

Calhoun's inventive spirit was driven by his desire to protect the slave power of the South and the extremely wealthy plantation owners who were his patrons. Clay was advancing a bill to charter the Bank of the United States, which the slave states strenuously opposed. Like many issues at the time that were not explicitly about slavery, such as territorial disputes, tariffs, and navigation rights, the fight over the bank was really about slavery. The South believed the national bank would centralize power in the federal government and strengthen Clay's "American system"—which Calhoun had passionately supported back in his unionist days—leading to an erosion of the slave states' power relative to the North.[27]

Organizing southern senators in opposition, Calhoun deployed them on the floor to make speech after speech against the bill, trying to stall it and back Clay up against the Senate's deadline for summer adjournment. A firsthand account of this filibuster crackles with the excitement of someone who realizes they are witnessing the birth of something new and important, and perhaps a little bit dangerous. The eyewitness was one of Calhoun's allies in the fight, Senator Thomas Hart Benton of Missouri, who recorded how he and his fellow obstructionist senators "became assailants" and "attacked incessantly."[28] One of Benton's early biographers, then-historian Theodore Roosevelt, would later note disapprovingly that Benton and Calhoun were acting "not with any hopes of bettering the bills, but for outside effect, and to annoy their opponents."[29] But Benton found the experience thrilling. "We kept their measures upon the anvil, and hammered them continually: we impaled them against the wall, and stabbed them incessantly," he enthused. Benton recounted how Calhoun's forces rallied friendly media outlets. "*The Globe* newspaper was a powerful ally," Benton recalled, "setting off all we did to the best advantage in strong editorials—and carrying our speeches, fresh and hot, to the people." The battle sparked a feeling of camaraderie among the minority of filibustering senators, even though they had no hope of actually defeating the bill. Their amendments were voted down again and again, but Benton seemed to enjoy every minute. "We felt victorious in the midst of unbroken defeats," he marveled.[30]

After several weeks, Clay, the Great Compromiser, decided that this proto-filibuster was such a severe threat to the Senate that it merited a restoration of the previous question rule, which would allow the majority to vote to end Calhoun's obstructionist "debate" and bring the bill up for a final passage vote. In his manual, Jefferson had warned against superfluous debate, and weeks of pointless delay clearly fit the bill. "Dreadfully harassed by the species of warfare," as Benton described him, Clay had never seen anything like what Calhoun was doing.[31] But when Clay moved to restore the previous question rule, Calhoun erupted. He invoked the loftiest of principles to cast Clay as a tyrant, and himself as the oppressed minority guarding Senate tradition. In full dudgeon, Calhoun decried the previous question motion as a "gag law." He demanded of Clay, "What is the difference, in principle between his [Clay's] gag law and the Alien and Sedition law?"[32] The Alien and Sedition Acts, of course, had empowered the federal government to jail dissidents, while Clay was simply seeking to restore a rule put in place by the Senate itself to end obstructionist debate. But Calhoun answered his own question, claiming that restoring the previous question rule would be "more odious" than the Alien and Sedition Acts.[33] Whipped up by Calhoun, Senator William King of Alabama joined the fray, asking Clay if he intended to introduce the previous question motion. When Clay affirmed that he did, King responded: "I will tell the senator, then, that he may make his arrangements at his boarding house for the winter."[34] Clay initially seemed to have the votes, but Calhoun's fervent opposition took him and his supporters aback. Clay backed down and let the debate continue.[35]

The bank bill eventually passed. It would be another century before the filibuster became powerful enough to reliably block bills altogether. In these early iterations of the filibuster, the majority could usually wait out the minority, who needed to continue occupying the floor for their filibuster to work.[36] Moreover, even as the filibuster emerged, the norm that the majority should eventually carry the day remained strong. As Benton recorded, once the obstructionists finally felt they had made their point, and once Clay had given up on restoring the previous question motion, "the loan bill was then taken up, and proceeded with in a most business style, and quite amicably."[37]

But Calhoun had created a bug in Madison's code. Fifteen years earlier, as vice-president, Calhoun had weakened one of the Senate's central protections against obstruction by undermining the presiding officer's power to call dilatory senators to order. Now he had shown how a determined minority could organize to frustrate and delay the majority. Even though Calhoun had failed to stop the bill, and even though no one knew what to call what they had just witnessed, he had invented the filibuster as we know it today. Equally important to what Calhoun had done was how he did it. While his true motive was protecting slavery and the South's powerful planter class, he had ostensibly unleashed the filibuster on the Senate in the name of something that had a much broader appeal: the principle of minority rights. "For the first time," Senate historian Richard Baker writes, "the principle of minority rights was applied in defense of extended debate."[38]

Madison had passed away in 1836. It did not matter that he had never intended for a minority of senators to be able to block the majority. Nor did it matter that in his decades of writing and correspondence, he'd never elevated unlimited debate as a pillar of the Senate; or that, to the contrary, he had overseen a series of tools to end debate when it became obstructionist, and warned against the dangers of letting a minority exercise a veto over the majority. Madison was gone, and Calhoun saw an opening. He took it, and from then on, naked obstruction in the Senate would be indelibly linked to higher principle.

WHILE HE CLAIMED TO be a champion of minority rights, Calhoun deployed his concern for the underdog only to help the overdog. Dubbing Calhoun "the Marx of the Master Class," the prominent twentieth-century historian Richard Hofstadter points out that his ideas were "designed specifically to protect a vested interest of considerable power."[39] Calhoun was the foremost political leader of the closest thing America had to an aristocracy, deriving his power from the support of the planter class of the antebellum South. By using that power to protect slavery, he prolonged the suffering of the most oppressed minority imaginable. For Calhoun, minority rights were a cloak for the interests of the wealthy, the powerful, and most of all, the white supremacist.

When the principle of minority rights conflicted with the slave power's interests, the slave power took precedence for Calhoun. Without hesitation, he would turn against minority rights with all the vigor and skill he used to champion them when they served the cause of slavery. In his 1841 filibuster against the bank bill, Calhoun had decried the previous question motion as an attempt to impose a "gag rule" on the minority. But years before, Calhoun had marshaled all his persuasive powers to urge the Senate to adopt an *actual* gag rule to protect slavery. In 1836, abolitionists were petitioning Congress for emancipation in the District of Columbia, where it had exclusive jurisdiction. To prevent the Senate from hearing their petitions, Calhoun proposed a rule that would bar the Senate from hearing not just the abolitionist petitions related to the District but all abolitionist petitions. Speaking on the Senate floor, Calhoun deployed his usual soaring rhetoric, but this time against minority rights, arguing that allowing the abolitionists to be heard would "sacrifice the Constitutional rights of this body."[40]

Calhoun won the fight to gag the abolitionists, but larger shifts were working against the slave states. By the 1830s, Britain had abolished slavery in its colonies. In America, the northern, industrialized economic model was proving superior to the southern, agrarian model. And westward expansion continued to force the issue of the balance of power in Congress. The moral, economic, and political winds all seemed to be blowing against the South. While racism was, of course, an oppressive fact of daily life everywhere in America, the rest of the country had little incentive to maintain slavery. For slavery's defenders, it was becoming increasingly difficult to explain why the entire country should continue tolerating an evil that no longer seemed necessary.

Amid these trying conditions, Calhoun did something no political leader of comparable stature had done before, and recast slavery from a necessary evil to a "positive good." In a speech on the Senate floor, Calhoun argued that slavery provided for racial harmony: "The two races have long lived in peace and prosperity, and, if not disturbed, would long continue so to live," he said. Slavery improved the lives of enslaved people, he contended: "There is no example in history in which a savage people, such as their ancestors were when brought into the country, have ever advanced in the same period so rapidly in numbers and improvement." Slavery was not just good, he argued, it was the highest condition people of African descent had ever experienced: "Never before has the black race of Central Africa, from the dawn of history to the present day, attained a condition so civilized and improved, not only physically, but morally and intellectually," he declared on the Senate floor. His case was so thorough, he also rebutted the argument, in wide circulation at the time, that slavery degraded the white race: "The white or European race has not degenerated. It has kept pace with its brethren in other sections of the Union where slavery does not exist," he contended. In summary, Calhoun said, "the relation now existing in the slaveholding states between the two [races] is, instead of an evil, a good—a positive good."[41]

As Calhoun sought to strengthen the South's position, the Senate's durable ethic of majority rule continued to pose a stubborn challenge. The expectation that after the minority had their say, the majority should rule persisted even among Calhoun's fellow filibusterers. In 1848, Calhoun and a group of southerners were filibustering a bill to organize a territorial government in Oregon because it barred slavery. For decades, the question of whether slavery should be expanded to new states and territories had been the most contentious issue in the country, in large part because the addition of senators from free states would overwhelm the South in the Senate.

The filibuster against the Oregon bill was fierce. But once it became clear that its proponents had secured a majority, the southerners yielded. As they explained, forcing a delay and applying pressure were acceptable tactics, but blocking the will of the majority was still a bridge too far—even for them. Senator William King of Alabama said that yielding to the majority "would comport better with the dignity of the Senate, with their standing in the country, and with public sentiment, than by persisting in opposing this resolution." Senator Thomas Rusk of Texas agreed, pointing out that "according to the course which had heretofore been pursued in the Senate, when a majority, a clearly ascertained majority, had agreed upon a measure, it was proper that he should yield, that they might have the opportunity of passing it, and assuming to God and their country the responsibility of the act."[42] Senator Henry Foote of Mississippi, another participant in the Oregon filibuster, said that he "felt authorized to declare that they [the minority] were now willing to yield and let the majority take the responsibility."[43] The filibuster was dropped, and the Oregon bill passed.

This acquiescence to majority rule, enduring even as obstruction rose, was echoed by another prominent filibusterer, Senator Thomas Hart Benton, who had documented the 1841 fight against the bank bill with such élan. Benton agreed with the prevailing wisdom that once debate had gone on for long enough, the Senate should be able to end it—although he had his own ideas for how to do it. In Benton's view, the British House of Commons had found "the best corrective" for obstruction in "its refusal to hear a member further when they are tired of him." He explained that in Parliament, when a member becomes tiresome, "a significant scraping and coughing warns the annoying speaker when he should cease: if the warning is not taken, a tempest drowns his voice: when he appeals to the chair, the chair recommends him to yield to the temper of the House." This method of ending debate "falls with just, and relentless effect upon the loquacious members, who mistake volubility for eloquence, who delight themselves while annoying the House [of Parliament]," Benton concluded approvingly.[44]

But even as his erstwhile allies embraced majority rule, Calhoun raged against it. He never accepted majority rule because he simply no longer believed in it. When his allies yielded on the Oregon bill, Calhoun complained that they were snatching defeat from the jaws of victory by standing down on the filibuster. "By the rules of the Senate, the bill was lost, and the majority well knew that," he groused.[45] Toward the end of his life he penned a treatise that was published posthumously, in 1851. Titled *A Disquisition on Government*, it laid out a theory of minority rule, a comprehensive alternative to Madison's vision. Calhoun's system relied on a concept he called "concurrent majorities," whereby all state legislatures could exercise veto power over every federal law, turning the United States into a loose confederation of nullifying states. Federal laws that survived the states' gauntlet would thereby demonstrate that they were supported by majorities in all states—hence "concurrent" majorities. Calhoun was not shy about his true aim, stating outright that the goal of his system was "to give to each interest or portion of the community a negative on the others."[46]

When Webster had accused Calhoun of wanting to return to the Articles of Confederation, he had hit the mark. In Federalist 75, explaining that requiring "more than the majority" to pass laws leads to "impotence, perplexity, and disorder," Hamilton had likened the Articles to foreign legislatures like the Diet in Poland, which he saw as embodying the dysfunction the Framers sought to avoid.[47] In his *Disquisition*, Calhoun cited the glacial Polish Diet as a success story for his system of concurrent majorities, providing "proof conclusive both of its practicability and its compatibility with the power and permanency of government."[48]

To Calhoun, the unworkability of minority rule was its selling point. In Calhoun's view, Madison's system had not given the minority sufficient power to defy the majority; one section of the

Disquisition is titled "Constitutional Limitations Insufficient to Check the Numerical Majority." But insufficiency was in the eye of the beholder. Calhoun's overriding goal was to preserve slavery and protect the planter class. By the time Calhoun wrote the *Disquisition* it had become evident that the limited minority protections the Framers had built were too weak to hold off the North's superior economic model and the creeping power of abolition. While the Senate's system of equal representation enhanced slave states' political power, Calhoun "did not consider this overrepresentation sufficient to guarantee the interests of slaveholders," writes James H. Read, a leading Calhoun scholar.[49] Madison's system had guaranteed the minority a voice, but a voice was not enough. To preserve slavery, Calhoun wanted a veto.

ONE DAY, America would find itself with a Senate where the minority wielded a veto over the majority, but Calhoun would not live to see it. It would take several generations, and new reactionary leaders, to get there. Indeed, it would be nearly a century before the Senate saw another obstructionist who could match Calhoun in stature and influence, and advance the power of the minority as much as he had. But in the meantime, workaday gridlock continued to tug steadily at the remaining restraints in the Senate. In the second half of the nineteenth century, filibustering began to be used with greater frequency: an authoritative study by political scientist Gregory Koger found a rise in the number of filibusters directly or indirectly related to slavery from the 1840s to the 1860s.[50]

As the use of the tool grew, so did the need to give it a name. In 1852 one senator thought another was talking for too long and accused him of "*cacoethes loquendi*." Somehow, it didn't stick. Historians disagree about exactly when the word "filibuster" first came into regular use, but it appears to have occurred in the 1850s and 1860s. In that period, American pirates were striking out for adventure along the Gulf Coast and into the Caribbean. They were known as "filibusters," derived from the Dutch *vrijbuiter*, which translates into English as "freebooter" and became Americanized as filibuster.[51]

The rising tide of obstruction took a toll on the Senate as the institution entered a period of steady decline. The period was marked by a shift of important action off the Senate floor and out of public view. When the most consequential questions of the day had hinged on the outcomes of Senate debates, those debates had often been substantive and soaring—what we like to think of as a high point of representative democracy—and the Senate floor had been the center of the political universe. But as the century wore on, senators began engaging in debate for debate's sake, "taking obvious pride in their sometimes extraordinary garrulousness," according to Baker, the Senate historian, and Neil MacNeil, the longtime Senate correspondent. In the "press and on the Senate floor, there was much talk of the 'degradation' of the Senate," they write in their indispensable history, *The American Senate*.[52]

The decline in quality of Senate debate coincided with a sharp increase in corruption.[53] In the Credit Mobilier scandal of 1874, the Union Pacific Railroad created a fake company and gave shares in it to senators, some of whom became millionaires.[54] The power of Senate committees rose during this period, moving much of the action off the floor and into committee rooms.[55] This made it easier for the rich to buy influence. Committee chairs wield dictatorial power over their committees, so bribing a committee chair effectively bought their entire committee, which controlled all legislation under the policy area of jurisdiction. Committees were also subject to less scrutiny: public hearings were irregular and hard to follow, and rarely attended by reporters. Nor were there public transcripts of committee proceedings, as there were for Senate floor debates.

By the end of the nineteenth century, the Senate had become fully branded in the public mind as the inscrutable and unaccountable redoubt of millionaires and monopolists. It was the target of editorialists' anger and the butt of cartoonists' mockery. The Senate's poor reputation crossed over into popular culture, inspiring the novel that defined the era.[56] Mark Twain's *The Gilded Age* was based in part on Twain's experience working for Senator William Stewart of Nevada, and one of its villains is based on Senator Samuel Pomeroy, who was busted paying off a state legislator in his native Kansas for a favor.[57]

Within the Senate, reformers believed rampant obstruction was contributing to the institution's decline and tried to reverse it.[58] Following in Clay's footsteps, the list of Senate reformers during the period reads like a "who's who" of the most prominent senators of the era: Stephen Douglas, Lewis Cass, Charles Sumner, Nelson Aldrich, and Henry Cabot Lodge all backed reform to restrict debate and reduce obstruction.[59] But in a rolling collective action problem, obstructionists were always able to derail reformers. As the leading scholars of the filibuster, historians Sarah Binder and Steven Smith, put it, "absent widely shared political incentives to revamp Senate rules, the exceedingly high threshold for change in the Senate foreclosed any real reform."[60]

Reformers did succeed in eliminating a wide range of delaying tactics that were softer targets than the filibuster. Obstructionists who lacked Calhoun's virtuosity often relied on chintzy tactics like disappearing quorums, disputes over rulings from the chair, and motions to postpone—all of which were eliminated by reformers.[61] The disappearing quorum, for example, was downright goofy. A quorum is the number of senators who must be present for a vote to be held. Under Senate rules, a majority forms a quorum, so if there are one hundred members in the Senate, fifty-one have to be present before a vote can be held. A *disappearing* quorum is exactly what it sounds like: when senators saw that they were going to lose a vote, they would bolt from the floor, causing the quorum to "disappear." By rule, the vote would be scotched. The use of this tactic forced the bill's proponents to ensure that a quorum was present on the floor for the duration of a vote, a difficult feat when senators liked to wander on and off the floor at will, and when there were no party leaders to coordinate schedules, no telephones to track down senators, and no spare staffers to fan out across the city and pull them from their homes or watering holes or mistresses' houses. To end disappearing quorums, reformers empowered the sergeant at arms, who is essentially the Senate's police chief, to "compel the presence" of absent senators by tracking them down himself. When this proved insufficiently intimidating, the sergeant was empowered to arrest senators if they resisted.[62]

But the filibuster had something going for it that these plainly ridiculous tactics did not: Calhoun's model made it easy for obstructionists to cloak themselves in high principles like debate and minority rights. This made the filibuster the hardest challenge for reformers. But at the end of the century, they came close to eliminating it.

It was 1891, and in what would be a regular occurrence in the coming decades, southern senators were filibustering a civil rights bill. Senator Henry Cabot Lodge of Massachusetts, who would become a giant of the Senate, had proposed a bill that would put the power to monitor elections for voter intimidation tactics, like poll taxes, into the hands of federal judges, thereby taking it away from the local elected officials who were the frontline enforcers of Jim Crow.[63] As the filibuster against his bill dragged on, Lodge and his allies grew frustrated. As Clay had in 1841, another leading light of the Senate rose to restore the previous question rule and reinstate the power to end obstructive debate. Senator Nelson Aldrich of Rhode Island was no one's idea of a wild-eyed radical. A creature of the East Coast establishment and one of the most influential senators of his time, he would write the plan that created the Federal Reserve and sponsor the Sixteenth Amendment, which established the federal income tax. His daughter, Abby, would marry John D. Rockefeller. At a time when the Senate did not have formal leaders, Aldrich was regarded as a de facto leader of the Republicans.

A founder and defender of institutions, Aldrich believed obstruction was harming the Senate.[64] When a procedural motion to advance his bill to restore the previous question rule came up for a vote, it passed 36 to 32, putting the Senate on record in favor of giving the majority the power to end debate.[65] Confident of victory, Aldrich and his allies adjourned for the weekend. As the *New York Times* reported at the time, they spent Sunday boasting that Aldrich's bill "was sure to pass."[66]

But Aldrich's opponents used their weekend differently. They "spent Sunday in planning a coup," according to the *Washington Post*.[67] Word got around that Aldrich had let one of the senators in his camp leave town without securing a "pair," or proxy, which would have ensured that his vote could still be counted even if he was not physically present. On Monday, Aldrich's opponents pounced, carrying one ally, Senator Daniel Voorhees of Indiana, "from his sick bed to the Capitol," while another, Senator James Eustis of Louisiana, "was brought from home," the *Post* reported. "Such action, it should be added, was never contemplated by the Republicans," the story noted dryly. Aldrich's opponents sensed that their side had the numbers. One of them gained control of the floor on an anodyne topic, then quickly gave the floor to another, who moved to call up a bill he had pending. If the vote to move to his bill passed, it would knock Aldrich's off the floor.

Aldrich had not been expecting any important votes until later, and his allies—including the one who had left town—were not all present. But his opponents were, and they won the vote to scuttle Aldrich's previous question bill by a single vote. Aldrich was unable to get his bill back to the floor, and his reform proposal was defeated, along with the Lodge bill to combat poll taxes. That was the closest the Senate would get to reforming its rules or passing civil rights for decades. After a narrow escape, the filibuster passed into the twentieth century unimpeded.

The defeat would prove portentous in another way, too. From its beginnings under Calhoun through the nineteenth century, the filibuster rarely stopped bills, usually only delaying them.[68] Obstruction was getting worse, but for the most part, bills still passed or failed based on whether they could muster a majority. Despite all Calhoun's effort, the minority had still not found a way to reliably stop bills the majority wanted to pass. That was about to change.

Chapter Three

DAWN OF THE SUPERMAJORITY

In Joseph Heller's absurdist masterpiece, *Catch-22*, the law that lets soldiers do whatever they want is the law that lets them do it. In the modern Senate, the rule that empowers the filibuster to stop bills is the rule that was supposed to weaken it. It is called Rule 22, and it is what Republicans used to block the 2013 background-checks bill in the name of further debate, even as they refused to debate it. Early in the twentieth century, well-intentioned reformers created Rule 22 as a tool for ending debate, but southerners bent on preserving white supremacy subsequently reinvented it as a weapon of mass obstruction. The story of that reinvention is the story of the rise of the modern Senate—of how it became paralyzed by gridlock, and how a chamber founded as a majority-rule body came to require a supermajority for everything it does.

The story starts with a guy named Fighting Bob.

In 1917, Senate obstruction triggered a historic wave of public anger. With German U-boats harassing American merchant ships, President Woodrow Wilson called on Congress to quickly pass a measure arming American vessels. On March 1, the House passed it overwhelmingly. But the Senate faced an immovable deadline to adjourn on March 3, which would wipe the legislative slate clean and force Congress to start over. Taking advantage of the time crunch, a small group of antiwar senators led by Senator Robert "Fighting Bob" LaFollette of Wisconsin filibustered Wilson's merchant ship bill for two days, past the deadline for adjournment.[1] The reaction was explosive. "Armed Ship Bill Beaten," blared a banner headline in the *New York Times*. "Without Remedy Until the Senate Amends Its Rules," it continued, in one of the few known instances of a banner headline about Senate rules.[2]

Wilson issued a blistering statement: "A little group of willful men, representing no opinion but their own, have rendered the great government of the United States helpless and contemptible." He demanded that the Senate reconvene immediately and reform itself. "The Senate has no rules by which debate can be limited or brought to an end. . . . The only remedy is that the rules of the Senate shall be so altered that it can act."[3] Responding to Wilson's call with alacrity, the Senate came back into session the same day the *Times* headline ran. Notably, LaFollette was neither a southerner nor a segregationist—he was a progressive pacifist. But his two-day filibuster against a bill widely viewed as tantamount to a declaration of war, proposed by a president who had won reelection by promising to keep America out of war, led to the biggest public backlash the Senate has ever seen.

With senators being burned in effigy across the country, the Senate responded to Wilson's call to change the institution's rules. A committee was quickly formed to recommend curbs on obstructionist debate. It promptly recommended a change that would, for the first time since the previous question motion was eliminated in 1806, provide senators with a tool to end filibusters. It was called Senate Rule 22, and it passed easily on a vote of 76 to 3.[4]

Rule 22 is similar to the previous question motion. It allows senators to call a vote to end debate—to tell the kids to wrap it up. In Senate parlance, that vote is known as "cloture," a derivative of "closure." But there is one major difference between Rule 22 and the previous question rule. Whereas the previous question rule had allowed a majority to end debate, Rule 22 set the threshold at a supermajority of two-thirds (it was later lowered to the three-fifths we know today). The decision to set the threshold at a supermajority was a close call; a majority of senators on the committee that devised Rule 22 wanted to set it at a majority.[5] But they compromised, a reasonable thing to do at a time when Senate norms still compelled minorities to eventually yield to the majority, as when Calhoun's allies had yielded on the Oregon bill. When Rule 22 was created only a handful of filibusters had ever succeeded in stopping bills altogether; of those few successful filibusters, a supermajority threshold seemed as if it would have been sufficient to end many of them.[6] It certainly seemed as if it would have been sufficient to cut off the most recent filibuster the Senate had witnessed. Senator Henry Cabot Lodge, the future chairman of the Senate Foreign Relations Committee and a supporter of Wilson's ship-arming bill, had counted seventy-seven votes for the bill.[7]

The committee that wrote Rule 22 was explicit about its intent, calling it a tool to "terminate successful filibustering."[8] It would later be repurposed by obstructionists, but at the time, every senator who voted for it "did so with a clear understanding that he was voting for an enforceable rule to close debate," according to a 1949 Senate report.[9] In theory, it was simply a procedural tool the majority could reach for when filibusters became excessive. Writing in 1940, the filibuster historian Franklin Burdette described Rule 22 as "the most important potential and actual curtailment of filibustering ever undertaken in the Senate."[10] It was not as strong as the reforms that Henry Clay, Nelson Aldrich, and other leading lights of the Senate had called for. But at the time, it seemed like it would be strong enough.

It was not to be. To the southern senators bent on preserving white supremacy, writing a supermajority threshold into Senate rules was like waving a red flag in front of a bull.[11] During the Constitutional Convention, the southern states had sought a supermajority threshold so they could block legislation that threatened slavery, but had been denied. In his time, Calhoun had tried to build the filibuster into a veto for the minority, but it required senators to continue filibustering indefinitely and defy norms compelling the minority to yield, which they were usually unwilling to do. Suddenly, at the height of the Jim Crow era, a supermajority threshold that could be applied to any legislation was on the books and within their grasp. There was the minor detail that the rule was designed to end obstruction, not empower it, and figuring out how to get around that would be a challenge. But it was one to which the sons of the South were prepared to rise.

AROUND THIS TIME, the Senate's bloc of southern white supremacists faced the prospect that if they did not build new weapons of obstruction—fast—civil rights bills were going to pass. Occupying about twenty Senate seats depending on the year, they had settled in as the federal government's in-house enforcers of Jim Crow. But between the wars, broad majorities of the public and Congress had coalesced around the need to take federal action on two civil rights issues: ending lynching and eliminating poll taxes. Bills to combat both were supported by majorities in the House and by presidents of both parties. In 1922, 1937, and 1940, anti-lynching bills passed the House and had presidents at the other end of Pennsylvania Avenue willing to sign them. The pattern was similar on poll taxes. In 1942, 1944, and 1946, bills to end poll taxes passed the House, and at least one of them (and possibly more) had presidential support.[12]

On at least two occasions, these bills also appeared to have the support of a majority of the Senate. More than a majority of senators were on record supporting at least one of the anti–poll tax bills and more than sixty senators supported at least one of the anti-lynching bills.[13] The reforms contemplated here were not sweeping, and their hypothetical ramifications are impossible to know. Still, some of the anti–poll tax bills were comparable to the first post-Reconstruction civil rights bill that passed in 1957 and which led to a series of stronger bills within eight years. The American people were ready, too: Gallup found 72 percent of Americans supporting federal anti-lynching laws in 1937 and 63 percent of Americans supporting anti–poll tax laws in 1941.[14] There was no reason to wait decades while millions of Americans suffered, except that a white supremacist minority in the Senate wanted to.

As it had done for Calhoun, the desire to continue oppressing black Americans spurred the southern senators of the Jim Crow era to innovate. They needed to improve on what Calhoun had built. Even deploying every tactic in Calhoun's repertoire against the civil rights bills coming over from the House, the most they would have been able to do was delay. But Rule 22 gave them an opportunity to turn the filibuster into something it had never been before: a tool powerful enough to allow a Senate minority to stop bills altogether.

Subverting the intent of Rule 22, southerners transformed it into a new, higher hurdle that the minority could throw in front of a bill's path to passage. I want to emphasize this point, because it's an important one: Rule 22 did not raise the threshold for bills to pass. To this day, the threshold for final passage in the Senate is technically still a majority. But in southerners' hands, Rule 22 became a way to block bills from ever reaching that final passage vote. Rule 22 had set the vote for cloture at a supermajority threshold on the theory that reasonable senators could agree to end debate when it soured from persuasion to obstruction. But if that reasonable cloture vote could be recast as something toxic, and combined with the other modes of pressure southerners had at their disposal, the supermajority procedural hurdle would become nearly impossible to clear.

During this period, southerners reversed the onus of the filibuster. Before the introduction of Rule 22, the majority could simply wait out a filibustering minority. It was tedious, and it created headaches for the majority, but it usually worked. After Rule 22, southern filibusterers could demand that the majority prove it had the votes to end debate by winning a vote on cloture. If cloture had remained the reasonable act of responsible senators, as its authors intended, this would not have been a problem. But during the Jim Crow era, southerners effectively branded cloture as a gross violation of high Senate principle, and backed up their soft-power appeal with more aggressive means of persuasion. As a result, it became nearly impossible for the advocates of a bill to move forward when the southern bloc deployed itself against them. Cloture became the Senate version of Chekov's gun: since it was there, the majority was expected to use it. It would take decades and a series of further innovations for the silent, absentee filibusters of today to emerge. But after the introduction of Rule 22, it slowly became the norm that if the majority wasn't going to force a cloture vote, the minority didn't have to hold the floor. If the majority wanted to end a filibuster, it was now on them to produce the votes for cloture.

This shift in power was not a foregone conclusion. It hinged on making the cloture vote toxic, which required overturning the long-standing ethic that the minority should eventually yield to the majority. To replace that deferential standard with one better suited to their purposes, southerners deployed the "gag rule" rhetoric that Calhoun had first hurled at Clay. The rhetoric had never disappeared, but southerners deployed it with renewed ferocity. In one civil rights debate after another through the 1930s and 1940s, southern senators elevated the idea of "unlimited debate" to a foundational principle akin to the First Amendment. "There is no greater bulwark of constitutional government than is [sic] freedom of debate in the Senate of the United States," Senator Richard Russell of Georgia declared on the Senate floor in 1948.[15] "Free speech and the Constitution of the United States won a memorable victory," Senator Tom Connally of Texas said, as he celebrated the successful defeat of a 1942 bill to end poll taxes. At the time, Texas was one of eight states that still had poll taxes on the books. But Connally dismissed the poll tax itself as a "mere incident."[16] The real issue, he contended, was protecting the minority's supposedly sacred right of unlimited debate.[17]

It is certainly possible that senators refused to vote for cloture out of a sincere commitment to the principle of unlimited debate. But there are three main reasons it is difficult to credit that explanation. First, the senators who defeated bills in the name of unlimited debate were not seeking to debate the bills further. The bills had already been debated to the point of exhaustion, often for months. Whenever southerners defeated cloture—thereby winning the right to continue debating a bill—they made sure the bill was immediately pulled from the floor. That is what happened to the anti–poll tax bill that Connally boasted about defeating in the name of free speech, for example. Neither Connally nor his allies had any interest in debating the bill; they just wanted to kill it.[18]

Second, the only issue where voting for cloture was consistently portrayed as a violation of Senate tradition was civil rights. Between the advent of cloture in 1917 and 1940, the Senate held thirteen cloture votes. On seven of them, a majority or more of the Senate voted for cloture, but never on civil rights. Four of those seven votes achieved the two-thirds threshold necessary to invoke cloture: seventy-eight senators voted to invoke cloture on the Versailles Treaty, sixty-eight on the World Court Protocol, sixty-five on a banking bill, and fifty-five on a Prohibition bill.[19] On these non–civil rights votes, between a quarter and half of the southern caucus voted for cloture. Thus, even when cloture was not invoked, a majority of the Senate, including many southerners, seemed perfectly comfortable with the principle of it. But on civil rights, cloture became apostasy. A 1938 vote on an anti-lynching bill, for instance, "presented the interesting spectacle of approximately two-thirds of the Senators ready to vote for the measure but less than a majority willing to close debate," according to Burdette, the filibuster historian.[20] The first time a southern filibuster against civil rights was broken was in 1964. In the eighty-seven years between the end of Reconstruction and 1964, the only bills that were stopped by filibusters were civil rights bills. On the rare occasion a non–civil rights bill ran into a filibuster, it eventually passed.[21] Only on civil rights did cloture become a matter of grand principle.

Finally, persuasive though they were, southerners' rhetorical campaigns on behalf of minority rights were backed up by raw power. The South was by far the most powerful bloc in the Senate, with its members possessing the dangerous combination of institutional authority, longevity, and long memories. The South had been solidly Democratic since the Civil War, with most southern states operating as single-party fiefdoms. Senate seats were tantamount to lifetime appointments for southern Democrats. In the Senate, influence lies in the committees, and at the time, committee assignments were based strictly on seniority. Southerners' lifetime tenure allowed them to rise to the helms of the most important committees. One senator described the committee system as an "interlocking directorate of southerners," able to control everything a senator needed to be successful.[22] If the South asked for another senator's help to defeat civil rights on cloture, and even went to the trouble of offering "minority rights" and "unlimited debate" as more palatable rationales for those who might be uncomfortable opposing civil rights on the merits, it was a bad career move to say no.

From the time Rule 22 was invented, southern senators used their combination of procedural savvy, rhetorical gloss, and thinly veiled threat to transform Rule 22 from a tactic to "terminate successful filibustering" into one that made the filibuster capable of stopping bills altogether. But the push for civil rights in the outside world kept growing stronger. If the southerners were going to continue preserving white supremacy, even with this powerful new weapon at their disposal, they were going to need a steady hand to guide them.

AMONG THE DAUNTING, craggy visages of the southern bloc, one face intimidated more than any other: that of Senator Richard Brevard Russell of Georgia. In 1948, Russell, a Democrat, believed the sitting president, Harry Truman—also a Democrat—was too liberal on civil rights, and sought to block him from securing the nomination as their party's standard-bearer. Russell was the recognized leader of the southern Democrats, and while his bloc was finding its fit within the party increasingly uncomfortable, he was not going to cede control without a fight.

At the time, the ideological composition of the parties looked very different than it does today. There were comparable numbers of liberals and conservatives in each party, and the most conservative members of the Senate were Russell and the southern Democrats. They were populists: they wanted to redistribute wealth to white, working-class people, while keeping black people oppressed. They were ardent New Dealers, and key allies of President Franklin Roosevelt. But the price of their support was cutting huge numbers of black Americans out of major New Deal programs, such as the G.I. Bill, the federally subsidized home loans that white families used to buy their houses in the postwar boom, and, to a large extent, Social Security.[23] While millions of white Americans used those benefits as a springboard to the middle class, southern Democrats made sure black Americans were left behind, exacerbating a massive racial wealth gap that continues to this day.[24] But even though black Americans benefited from the New Deal far less than white Americans, the economic recovery under Roosevelt generally helped them. During his administration black Americans began to shift away from the party of Lincoln, and toward Democrats.

Russell and the southern Democrats did not want the Democratic Party to court black voters. Truman, while vacillating a good deal on civil rights, was significantly more progressive. In 1945, he and Russell had clashed over legislation governing a federal commission to combat employment discrimination, called the Fair Employment Practices Commission. Roosevelt had created it in 1941 via executive order, but it required legislation to be made permanent. In 1945, Truman backed legislation to create a permanent FEPC, but was blocked by Russell and Senate Democrats—another civil rights bill defeated by a southern filibuster. In 1946, Truman appointed a presidential commission to study civil rights. Its landmark report, *To Secure These Rights*, was issued in 1947, and Truman sent a special message to Congress backing many of its recommendations.

Tentative as these steps were, to Russell they amounted to a dramatic lurch to the left.[25]

Russell's efforts to block Truman came to a head at the Democratic Convention in the summer of 1948. Since convention delegates are mostly controlled by state-level party machines run by governors and other local officials, Russell had little actual power. But to demonstrate the South's opposition to Truman, he allowed his own name to be placed in nomination. Russell had little hope of winning (he would run for president in earnest in 1952), but he wanted to send a message. He did, winning all of the South's delegates—about a quarter of the total, and enough to demonstrate that the party was not united behind its nominee.[26]

Meanwhile, in an un-air-conditioned Philadelphia convention hall where temperatures reached the nineties, a fight was unfolding over how strong the civil rights plank in the platform should be. Russell and the southerners wanted it to be as weak as possible, which meant simply keeping the same thin plank the party had backed for years. At first, it looked like they were going to win. But on the last day of the convention, the young, telegenic mayor of Minneapolis, Hubert Humphrey, came to the podium and confronted the South. "To those who say that we are rushing this issue of civil rights, I say to them we are 172 years late," Humphrey declared. As the southerners fumed, Humphrey issued a challenge: "The time has arrived in America for the Democratic Party to get out of the shadow of states' rights and to walk forthrightly into the bright sunshine of human rights."[27] In what the *New Republic* described as "the most sweeping change made in a Democratic platform since Repeal [of Prohibition]," the delegates rallied behind Humphrey and replaced the weak civil rights plank with a stronger one.[28] In protest, the Mississippi delegation and half of the Alabama delegation walked out of the convention, later forming the Dixiecrat Party and nominating Strom Thurmond for president; in November, Thurmond carried four states, all southern. It would be several decades before the parties fully sorted themselves by ideology, with conservatives migrating to the GOP and liberals to the Democrats. But 1948 marked the end of the "solid South" Democrats had enjoyed since Reconstruction.[29]

Despite the divisions, the convention was a success. Around 1:45 a.m. on the last night, Truman took the stage. Lagging in the polls, he surprised a dispirited audience that was ready to give up on him by rallying them against the Republican-led Congress. The Constitution empowers the president to call special sessions of Congress, and Truman availed himself, calling one and demanding that Republicans use it to pass his agenda. "They can do this job in 15 days, if they want to do it," he said.[30]

When the special session convened, Republicans brought up a bill to end poll taxes, which they and Truman supported but southern Democrats opposed. In response, southern Democrats "immediately aligned themselves for perhaps the most determined filibuster in history," the *New York Times* reported. Russell, their leader, brushed aside the support of a president of his own party and vowed to fight the bill "to the limit."[31] He did, and won. But Truman got what he needed out of the session, politically. Since Congress didn't pass anything during the special session, Truman labeled it the "do nothing Congress" and the phrase caught on. Truman rode a wave of public anger at this Republican Congress, which had tried to deliver him a bill ending poll taxes but been blocked by a Democratic filibuster, to one of the biggest upsets in American political history.[32]

RICHARD RUSSELL WAS a lonely man. His one major regret was that he never married. But as he claimed his father told him, "He who travels, travels fastest alone."[33] Russell lived by himself, taking up residence at one point in the Woodner apartment building.[34] A midcentury marvel in the Mount Pleasant neighborhood of Washington, DC, tucked between the central artery of Sixteenth Street and the green expanse of Rock Creek Park, the Woodner was hailed as a "city within a city" when it opened in 1951, complete with a cocktail lounge, a grocery store, a restaurant with views of the park, and "sun decks for sunbathing and starlight dancing."[35] Men in tuxedos and women in sparkling gowns roamed the hallways. When Jayne Mansfield and Louis Armstrong performed at the nearby Carter Barron amphitheater, they stayed at the Woodner.[36]

But starlight dancing was not for Russell. To those who knew him, his work was his love. A handsome man with an aquiline nose and a patrician gaze, he had little in the way of a social life and few friends. He "turned down scores of dinner and cocktail invitations from women who considered him one of the most eligible bachelors in the nation's capital," according to his biographer, Gilbert Fite. Instead, he devoted his weekends to the stacks of books he brought home from the Capitol, where the librarian occasionally had to remind him to return those that were overdue.[37]

Russell ate breakfast most mornings in the Senate dining room, arriving at his office by 9 a.m. In the evening, his appointments usually ended around seven o'clock, at which point he'd pour himself a drink from the bottle of Jack Daniel's he kept in his drawer. His staff, who admired Russell but were not close to him, wished he would get married so he'd leave the office earlier.[38] His favorite dinner spot was O'Donnell's Seafood Grill on E Street, where he would eat alone at the counter before heading home to his books. If there was a baseball game on, he'd try to catch it—he was a fan of the Washington Senators and would inundate friends with statistics.[39] Sometimes he felt that he drank too much and would occasionally tell acquaintances that he was back "on the wagon." He paid his staff at the low end of the scale set by the Senate, and when he gave to charity, it was usually less than ten dollars.[40]

Russell held no formal leadership role among Senate Democrats. He "could have been elected majority leader had he chosen to seek the office," Senator Robert Byrd recounted in his history of the Senate.[41] But at a time when the leader was little more than a figurehead, it was not a job worth pursuing—and anyway, Russell controlled who got it and what they were able to do with it. An unmatched parliamentarian, he knew the Senate's rules and levers of power like no one else. He was the "high priest of the legendary Senate Establishment," as the *Saturday Evening Post* described him in a 1965 profile.[42] But Russell's real power came from his status as the leader of the Democrats' southern caucus.

White supremacy was not an avocation for Russell, it was his life's purpose. "White supremacy and racial segregation were to him cardinal principles for good and workable human relationships," according to his biographer.[43] Russell did not miss a chance to advance his cause. On the Senate floor, Russell argued against racial intermarriage on the basis that it would lead to "miscegenation" and a "mongrel race."[44] He opposed integration in every arena, arguing that integrating the armed forces, for instance, was "sure to increase the numbers of men who will be disabled through communicable diseases."[45] Russell wrote and proposed a bill to provide financial incentives for black Americans to leave the South. Since southern states had much higher black populations, proportionally, than states in any other region, Russell argued that relocating black Americans elsewhere would "assist in equalizing our racial problem."[46] Pressed about his views on race by *Time* magazine, Russell conceded that there are "some very distinguished Negroes," but added that "whether they are entitled to the credit, or whether the white people are entitled to the credit, is something I have never weighed."[47] His racism was laced with threat. Since a burning cross atop Georgia's Stone Mountain had heralded the twentieth-century revival of the Ku Klux Klan, Russell's meaning was clear when he said, "Should some real menace from the negro present itself, I still believe that the white manhood not only of Georgia, but the entire South, would rise en masse immediately and again assert itself."[48] Russell cast white supremacy in the same terms that President John F. Kennedy would later cast freedom, professing that he was "willing to go as far and make as great a sacrifice to preserve and insure white supremacy in the social, economic and political life of our state as any man."[49] He summed up his philosophy in the belief that "any southern white man worth a pinch of salt would give his all to maintain white supremacy."[50] And he backed up his words with action, filibustering more civil rights bills than anyone from the 1930s through the 1960s.[51]

As Russell sat alone in his impersonally furnished apartment with his whiskey and his books, much of what he read about the march of civil rights disturbed him. It was not only black "agitators" calling for reform—even members of the white southern elite were resigning themselves to it. In July 1948, the influential Ralph McGill of the *Atlanta Journal-Constitution* wrote in an editorial that civil rights and integration were inevitable. Calling on southerners to "face another fact, which is uncomfortable to many," McGill contended that "civil rights measures are coming in one form or another." All the South could do, he concluded, was to "put our own houses in order."[52]

Russell's own allies were not helping the cause. The ham-handed use of the filibuster by other southern senators had begun to make the South look bad. The less sophisticated members of the southern caucus did not seem to understand that the first rule of filibustering on behalf of white supremacy was that there was no filibuster on behalf of white supremacy—only principled stands to protect "minority rights" and "unlimited debate." Senator Theodore Bilbo of Mississippi, author of the 1947 book *Take Your Choice: Separation or Mongrelization*, had a habit of saying things on the Senate floor such as, "Once the flat-nosed Ethiopian, like the camel, gets his proboscis under the tent, he will overthrow the established order of our Saxon civilization."[53] On another occasion Bilbo claimed that "there is a certain class of Kike Jews in New York, organized with the CIO and the Negroes."[54] These were unacceptable violations of the white supremacist omertà. Russell prided himself on being cut from a more refined cloth than Bilbo, so he was horrified when a constituent wrote to say he was "becoming synonymous" with the Mississippian (it was not meant as a compliment).[55]

The success of the South's obstruction against civil rights depended on its ability to maintain a gloss of respectability on its cause. In the late 1940s, Russell began using his influence as the leader of the southern caucus to rein in the blatant racists like Bilbo. He urged his fellow southerners to elevate their tone and focus on issues of principle. They were welcome to filibuster, he counseled, but they should concentrate on the merits of the bill instead of embracing obstruction for obstruction's sake.[56] They took his advice, and keen observers soon noticed. "Newsmen covering the Senate say that under Russell, filibuster oratory has improved greatly in quality," the *Saturday Evening Post* reported in 1951. "The Negro, who is at the heart of the Civil Rights issue, is never mentioned, and none of the Southern coalition, which reporters have irreverently dubbed Dick Russell's Dixieland Band, ever breaks into the demagogue ranting of a Bilbo or a Rankin. Discussion swirls around the parliamentary procedure at issue, and the speeches, though interminable, are germane. The day seems past when a hoarse-voiced filibusterer could hold the floor by reading the telephone book or discussing, ad infinitum, a recipe for making pot likker."[57]

A new coat of paint was important, but Rule 22 remained the foundation. Without it, the civil rights movement would overtake him and the entire South. And in the years to come, Rule 22 would come under threat as never before.

In 1948, Russell was forced to decide which kind of filibuster he wanted: the talking filibuster of Calhoun's era or the post–Rule 22 version. His choice was revealing and would shape the future of the Senate.

By this time, a loophole had been discovered in Rule 22 that let senators have the filibuster both ways. The loophole rendered filibusters on the motions to bring up bills (called "motions to proceed") immune to cloture. In practice, this meant that senators could filibuster the old way of the Calhoun era on motions to proceed, delaying a bill by holding the floor interminably; if they did, cloture could not be imposed even if their opponents had the votes. Meanwhile, on bills themselves, senators could deploy the filibuster of the post–Rule 22 era, and force their opponents to secure the votes for cloture. Obstructionists could choose which method they preferred (or use both), depending on what they thought would be most effective.

As Russell was filibustering Truman's poll tax bill in early August 1948, Senator Arthur Vandenberg of Michigan, the presiding officer, was sustaining a point of order when he surprised the Senate by ruling that the loophole rendered Rule 22 moot. Because the loophole let senators evade cloture at their discretion, Vandenberg ruled, "the Senate has no effective cloture rule at all."[58]

Vandenberg's ruling left reformers in a muddle. On civil rights, cloture had been transformed into a powerful tool of obstruction. But most senators did not see the world through the prism of civil rights. And Rule 22 still represented the most significant reform of Senate rules since the previous question motion was eliminated in 1806. If they got rid of it, they would be going back to the time when there was no way to end debate at all. As bad as things had become, reformers could not seem to decide if getting rid of Rule 22 would improve the situation or make it worse. Rule 22 needed to be strengthened, they believed, and its threshold needed to be lowered. But they were loath to get rid of it altogether. Since it was late in the summer in an election year, reformers punted, vowing that they would figure out what to do after the election.[59]

Richard Russell's view of Rule 22 was not muddled: he wanted to keep it. This was telling. If Russell's concern had truly been for the unlimited debate he and his fellow southerners claimed to defend, he should have celebrated Vandenberg's ruling, since it eliminated the only restriction on debate that the Senate had put on the books in more than a hundred years. This was supposedly what Russell wanted: a return to the days before Rule 22 when there was no way to end debate at all. But if that had ever been what Russell wanted, it wasn't anymore. Rule 22 had given him something new: a way for the minority to block bills favored by the majority. That was better, and he meant to keep it.

As soon as the new Senate convened in January 1949, liberals called a Rules Committee hearing to consider options for reform. With a pro-reform president in Truman riding stellar post-election approval ratings and boasting a bipartisan reform coalition in the Senate, reformers had the upper hand. On the other side of the fight stood Russell and the South. The previous year, southerners had announced to reporters that they were formally submitting themselves to Russell's "generalship." Now it was up to him to set their strategy. At the hearing, Russell revealed how much importance he invested in the issue, declaring, "All that we can do, Mr. Chairman, under those circumstances, in self-defense, is to undertake to gird up our loins and shout the cry of the centuries when the enemy comes, 'To your tents, oh, Israel.' "[60]

Russell turned the debate into a question of whom his colleagues trusted: him, the human embodiment of the Senate and defender of its traditions, or Truman, the head of the suspect executive branch who was trying to tell them how to run their chamber. The majority leader at the time was Scott Lucas, who was allied with Truman and the reformers. But the majority leader was a figurehead back then, and Russell used Lucas's powerlessness against the reformers, arguing that Truman was the one pulling the strings. On the left, advocates like the group Americans for Democratic Action were pushing reformers to lower the threshold for invoking cloture to a majority. In the Senate, reformers coalesced around a more modest set of proposals, ranging from simply restoring Rule 22 and closing the Vandenberg loophole, to lowering the threshold to three-fifths instead of two-thirds. Russell slyly argued that the reformers were using the moderate proposals as a Trojan horse for the more aggressive proposals advocated by the ADA. At Truman's behest, he argued, they would pretend to favor the more modest proposals, then quickly vote to lower the threshold to a majority, where the leftist advocates wanted it.[61]

On February 28, Russell put on a show on the Senate floor, humiliating Lucas in front of their colleagues. Lucas rose to deliver a stilted statement in favor of reform: "After a careful examination and consideration of the resolution which has been reported, it seems to me that the supporters of the proposal for limitation of debate are advocating only a very reasonable step," he began. As Lucas started reading quotes validating his position, Russell interrupted. "Will the Senator yield?" he asked. Lucas said he would. "I should like to ask the Senator whether he is reading a statement he has prepared, or whether he is reading from the remarks of someone else," Russell queried. Lucas, stammering, pointed out that he was quoting Alexander Hamilton and Senator Henry Cabot Lodge, who happened to be a Republican. Russell responded, "I should like to ask the Democratic leader whether he cannot quote some Democrats on that point." The chamber erupted in laughter.[62]

After playing cat-and-mouse with Lucas a little while longer, Russell got to the point, which was to show his fellow senators that Lucas was just a front for Truman's radical designs. Continuing to command the floor, Russell told the chamber he had been informed by members of the press that Lucas had just come from the White House. Since Lucas had just spoken with Truman, Russell asked, could Lucas tell the Senate whether the president favored the more radical proposal, the one "advocated by the Americans for Democratic Action, the PAC, and other minority groups?" Lucas stalled.[63] Senator Francis Myers of Pennsylvania, who as the Democratic whip was Lucas's second in command, stepped in to try to rescue him, and Russell coolly turned his cross-examination onto Myers. Noting that Myers was the lead sponsor of a moderate reform proposal, Russell asked him "to tell us whether or not that embraces the views of the President of the United States." Myers replied, lamely,

"I have never discussed this problem with the President of the United States." Lucas quickly moved the Senate onto other business.[64]

It is hard to tell if Russell's gambit would have worked on its own. But days later, Truman confirmed every suspicion Russell had planted. Still flush with his upset victory, Truman had been exhibiting a "post-election self-confidence which friends hail as 'bold leadership' and opponents brand as 'reckless brashness,'" observed the veteran political correspondent Richard Strout of the *Christian Science Monitor*.[65] Badly misreading the situation, and perhaps frustrated with Lucas's leadership, Truman stormed into the fight, telling reporters that he did, indeed, support the radical proposal—just as Russell had said. Truman's statement was a disaster for reformers. "Truman Drops Grenade into Senate Filibuster," declared one headline, noting that his Senate allies "were taken aback."[66] His statement had "a chilling impact" on the negotiations, the *New York Times* reported, with Russell and the southerners "plainly jubilant" at its impact.[67] Trying to salvage the reformers' position, Lucas immediately broke with Truman, telling the press, "I regret to be compelled to disagree with my chief."[68] Senator Carl Hayden of Arizona, the chair of the Rules Committee and a leading advocate of the moderate reform proposal, labeled Truman's plan "extremist" and called on all involved to renounce it.[69] Trying to rally their side, reformers held a closed-door meeting where "an extraordinary move was made to strengthen their perilous tactical position by disassociating themselves from President Truman's stand," according to the *Times*.[70]

Russell sat back like a Cheshire cat, watching the reformers panic. "The President has now justified every statement that we have made," he told the press.[71] Lucas floated a peace offer. "All I am asking the senator to do is to think about it," he begged on the floor.[72] Russell batted it away, telling reporters he was not inclined to talk peace.[73] Senator J. William Fulbright of Arkansas, a rising star on international affairs who would go on to be the longest-serving chairman of the Senate Foreign Relations Committee, but who also moonlighted as a member of Dick Russell's Dixieland Band, twisted the knife, openly questioning Lucas's credibility on the floor. As Lucas urged Fulbright to consider the reform proposal, Fulbright dismissed him. "I have been led to believe, and I am subject to correction, that that is what the Senator might do next week, but that following next week, if he so desired, he might change it." All Lucas could do was plead with Fulbright to "have in mind the great legislative program that is before the country, including his bill for oleomargarine."[74]

It was a rout, but, more importantly, it was a chance for Russell to tailor Rule 22 to his liking. With the reformers' cause in ruins, he offered what seemed like generous terms of surrender. He agreed to close the loophole in Rule 22 that Vandenberg had identified, effectively reinstating Rule 22 and applying it to everything the Senate did, including the motions to proceed to bills that had previously been exempted. Russell even included nominations, which had not previously been covered by Rule 22. As the benevolent victor, all he asked in return was that Rule 22's supermajority threshold be made a little harder to clear. He proposed keeping the threshold at two-thirds, but instead of pegging it to the number of senators who appeared in person for a given vote, as it had been, it would be pegged to the total number of senators who were in office. (At the time, it was common for senators not to show up for votes, which lowered the threshold; but if the threshold was pegged to the number of senators who held office, it would remain high no matter how many senators showed up.) Finally, Russell threw in one more supposedly modest suggestion. To senators tired of debating Senate rules, he suggested that they make it nearly impossible to alter Rule 22 in the future. Under Russell's suggestion, Rule 22 would be placed in a special category, immune to any form of cloture.[75] By this point, it was March, and the Senate was entering its third month of debating its rules. Other work was piling up. Senators were ready to trust Russell and move on. His rewrite of Rule 22 passed easily.[76]

Soon, it would become clear that the concessions Russell had made were not concessions at all. Reinstating his precious Rule 22 after Vandenberg decimated it was more likely his goal than a give to reformers. Plugging the loophole empowered obstructionists, not reformers, by allowing them to apply supermajority thresholds to the motions to bring bills to the floor in addition to the bills themselves, thereby placing even more hurdles along a bill's path to passage. By bringing nominations under Rule 22, he ensured that all executive branch and judicial nominations would now be subject to a supermajority threshold, too. And if future senators did not like this state of affairs, the special status his rewrite had bestowed on Rule 22 made changing it nearly impossible.

Russell had not just won a skirmish over an obscure rule, he had chosen the Senate's future. Calhoun's dream, as outlined in his *Disquisition* toward the end of his life, was a Senate that would "give to each interest or portion of the community a negative on the others."[77] The well-intentioned reformers who wrote Rule 22 had inadvertently handed an obstructionist minority the veto power Calhoun had described. By repurposing Rule 22, the white supremacist senators of the Jim Crow era figured out how to do something that had never been done before, and force bills to clear a supermajority threshold. Appalled at this trend, a bipartisan group of reformers and a hapless president had sought to reverse it. But with his deft maneuvering, Russell strengthened it instead, and ensured that the supermajority Senate would become an enduring feature of modern American life.

Chapter Four

AN IDEA WHOSE TIME HAS COME

DURING THE FIGHT OVER Rule 22, a new senator auditioned for Dick Russell's Dixieland Band. As his song, he chose the ballad of the filibuster, a surefire crowd-pleaser among his target audience. He had been elected in 1948 in what many rightly considered a stolen election, and this was his maiden speech on the Senate floor. He took up the South's cause with gusto, defending the filibuster as the "last defense of reason, the sole defense of minorities who might be victimized by prejudice." He said the quiet part out loud: "When we strip away the trappings of rhetoric and theory and legend which surround the arguments here against the filibuster, we have left the simple fact that we are debating the so-called civil-rights legislation." By using the filibuster to maintain Jim Crow, he explained, the South was actually looking out for the best interests of black Americans. "We are not speaking against the Negro race," he said. "We are not attempting to keep alive the old flames of hate and bigotry. We are, instead, trying to prevent those flames from being rekindled. We are trying to tell the rest of the nation that this is not the way to accomplish what so many want to do for the Negro." He placed the right to filibuster above all other freedoms. "If I should have the opportunity to send into the countries behind the iron curtain one freedom and only one, I know what my choice would be," he said. "I would send to those nations the right of unlimited debate in their legislative chambers."[1]

He had given Richard Russell a copy of the speech ahead of time. Russell liked it so much, he contacted the other members of the southern caucus and made sure they were on the floor to hear it. He alerted reporters, too; here was a rising star. The speech was a hit with the southerners. As soon as it was over, they lined up to shower this junior senator with praise, to offer congratulations and handshakes, to put themselves, not for the last time, in the grip of the big, powerful hands of Senator Lyndon Baines Johnson.

JOHNSON WANTED TO BE president, and his drive to get to the White House changed the Senate. To accomplish his goal, he needed to present himself as a unicorn of midcentury American politics: a southern senator whom liberals could embrace. In the 1950s, southern Democrats were anathema to liberals. Russell had learned this the hard way. At the start of 1952, Russell was enjoying large crowds at parades and speeches, and it was not uncommon for people of stature and influence to tell him he should be president. At a parade in Atlanta, the band had rewritten the Georgia Tech anthem "The Ramblin' Wreck," singing, "The Senator from Georgia / Dick Russell is his name," and, "His Years of Public Service Devoted to Our Nation / Will Lift Him from His Senate Seat / The Presidential Station!"[2] Despite his differences with Truman, Russell cherished a note the president had written him in 1945, saying, "Dick: I hope you [will] be recognized next."[3] Russell took these accolades at face value and ran for the Democratic nomination in 1952. His campaign was humiliating. He won just one primary and got passed over at the convention in favor of Illinois governor Adlai Stevenson, a liberal. Russell's pride would never fully recover.[4]

Johnson's path to the presidency involved three steps, each of which would have taken a person of less Olympian drive a lifetime to achieve. First, he had to rise rapidly in the Senate, an institution designed to make such a rise nearly impossible. Second, he needed to keep the South convinced he was committed to the Lost Cause, since they would continue to be the source of his power even after he rose. Third, and in direct conflict to steps one and two, he needed to make inroads with the ascendant liberal wing of the Democratic Party, the enemies of the South.

The first two steps required sticking close to Russell, a task Johnson was cut out for. He had a talent for ingratiating himself with older men, especially lonely ones. He had displayed it since his college days, when he flattered professors at Southwest Texas State Teachers College, leading his acquaintances to call him the "professional son." Johnson had come to the Senate from the House, where he had quickly set himself apart from other junior members by becoming a favorite of the Speaker, the stocky, severe Sam Rayburn. The most powerful Speaker of the twentieth century, Rayburn still holds the tenure record at seventeen years. He shepherded landmark legislation through Congress under presidents Franklin Roosevelt, Truman, Eisenhower, and Kennedy.[5] But to Johnson, he was "Mister Sam." Rayburn didn't have children, so Johnson and his wife, Claudia—better known by her nickname Lady Bird—began inviting Rayburn to their house regularly for dinner, and Johnson made a point of telling anyone who would listen that Rayburn was "just like a daddy to me."[6]

In the Speaker's inner sanctum in the Capitol, Rayburn hosted a drinking club nicknamed the "Board of Education." In a chamber of over four hundred members, gaining access to this rarefied circle was a prize. The club's mostly senior, powerful members were surprised when Johnson, who was a junior, rank-and-file member with no clout to speak of in a body that parsed status with an accountant's focus, started showing up. And they were downright shocked when Johnson would walk across the room and kiss "Mister Sam" on his big, bald head.[7] Through Rayburn, Johnson met President Franklin Roosevelt. Together, Rayburn and Roosevelt helped Johnson deliver for his congressional district in the Hill Country of Texas, producing tangible benefits such as a rural electrification program that positioned Johnson to run for an open Senate seat in 1948.[8] He won the race with the help of 202 ballots that appeared in Texas's 13th precinct, in a town called Alice, six days after the election—when Johnson happened to be down by about 150 votes. All of these late votes were cast for Johnson, and miraculously, the voters had all managed to cast their ballots in alphabetical order.[9] His election became a curiosity, and as he ascended to the upper chamber he acquired the nickname Landslide Lyndon.[10]

In the Senate, Johnson wasted no time applying the same approach to Russell that he had used on Rayburn. He came up with a nickname for Russell: the Old Master. He started imitating the courtly Georgian's mannerisms and the way he dressed. It was a big change. Russell's sartorial choices befitted a country lawyer from Winder, Georgia, his hometown. Johnson, ever the Texan, favored loud suits and ties, and had the personality to match. He dominated conversations, which he laced with references to sex and bodily functions. He would make a show of scratching his testicles in public, and would urinate and defecate in front of his staff, sometimes while making them take dictation.[11] But as he courted Russell, Johnson reined in his trademark crudeness, and started dressing and acting more like the older senator.[12] He toned down his appearance and behavior, and "learned to observe amenities with Senator Russell," according to Bill Jordan, a longtime aide to the elder statesman.[13] With his courtship of Russell in full swing, a 1951 *Newsweek* profile described Johnson as "quiet and gentle" and noted that "everything he does, he does with great deliberation and care," a description that surprised those who knew him.[14]

As he had done with Rayburn, Johnson started inviting Russell over to his home. He told historian Doris Kearns Goodwin that he knew Russell was lonely on Sundays, which he called "a tough day for a politician" who spent the week inundated with the attention of supplicants, "especially if, like Russell, he's all alone." Johnson would invite Russell over "for breakfast, lunch, brunch, or just to read the Sunday papers," he said. "He was my mentor, and I wanted to take care of him."[15]

But Russell was a harder case to crack than Rayburn. Russell didn't just want adulation. What Russell prized most was loyalty to the cause to which he had dedicated his career: upholding white supremacy.[16] As Robert Caro writes in *Master of the Senate*, "Fondness alone would never have gotten Johnson what he wanted from Russell. . . . He would have to prove to him that they had the same feelings on the issue that dominated Russell's life."[17]

For his part, Russell's feelings about Johnson were complicated by his dawning realization that he might never make it to the White House himself. Russell believed that electing a southern president was necessary to heal the wounds that still lingered from the Civil War—although to him, that meant uniting the country behind the South's vision of racial hierarchy. After his own ill-fated bid for the presidency in 1952, Russell started to think of Johnson as the acolyte who could achieve this dream. Since Russell's own experience had shown him that any southerner would need at least some support from liberals to win the Democratic nomination, he started making exceptions for Johnson, giving him leeway that he denied other members of the southern caucus. He even let Johnson keep his participation in the caucus a secret. Once, when a reporter caught Johnson leaving a southern caucus meeting, the big Texan rushed into his office and slammed the door, bracing himself against it from the inside and shouting "No, no. No, no," until the reporter went away. To an astonished staffer in his office, Johnson explained, "That little shit from the AP wanted me to comment."[18]

With Russell's support, Johnson quickly rose to the top of the Democratic leadership. In 1951, Russell's endorsement got Johnson the job of whip, the second-highest ranking position in party leadership. Then the reigning Democratic Senate leader, Ernest McFarland of Arizona, stood up to a demagogic first-term senator from Wisconsin named Joe McCarthy, who was stoking false fear of communist infiltration within the federal government. When "Tail

Gunner Joe" (who had never been a tail gunner) returned fire during McFarland's 1952 reelection campaign, the Democratic leader lost to his Republican challenger, a young conservative named Barry Goldwater.[19]

In January 1953, with Russell's backing, Johnson was named leader—minority leader at first, but Democrats would retake the majority in 1954. Prior decades were littered with the political corpses of failed Senate leaders. But in recent years, a big reason the job had been more likely to humiliate its occupants than empower them was that the real power lay with Russell, and the "leader" only had as much leash as Russell chose to give him. Johnson had only just arrived in the Senate when Russell eviscerated then–majority leader Scott Lucas in the 1949 fight over Rule 22. Now, as leader himself, Johnson embraced Russell's power. He had told Russell he would take the job under one condition: that Russell move his desk behind his own, ostensibly to make it easier for him to ask Russell's advice. On the floor, the leader's desk is front row center, nearest to the "well," the kidney-shaped space in the front of the chamber where senators stand to cast their votes, and where no staff member can set foot, other than the young pages and the clerks who record the votes. Russell agreed to his protégé's condition. In a demonstration whose significance no senator could miss, he moved to sit behind Johnson when the new session convened.[20] For the first time in recent memory, the titular and de facto Democratic leaders formed a unipolar center of power.

Johnson did not just need Russell's backing to rise to power, he needed it to wield power as well. Through creativity and force of will, Johnson would build the leader's job into one worth having, endowing it with more influence than it had ever held (how he did so will be discussed in Chapter Seven). But some of the key moves that strengthened the leader's role could not have happened without Russell's continued support. Johnson would eventually need to court the liberals, and his association with Russell would badly damage that effort. But he could worry about that later. For the time being, maintaining Russell's support was essential to Johnson's power. And the only way to maintain it was to prove his commitment to the intertwined issues Russell cared about above all else: blocking civil rights and protecting Rule 22.

THE DEMOCRATIC PARTY of the 1950s was split. On one side, Johnson had risen to become the Senate's leader on the strength of his southern support. On the other side, a liberal wing was coming into its own on the national stage, dominated by dashing young senators who seemed more likely than Johnson to represent the future of the party. Hubert Humphrey, the Minneapolis mayor who had rallied Truman's convention behind a stronger civil rights plank, was now Senator Humphrey, arriving in the Senate the same year as Johnson. The incoming Senate class that year included other liberal champions like Paul Douglas of Illinois and Clinton Anderson of New Mexico. Even the South elected a liberal in Estes Kefauver of Tennessee. Media savvy and determined to take on the Senate establishment, these senators were a new generation of reformers.[21] And one of their top targets was Rule 22.

In what Douglas called the "biennial struggle over the filibuster," he and his fellow reformers waged a relentless attack on Rule 22, going after it in every two-year session from 1949 until the passage of the Civil Rights Act in 1964.[22] In his 1949 rewrite of Rule 22, Russell had placed it in a protected category, so changing it through the normal legislative track was now virtually impossible. Reformers adjusted accordingly. They developed a theory that the Senate was not technically a continuing body, and instead was disbanded and formed anew after every election. If they could convince a majority of their colleagues to vote to endorse this theory, the Senate's rules would be wiped clean at the outset of a new session. The Senate would then revert to standard parliamentary procedure, which dictated that all votes were to be held at a simple-majority threshold, and rewrite its rules from there. This return to a primordial state would remove Rule 22 and the other entrenched advantages the South had built over the years, allowing reformers to install a more reasonable cloture procedure.

When reformers tried this approach in the early 1950s, Johnson defeated them with relative ease. There were numerous problems with their strategy, the main one being that they were asking their colleagues to throw the entire structure of the Senate up in the air for the sake of changing Rule 22. But there was a more mundane problem as well: Johnson was aggressively punishing senators who sided with the reformers. By definition, the reformers' effort had to occur at the beginning of a session, before the Senate adopted its rules. This also happened to be before committee assignments and leadership posts were awarded. That made it easy for Johnson to watch how senators voted on reforming Rule 22, and dole out rewards and punishments accordingly. Years later, after Johnson was out of the Senate and stuck in what appeared to be a dead-end vice-presidency, Senator Joseph Clark of Pennsylvania, a liberal ally of Humphrey and Douglas, took to the Senate floor and delivered a lengthy address describing the pressure tactics Johnson had deployed to prevent senators from siding with reformers on Rule 22. Submitting charts and memos into the *Congressional Record*, Clark detailed how senators were systematically "rewarded or punished on the basis of their behavior on this critical issue."[23] In his memoir, Douglas concurred. Senators who sided with Johnson and opposed reformers on Rule 22 "were given good committee assignments and, later, generous appropriations, together with favorable legislation for their states," he recalled. By contrast, Douglas sighed, the reformers "could offer only the rewards of good conscience."[24]

In 1956, liberals tried another maneuver against Johnson and the South. In a pattern that was by then familiar, a civil rights bill had passed the House and was destined for the Senate. Typically, such a bill would be referred to the Judiciary Committee, which like most powerful committees was run by a southern Democrat. In 1956, the chair was Senator James Eastland of Mississippi. An ardent segregationist, Eastland had been described by Clarence Mitchell, the longtime spokesman for the NAACP, as "a mad dog let loose in the streets of justice."[25] Eastland reveled in his image as an enemy of civil rights, boasting that he had "special pockets" put in his pants for stashing away the civil rights bills that landed in his committee.[26]

But this time, the reformers had a plan. To prevent the bill from being sent to Eastland's committee, they would object to the motion to refer it, sending the bill to the Senate calendar instead, where it would become available for any senator to call up at any time. It was just a first step, but it would save the bill from the certain death that awaited it in Eastland's committee. While the process may sound simple, it is easy for senators to miss the opportunity to object. There is no schedule telling senators when a bill will arrive from the House, and the process of referral takes only a few minutes at most: the presiding officer reads the title of the bill (twice, to make sure the Senate is aware of what the House has sent them) and then the leader makes the referral. To spring a surprise objection, senators need to be diligent enough to know when the bill is arriving and stealthy enough to prevent the leader from seeing their objection coming.

The reformers thought they had it figured out. When a bill comes to the Senate from the House, a physical copy is carried by a clerk across the hallway that connects the House and Senate in the Capitol building. (It still works this way today.) To make sure they did not miss their chance to object, the reformers planned to stay with the bill, physically, from the moment it left the House to when it entered the Senate chamber. On the day the House passed the bill, Douglas walked across the Capitol building, intending to find the House clerk who would carry the bill to the Senate and escort them over to the upper chamber.[27] Meanwhile, on the Senate floor, reformers stationed a sentry, Senator Herbert Lehman of New York, in case the bill snuck past Douglas.

As usual, Johnson was a step ahead. He had gotten wind of the reformers' plan and contacted Rayburn, who made sure the bill was printed faster than usual in the House and hustled out a side door.

By the time Douglas arrived on the House floor, the bill was already on its way to the Senate; he might have passed the clerk carrying it on his way over. But it took Douglas some time to figure this out, because he had trouble getting a straight answer from the House clerks, who feigned ignorance about the bill's location. When Douglas realized what was happening, he raced back across the Capitol building, through the rotunda where tourists gawk up at the Capitol dome, and back to the Senate. But it was too late. Johnson had put Senator Lister Hill of Alabama, who was known as "the south's fastest talker," in the presider's chair. When Lehman, the liberals' sentry, had been "briefly decoyed" off the floor, Hill read the bill twice and referred it to Eastland's committee.[28] As Douglas burst into the chamber, a smile crossed Hill's face. "Paul, my dear boy," Hill said, "we move in accordance with the time-honored rules and procedure of the Senate."[29]

Johnson was not content just to beat Douglas and the liberals. He wanted to teach them a lesson. When Douglas pressed the issue the next day, Johnson forced a meaningless procedural vote, but made clear that it was a "leadership matter," telegraphing to senators that it was a test to see whose side they were on.[30] Under pressure, many of Douglas's allies, including Humphrey, abandoned him and sided with Johnson. The vote was, for Douglas, a harsh 76 to 6. Douglas slunk off the floor. At the elevators, he asked an aide to punch the button three times—the signal to the elevator operator that a senator was waiting—muttering, "Let's pretend I'm a senator." When he got back to his office, he closed the door and wept.[31]

By proving himself to the South, Johnson was accomplishing the second part of his plan to become president. Now, all that was left was winning the loyalty of the liberals—like the one he had just humiliated on the Senate floor.

THE DIVIDE BETWEEN the liberals and the southerners that Johnson had to bridge was only getting wider. In the 1950s, southerners escalated their tactics from blocking civil rights bills to calling for the open defiance of federal laws. In response to the Supreme Court's *Brown v. Board of Education* decision in 1954, southern Democrats produced the foundational text of the white backlash movement known as "massive resistance." With Russell's guidance, southern senators titled the document the "Declaration of Constitutional Principles," but it was more commonly referred to as the Southern Manifesto. In anodyne legal language, it urged states to defy the *Brown* ruling. Senator Harry Byrd of Virginia, a leading member of the southern caucus, directed the most aggressive rejection of *Brown* in the nation. His "Byrd machine" controlled Virginia, and loyalists in the state legislature passed a series of laws that shut down Virginia's public schools while providing vouchers to white families, enabling many of them to send their children to private schools that came to be known as "segregation academies." Federal courts eventually overturned much of the Byrd machine's work, but public schools in Virginia's Prince Edward County stayed closed for five years.[32]

As Senate Democrats sought to oppress black Americans, Republicans were working to win their loyalty. By 1956, President Dwight Eisenhower could point to a record on civil rights that was arguably stronger than the records of Truman and Roosevelt. Eisenhower's Supreme Court nominees included Chief Justice Earl Warren, who wrote the *Brown* decision and presided over the most favorable stretch of civil rights rulings in American history. His administration had worked to desegregate the District of Columbia, where the federal government had exclusive jurisdiction. While Truman had issued an executive order desegregating the armed forces, he did not enforce it aggressively; Eisenhower did. He also desegregated the Veterans Administration and created a presidential commission dedicated to ending discrimination by federal contractors, a successor to the defeated FEPC.[33] Some of the progress was the work of Eisenhower's attorney general, Herbert Brownell, an aggressive advocate of civil rights, who occasionally pushed the administration further than it wanted to go.[34] And the administration's record did not amount to a sea change. But it was more than Democrats were offering.

Many black Americans responded favorably. During the 1956 election, Clarence Mitchell of the NAACP campaigned for Eisenhower, urging black Americans to vote Republican because GOP control of Congress would "automatically eliminate twenty-one Southern chairmen from the key committee posts they now hold."[35] Democratic congressman Adam Clayton Powell, who represented Harlem and remained the pastor of the historic Abyssinian Baptist Church, endorsed Eisenhower.[36] In the election, Eisenhower stunned Democrats by carrying 39 percent of the black vote on his way to sweeping forty-one states.[37] Afterward, Gallup reported that "of all the major groups in the nation's population, the one that shifted most to the Eisenhower-Nixon ticket was the Negro voter."[38]

For Johnson, the 1956 election also served as a painful reminder that there was no way around the third step in his plan: winning over the liberals. As Russell had before him, Johnson misread a run of positive national attention and made an ill-advised run for the Democratic presidential nomination, which immediately ran aground on liberal antipathy. Ignoring those around him who could see his bid was doomed, Johnson stuck in the race all the way to the convention. When it became clear that Adlai Stevenson was going to win the nomination again, Johnson refused to release the small number of southern delegates he had in his corner to make the nomination unanimous. By the time it was over, he had shown himself to be a sectional candidate with no national appeal, and a sore loser besides. In the assessment of the nationally syndicated columnist Drew Pearson, "Lyndon ended up looking like a cellophane bag with a hole in it."[39]

IN EISENHOWER'S SECOND TERM, Senate reformers gained a new ally in their push to gut the filibuster and pass civil rights: the vice-president, Richard Milhous Nixon. In 1956, Nixon had helped lead the Eisenhower campaign's successful outreach to black Americans while advocating for civil rights and railing against the filibuster. Campaigning in Harlem, Nixon declared that civil rights legislation would never pass "as long as the filibuster exists in the Senate."[40]

In January 1957, fresh off Eisenhower's landslide reelection, Nixon joined leading Senate reformers like Humphrey and Douglas to launch a coordinated assault against Johnson, Russell, and Rule 22. This bipartisan axis of reformers would pursue the same strategy reformers had used earlier in the decade, and seek to rewrite the Senate's rules at the beginning of a session. But this time, they had a powerful new advantage. As vice-president, Nixon would preside over the Senate and deliver a ruling endorsing the idea that a majority of the Senate could change its rules. In itself, this ruling would not end Rule 22, since the Senate could then decide whether to endorse or reject the ruling. But even if reformers lost that vote, the ruling would strengthen their cause; as the Calhoun and Vandenberg episodes demonstrated, precedents set by the presiding officer could have lasting impacts. If the reformers picked up more votes than they'd secured on their efforts earlier in the decade, they could also demonstrate momentum for their cause. For Nixon, it was another opportunity to make inroads with black voters, which at the time was a central part of his strategy to win the presidency.

There was not much Johnson could do to stop the reformers from securing this ruling. When the Senate convened in January, it was widely known that the reformers would make their play, and the chamber was filled with anticipation. Nixon sat in the presider's chair on the dais at the front of the chamber, and the reformers asked him for a ruling on whether, at the beginning of a Senate session, the chamber could use a simple-majority vote to begin the process of changing Rule 22 (instead of having to slog through the impossible path Russell had created in 1949). Nixon delivered: "This constitutional right is lodged in the membership of the Senate and it may be exercised by a majority of the Senate at any time," he stated. Since every new session of the Senate had the constitutional right to make its own rules, Nixon said, Rule 22 could not bind them unless they chose to let it: "The right of a current majority of the Senate at the beginning of a new Congress to adopt its own rules, stemming as it does from the Constitution itself, cannot be restricted or limited by rules adopted by a majority of the Senate in a previous Congress."[41] In effect, Nixon's ruling held that the Constitution trumped Richard Russell. It gave every new group of senators the right to make their own rules on a majority-vote basis, and declared that the actions of past senators could not bind them to a more restrictive standard, as Russell had tried to do.

Now senators had three options on how to respond: they could open a debate on changing the Senate's rules, giving the reformers a shot at formally changing Rule 22; they could vote to overturn Nixon's ruling; or they could set the ruling aside and move on to other business, a split decision that would let the ruling stand but head off the reformers' efforts to actually change Rule 22. It was Johnson's call on how to proceed. He started by letting Russell work the audience of senators as only he could. In his courtly but mildly threatening way, Russell explained that if the Senate went ahead with a debate over its rules, he would take his time reexamining *all* of the Senate's rules, which could easily take months. "We shall be opening a Pandora's Box," he warned on the Senate floor.[42] Senators knew he meant it. Meanwhile, Johnson made clear to senators that "leadership had an interest" in the vote on reform. Senators knew he meant it, too. At least, most did. Newly elected Senator Frank Church of Idaho did not get the message and sided with the reformers. As retribution, Johnson began to ignore Church, turning away from him whenever he approached, and denying Church his longed-for seat on the Foreign Relations Committee—until Church found a way to make it up to him.[43]

The Senate chose the third option, deciding to "table" the issue and move on to other business while leaving Nixon's ruling in place.

It was far from reformers' ultimate goal of undoing Rule 22, but it was a significant victory nonetheless. On the vote to table, reformers got thirty-eight votes, just thirteen shy of victory and a thirty-four-vote swing in their favor from a similar effort in 1953.[44] Nixon's ruling stood both as a tool for future efforts and as a marker that Johnson and Russell had been unable to muster the votes to overturn it. As the *New York Times* reported, reformers "were elated over their show of strength."[45] It was also a win for the canny Nixon. His ruling set the town abuzz, stirring "much cloakroom talk." The man who would one day pioneer the racist politics of Republican realignment, drawing the segregationists out of the Democratic Party and into the GOP, had, according to the *Times*, "solidified his position in the Republican party's liberal wing."[46]

JOHNSON HAD ONCE AGAIN delivered for the South, but in the process he had dealt a blow to his own goal of becoming president. His success at achieving the first two steps of his plan seemed to have made the third step impossible. He had risen rapidly in the Senate and won the loyalty of the South. But those steps had meant blocking civil rights, defending Rule 22, and alienating the liberals. The day after he fought reformers to a draw in January 1957, the front page of the *New York Times* carried the story of the rules fight next to a picture of Eleanor Roosevelt, Harry Truman, and Adlai Stevenson, above the headline "Democrats Demand More Militant Leaders."[47]

Events only increased the tension. Beyond the Capitol dome, the fight for civil rights was becoming increasingly urgent. The 1956 civil rights bill that Johnson had sent to die in Eastland's committee was coming back to the Senate with a head of steam in the summer of 1957, passing the House by a vote of 286 to 126 in June.[48] Across the country, columnists and commentators agreed that this would be the year civil rights would finally pass.[49]

Johnson had to make a move, and little by little he developed a plan. First, he got Russell to agree that he would not lead a filibuster of the House-passed civil rights bill as long as Johnson didn't force his hand by advancing the bill; it was the Senate version of a no-first-use agreement.[50] For Johnson, avoiding a filibuster was essential because if the South launched one he'd face an impossible choice: side with the South against a marquee civil rights bill and lose any hope of becoming president, or side with the liberals, alienate the South, and lose his power in the Senate. Unsure of what to do next, Johnson stalled while Russell and the southerners sniped at the bill.

Russell had his own interest in declining to filibuster. His retreat furthered his project of putting a more respectable face on southern opposition to civil rights. He wasn't going to let a strong civil rights bill pass, and he could always filibuster if he needed to. But he calculated that with time, he could gut the bill to an acceptable level without being forced into a filibuster. On July 3 he called a meeting of the southern caucus in his office to go over the strategy. The firebrand Thurmond rejected Russell's toned-down approach, proposing that the southerners "march in a body" to the White House and demand that Eisenhower pull the bill. But Russell reminded the group that they needed to be conscious of public opinion, in order to more effectively defy it. "We've got a good case on the merits," he said. "Let's see if we can keep our speeches restrained, and not inflammatory."[51] For the most part, the caucus followed his lead. "Dixie senators in general, while maintaining their undying dislike for the legislation, put a more restrained curb on their tongues," the Associated Press observed of the debate that summer.[52]

Toward the end of the bill's saga, Thurmond broke from Russell's strategy and launched a twenty-four-hour filibuster that, to this day, remains the longest ever recorded. Despite its notoriety, Thurmond's effort had little impact other than to annoy his colleagues. As Thurmond knew, by the time he began talking, the bill had been gutted to Russell's satisfaction and passage was assured, with southern cooperation. The leaders had even designated floor time for senators to speak in opposition to the bill, and that was the

time Thurmond used.[53] William White, the longtime Senate correspondent for the *New York Times* and a veteran of many southern
filibusters, judged Thurmond's filibuster to be so ineffectual that
it was not worthy of the name. "It was simply a one man demonstration without the organized and collective characteristic that
is indispensable to a true filibuster," White scoffed. Not only was
Thurmond on his own, he enraged his fellow southerners. He made
them look like weak-kneed compromisers to their white supremacist supporters back home, "leaving in the South a public image of
a single Southern senator standing at the barricades that had been
deserted by the others," according to White.[54] And he exacerbated
the ever-present fear that unnecessary, theatrical filibusters would
strengthen reformers' side in their war against Rule 22. As another
account reported, Thurmond's speech sparked "resentment among
Southern Senators who fear that such tactics may stimulate an all-
out effort to tighten the closure rule."[55]

To be fair to Thurmond, even Russell struggled to keep his rhetoric restrained during that summer. In a July speech, Russell had
compared the federal government to Nazis and hinted at violent
resistance. In his smooth Georgia drawl, he assured his listeners
that "what I now say is in no sense a threat. I speak in a spirit of
infinite sadness." But what he said next sounded like a threat: "If
you propose to move into the South in this fashion, you may as well
prepare your concentration camps now, for there are not enough
jails to hold the people of the South who will today oppose the use
of raw federal power to forcibly comingle white and Negro children
in the same schools."[56]

By the end of the summer, though, there was no longer any potential that the civil rights bill would integrate the South—or have
much impact at all. What had started out as a strong bill had been
eviscerated by Johnson and Russell. The summer stall gave Johnson
time to forge an ingenious alliance between southern segregationists
and western liberals. He brokered a trade: first, southerners would
support western liberals' efforts to build a federal dam at Hells

Canyon. Water rights were a pressing concern in the Mountain West. With private companies circling, a federal dam at Hells Canyon would put a large proportion of water rights and electric power under federal control, an achievement that was the top priority for many western liberals. In exchange, the western liberals agreed to support the South's efforts to weaken the civil rights bill. Once it had been weakened to the South's satisfaction, both groups would come together to make sure it had the votes to pass, and southerners would not filibuster it (Thurmond's stunt notwithstanding).[57] A key western liberal was Frank Church, the young Idaho senator whom Johnson had punished by denying him a spot on the Foreign Relations Committee after Church supported the reformers on Rule 22 that January. Over the summer, Church helped Johnson strike the civil rights deal and was rewarded with his coveted Foreign Relations seat. Church and the other western liberals acquiesced in the extraction of all of the bill's teeth, leaving just a weak voting rights provision with no enforcement power. The Hells Canyon bill they traded for would fail in the House, and never become law.[58]

The resulting civil rights bill passed the Senate on August 29, 1957, by a vote of 60 to 15, and was signed by President Eisenhower.[59] It was the first civil rights bill to become law since Reconstruction, but some prominent civil rights leaders struggled with whether to endorse it. The *Chicago Defender*, the historic black-owned newspaper, criticized black leaders who did as committing "the gravest tactical blunder that has ever been made."[60] But one of the leaders who thought the bill was worth supporting was Martin Luther King Jr. "After considering all angles I have come to the conclusion that the present bill is far better than no bill at all," he wrote to his ally, Nixon, who had joined King in lobbying for a stronger bill than the one Johnson delivered. "Let me say," King noted, "how deeply grateful all people of goodwill are to you for your assiduous labor and dauntless courage in seeking to make the Civil Rights Bill a reality."[61]

Johnson's maneuvering in the summer of 1957 is rightfully considered a historic feat of personal persuasion, tactical brilliance, and strategic acumen. But only months before, Johnson had defeated an effort that might have rendered much of it moot, along with the gutting of the bill that resulted. By blocking the bipartisan coalition of reformers led by Nixon from reforming Rule 22 in January, Johnson preserved the South's ability to credibly threaten the civil rights bill with a filibuster, making it necessary to gut the bill and win their cooperation. The January push to reform Rule 22 had come up just thirteen votes shy, leaving little doubt that reformers would have succeeded if Johnson had backed them instead of aggressively punishing senators who joined them. If the reformers had succeeded in their professed aim of lowering the cloture threshold, it is likely that a stronger civil rights bill would have passed the Senate. The strong bill proposed by the Eisenhower administration passed the House intact, by a wide margin. It was backed by a president who had won a landslide reelection less than a year earlier. Most importantly, a majority of the Senate appeared to support it. That summer, the Senate had held a vote that tested support for the bill before it was gutted. At a point of frustration, before the alliance was forged to weaken the bill, southerners moved to refer it to the graveyard of Eastland's committee. It was just a vote to protect the bill, not to pass it. But the southerners were defeated, with fifty-four senators going on record supporting the strong bill.[62]

Ultimately, what would have happened if the strong civil rights bill had only needed a majority for passage is unknowable. But in 1964, after seven years that saw Bull Connor's dogs, the murder of four little girls in the bombing of the 16th Street Baptist Church in Birmingham, and the assassination of Medgar Evers, among countless other atrocities, the Senate would pass a civil rights bill very similar to the one that a majority of the House, a majority of the Senate, and a popular Republican administration supported in 1957.

POLITICALLY, the passage of the 1957 bill completed the third step in Johnson's plan, making him a hero to many liberals. Within the

Senate, it was the accomplishment that gave him the authority to finally stand on his own, apart from Russell. He would need it. Passing the bill with southern acquiescence had allowed him to delay his inevitable break with the "Old Master." But the break would come.

In 1960, another civil rights bill arrived on the Senate floor. Russell had hoped that the 1957 bill would ease calls for change, but they had only increased. This time, there was no way around open conflict. Russell launched a filibuster, and Johnson moved to break it. It quickly became a tactical arms race. Russell organized the southerners into groups that would each handle four-hour-long blocks. Johnson, now directing the liberal Democrats and Republicans within the chamber, organized his troops, too, ordering dozens of army cots and setting them up in the old Supreme Court chamber, a windowless crypt a few steps from the Senate floor. Johnson's forces would keep the pressure on Russell, and if any of Russell's men made a slip, they would be there to take advantage. Johnson kept the Senate in session for 125 hours straight, a record that has never been broken. Once again, a majority of the Senate appeared ready to vote for a civil rights bill. A test vote on cloture ended 53 to 42, meaning a majority of the Senate wanted to end the filibuster and move forward with the strong bill.[63] But because of Rule 22, a majority was not enough. As in 1957, the delay allowed Russell to gut the bill, and southerners allowed a toothless version to pass, ending their filibuster once the bill had been sufficiently weakened.

In the end, Johnson's Herculean political feat of rising rapidly in the Senate, securing the trust of the South and then, in quick succession, the liberals, would not be enough to gain the presidency on his own. But it was enough for John F. Kennedy to pick him as his vice-president in the 1960 presidential race. Early in the campaign, the issue of civil rights was a political muddle, and Kennedy spent much of it reassuring segregationist Democrats that he would take a conservative approach on the issue.[64] But when a crucial moment presented itself, Kennedy seized it while Nixon froze. In October, Martin Luther King Jr. was arrested in Georgia and taken to jail.

Terrified that he might not make it out alive, Coretta King was sick with worry. On the advice of his aides, Kennedy called her, and word leaked to the press. The national attention helped build pressure on Georgia's governor to release King.[65] In the election, black Americans swung to Kennedy, and he edged out Nixon in the closest contest since 1916. "On Election Day, if blacks hadn't turned out for him in large numbers, Kennedy might have had to deliver a concession speech," journalist Steven Levingston wrote.[66] Three years earlier, Nixon had worked closely with King to push for a strong civil rights bill that Johnson had eviscerated before riding its passage to the vice-presidency. Now Kennedy had outmaneuvered Nixon on civil rights, too. That would be the last America would see of Richard Nixon, civil rights champion.

The years from 1960 to 1964 made painfully clear that the weak civil rights bills of 1957 and 1960 had not been enough. After Evers was assassinated in June 1963, Kennedy introduced a new, stronger civil rights bill. When Kennedy was assassinated that November, Johnson took up the cause. Shortly after Kennedy's assassination, Johnson sat at his dining room table, huddling with his advisers about which parts of Kennedy's agenda he should adopt. His advisers warned him against taking up civil rights, arguing that it was a lost cause. "Well, what the hell's the presidency for?" Johnson shot back.[67]

The 1964 civil rights bill would be Johnson's decisive showdown with Russell. Up to that point, neither Johnson nor anyone else had been able to use Rule 22 to break a southern filibuster against civil rights (in 1957 and 1960, the South had let the bills pass after weakening them). Now, Johnson was determined to use his former mentor's treasured rule to defeat him on the cause of his life. Johnson would not accept a weak civil rights bill; he would command passage of a strong one. Instead of negotiating with Russell, he would whip the votes to invoke cloture. No longer seeking a truce, he demanded unconditional surrender.

It took all of Johnson's drive and knowledge of the Senate just to get the civil rights bill to the floor. In 1963, Johnson had advised

Kennedy not to let the civil rights bill get stuck behind the president's top economic priority, a tax-cut bill. Johnson knew the southern committee chairmen would hold the tax-cut bill hostage until the end of the session, threatening to kill it if Kennedy pressed them to move on civil rights. Reflecting Johnson's low standing in the administration (the Ivy Leaguers who populated Kennedy's White House nicknamed him "Rufus Cornpone"), Kennedy hadn't listened, and the civil rights bill got stuck just as Johnson had predicted. As Roy Wilkins of the NAACP summed it up, "Kennedy was not naïve, but as a legislator he was very green."[68] To clear the way for civil rights, Johnson finessed the passage of the tax-cut bill by leaning on his relationship with Senator Harry Byrd, of the Virginia Byrd machine and massive resistance, who chaired the Senate Finance Committee. Johnson negotiated a deal with Byrd to release the tax-cut bill from his committee, and it passed in February.[69]

Now there was nothing blocking the civil rights bill except Dick Russell and his Dixieland Band. Russell proceeded to launch one of the longest coordinated filibusters in Senate history. A nation watched, riveted, for three months, as Johnson and Russell maneuvered against each other. Johnson would not accede to Russell's demands to gut the bill as he had in 1957 and 1960, and Russell's minority would not yield. That meant Johnson needed to secure a supermajority to invoke cloture and break the filibuster—to use Rule 22 to "terminate successful filibustering," as its creators had intended. When the head of CBS News proposed to Roger Mudd that he report on the filibuster nightly, Mudd recalled, "My initial reaction was less than enthusiastic. It sounded more like a flagpole-sitting stunt."[70] But in the weeks to come, Mudd's nightly updates from the Capitol steps would make him a star, as viewers hung on every detail. In addition to working with the Democratic Senate leader, Mike Mansfield, Johnson worked closely with the Republican leader, Everett Dirksen, to whip the votes for the bill. In June, when they finally believed they had secured a supermajority, Mansfield reached for Rule 22 and filed cloture.[71] On June 10, with the galleries packed and hundreds waiting outside, Senator John Williams of Delaware, nicknamed "Whispering Willie" because no one could ever hear him, cast the deciding vote to invoke cloture and end debate. As Mudd recalled, "All of us at that moment realized we were the only ones in history who had ever witnessed the breaking of a civil rights filibuster."[72]

In total, seventy-one senators voted to invoke cloture. "A lynch mob," Russell spat on the Senate floor.[73] Later, Senator John Stennis of Mississippi, another ardent white supremacist, wrote to Russell, trying to console him with the reminder that "except for you and your fine leadership," a strong civil rights bill would have passed long ago.[74] It was cold comfort and Russell was never the same. "About the only satisfaction Russell could gain from his years of resisting civil rights legislation was the knowledge that he had delayed passage of the law," Fite, his biographer, writes. He continues, "There is no doubt that Congress would have enacted a comprehensive civil rights bill much earlier if it had not been for Russell and the Southern Bloc."[75] The South had finally fallen, toppled by the very rule that had allowed them to stave off the will of the majority for nearly a century. "Cloture at last!" the Leadership Conference on Civil Rights wrote to its members.[76]

On the day the South's filibuster was defeated, Dirksen quoted Victor Hugo on the Senate floor, declaring that "stronger than all the armies is an idea whose time has come."[77] It was a powerful message that doubled as a vote of confidence in the Senate's ability to deal with tough issues, as it is sometimes invoked today. If you don't press too hard, the idea holds up. After all, the rule that had been invented to "terminate successful filibustering" had finally terminated a filibuster on civil rights. But rather than acting as the "cooling saucer" of Senate myth, the eighty-seven-year wait enforced by the filibuster—a delay that continued long after majorities in Congress and the public were ready for action—had exacted a toll of incalculable human suffering and inflamed the "violent passions" that Madison had intended the Senate to cool.

While America waited for the Senate to decide that civil rights' time had come, the institution applied a different standard to every other issue. During this period, the U.S. government passed the laws it needed to fight and win two world wars, build a social safety net, come back stronger from a Great Depression, bust trusts, create an interstate highway system and a nationwide network of national parks, go to the Moon, and much else, all while building the most dynamic middle class in the world. The policy solutions to many of these challenges were controversial and hard-fought at the time. But none of them faced systematic filibusters or—after southerners repurposed Rule 22—a de facto supermajority threshold. On the rare occasion a non–civil rights bill encountered a filibuster, the filibuster was dropped and the bill passed. From the end of Reconstruction in 1877 until 1964, the only bills that were ever stopped by filibusters were civil rights bills.[78]

After southerners' blockade of civil rights was finally broken in 1964, the Senate stood at a crossroads. It could have decided that giving the minority veto power on civil rights had been a disaster and taken steps to ensure that no future issues would face the same hurdles. Since Henry Clay in 1841, leading voices in the Senate had been calling for just such reform to restore the Framers' balance between minority protections and majority rule. Or the Senate could make a different choice, and start applying the standard it had used on civil rights to all issues, and give the minority a veto over every challenge the nation faced—exactly as Calhoun had called for in his *Disquisition* a century earlier. In the decades ahead, new innovations and the same old impulse—the desire of a conservative minority to impose its will on the majority—would steer the Senate inexorably toward the second path. For nearly two hundred years, the visions of Madison and Calhoun had struggled for supremacy in the Senate. In the decades after Dirksen invoked Hugo on the Senate floor, it would become clear that Calhoun's vision of minority rule was also an idea whose time had come.

Part II

TYRANNY OF
THE MINORITY

Chapter Five

THE SUPERMINORITY

THE STORY OF THE SENATE through the 1960s was, in large part, the story of a white supremacist minority's struggle to acquire veto power through the filibuster. Once they did, it was hard to use, and was only consistently deployed to maintain the oppression of black Americans—since that alone provided sufficient motivation. The second half of this book brings in the story of the Senate today, showing what happened when the filibuster was streamlined so that it could be used against any (and in recent years, every) issue, by leaders wielding unprecedented top-down control, awash in dark money, in a country more polarized than ever before. This is the story of the rise of the modern Senate. As the minority extended its veto across all issues, it helped to create the broader state of minority rule that has become a defining feature of twenty-first-century America. Changes in Senate rules provided the tools, but underlying shifts have imbued them with new power.

In our democracy, power is derived from the people, but structures empower some people over others. The Senate empowers a minority of predominantly white, conservative voters to elect enough senators to block the will of the majority. Over the past few decades, changes in the Senate's rules have meant that senators representing as little as 11 percent of the population can deliver the obstructionist agenda these white, conservative voters desire, blocking progress across most issues. This dynamic renders these voters abnormally powerful. This group is not just a minority, it is a superminority.

The Senate has been divided over the question of minority rights and majority rule since the very beginning, when Madison opposed the Great Compromise. Since Henry Clay in 1841, reformers have been pressing the case that the delicate balance struck by the Framers has tilted too far toward the minority. They called for the Senate to reverse the shift and take steps to restore the limits on minority rights the Framers had put in place. Chief among those reforms was the power to end debate when the minority veered into obstruction, a power that the majority used to possess through the previous question rule. When I was in the Senate, for the first time in the institution's history a leader implemented some of the changes sought by reformers from Clay to Nelson Aldrich to Paul Douglas, forever changing the Senate and triggering a rolling dispute that is unlikely to end anytime soon. The move was what has become known, in the melodramatic parlance of our time, as "the nuclear option."

THE *WASHINGTON POST* broke the news. "Harry Reid Is Set to Go Nuclear," the headline read on November 19, 2013. The story quoted a senior aide to Senate majority leader Harry Reid, who said, "Reid has become personally invested in the idea that Dems have no choice other than to change the rules if the Senate is going to remain a viable and functioning institution." The author, journalist Greg Sargent noted that this was "a long journey from where Reid was only 10 months ago, when he agreed to a toothless filibuster reform deal out of a real reluctance to change the rules by simple majority." The aide explained, "It's been a long process. But this is the only thing we can do to keep the Senate performing its basic duties."[1] When the story hit, the reaction was immediate. I was inundated with requests from other reporters to confirm the scoop. Organizations on all sides of the spectrum, including left-leaning groups who had been pushing for this change for years, called our office asking if it was true. As the aide in the story, I was able to confirm that it was.

Two days later, as I turned my Honda Civic left on Pennsylvania Avenue, the Capitol dome came into view. It had been seven months since Republicans blocked the background-checks bill in the wake of the Newtown mass shooting, and, aside from an immigration bill that was passed by the Senate but quickly put on ice by the Republican-led House, the year had been one of unrelenting obstruction, including what at the time was the third-longest government shutdown in American history.[2] After President Obama's reelection in 2012, there had been a brief hope that the Tea Party "fever," as he called it, would break.[3] That had not happened. Obama continued to face implacable obstruction, of a degree and kind never before experienced by any president of either party. That day, we were going to do something about it.

The term "nuclear option" describes the process of changing the Senate's rules by a simple-majority vote.[4] Born of senators' frustration with the way Rule 22 put the changes made by one group of senators out of reach for future generations, it was used at least eighteen times between 1977 and 2013.[5] It was controversial because it circumvented the supermajority threshold set by Rule 22, and because whichever party opposed its use at a given time portrayed it as an extreme step. But the main reason the term stuck was that reporters liked it. "Nuke this morning?" one reporter emailed. "Yes," I replied.[6] The buzz-saw guitars of Nirvana's "Scentless Apprentice" came on the car stereo. I turned the volume up.

For Senator Reid, it was a normal day. He woke up before dawn and took a walk through Rock Creek Park. On his walks, he'd wear sunglasses and a baseball cap pulled low over his eyes. We would joke that he looked like Whitey Bulger on the lam. He wore headphones, usually tuned to National Public Radio. Two plainclothes members of his Capitol Police security detail trailed a few feet behind him, wearing workout clothes but moving at the pace of a seventy-three-year-old man. Reid was one of the three most power-ful elected officials in the country, but no one ever recognized him.

On his walk, he called into the press office, where two young staffers, Christopher Huntley and Hannah Hurley, split shifts, most days from 4:30 a.m. to 7 p.m. Alternating morning duty, they arrived early to read the news and brief Reid when he called in. He was an early riser, especially if he had trouble sleeping, and sometimes he would call as early as 5 a.m., before his walk. On that day, he called in at the normal time, around 6:30 a.m. Hannah read him the news. He listened politely and didn't press on any particular topic.

Around 8:30 a.m., Reid arrived at the Capitol, his motorcade of two black SUVs turning right off Constitution Avenue, past a col-lapsible barricade installed after 9/11 and Capitol Police officers standing on either side with assault rifles slung across their chests. The two cars pulled up to the Senate's carriage entrance, a cavern-ous stone archway with marble steps leading up into the building. Reid got out, flanked by two officers in suits, and together they walked into the Capitol.

Inside the carriage entrance there is a bank of six elevators where reporters loiter in order to catch senators coming and going. The usual crew was there that morning. They wanted to hear the news from Reid himself. They walked alongside him, lobbing questions: "Are you going nuclear, Senator?" "Do you have the votes, Senator?" Reid gave a confident grin and continued on, through the hallways called the Brumidi Corridors, named after the nineteenth-century Italian artist who designed them, painted with birds and fruit arrayed amid classical motifs. After ducking into a conference room to spend a few minutes greeting a group of his constituents from Nevada—a weekly event he called "Welcome to Washington"—Reid stepped back into the ornate halls and hung a left past a wooden sign that read "Senators only" in gilt lettering, leaving the reporters behind as he stepped into an elevator; the red digital sign above it also read "Senators only." He took it up one floor and exited into a grand space adjoining the Senate floor. Known as the

Ohio Clock corridor, it's named after an eleven-foot-tall clock that was in fact made in Philadelphia, and, rumor has it, used to stash senators' booze during Prohibition. Sometimes, reporters would run up the nearby marble stairs to meet Reid as he left the elevator. That day none did, as they seemed to know they had gotten all he was going to give them: a smile.

A few minutes before 10 a.m., Reid got up from the desk in his office, a piece of carved wood with a leather top as big as a billiard table that dated to the presidency of Abraham Lincoln. He opened the tall wooden door that led into his office and walked past the four assistants and schedulers who sat just outside. Without looking, he grabbed a shiny blue folder embossed with a Senate seal off the desk of his speechwriter, Phoebe Sweet, who had finished the last edits a few minutes prior, and strolled past a Gilbert Stuart portrait of George Washington on his way to convene the Senate for the day's session. The two Capitol police officers who formed his security detail were stationed on either side of the entrance to his office, but they barely moved as he walked the dozen or so steps from his suite to the Senate floor, a space the officers were not supposed to enter except in emergencies. As Reid ascended the two marble steps that led up to the chamber, I thought I detected a spring in his step.

REID WAS CALM because he knew he had the votes. Since Henry Clay, Senate leaders had tried to restore the rule—the previous question rule—that the original Senate included to allow the majority to cut off debate when it devolved from thoughtful consideration of issues to obstruction. Many veteran Democratic senators, including Barbara Boxer of California, Patrick Leahy of Vermont, and Chuck Schumer of New York, had opposed doing so via the nuclear option earlier in their careers, as had Reid himself. To some degree, senators' views depended on whether they were in the majority or the minority; "Where you stand depends on where you sit," as the saying goes. But a group of younger reformers led by Senators Jeff

Merkley of Oregon and Tom Udall of New Mexico had taken up the cause of reform, soberly making the case for years.

Eventually, the sheer scale of Republican obstruction made it impossible for Senate Democrats to do anything other than side with the reformers. The "appointments clause" of the Constitution states that the president "shall nominate, and by and with the Advice and Consent of the Senate, shall appoint Ambassadors, other public Ministers and Consuls, Judges of the supreme Court, and all other Officers of the United States." For centuries, the norm was for senators of both parties to treat presidential nominees with deference, on the theory that presidents should get to pick their team. Judicial nominations were more contentious, but even so, fights generally arose only over ideologically extreme or ethically challenged nominees. A president who faced a Senate controlled by the opposing party would often have a harder time getting their nominees confirmed and have to tailor their selections accordingly. Even then, the expectation was that mainstream nominees who were qualified and had clean ethics records would be confirmed in a timely fashion.

Under President Obama, Republicans laid waste to that norm.[7] They obstructed his nominees with unprecedented frequency. By the time Reid went nuclear, half of all filibusters against nominees in the history of the United States were waged by Senate Republicans against Obama's.[8] There was nothing unusual about Obama's nominees. As presidential nominees tend to be, they were generally highly qualified professionals in the ideological mainstream of their party with clean ethical records. But Republicans' opposition to Obama's nominees often had little to do with qualifications. In 2013, Obama nominated one of their own as defense secretary: Republican senator Chuck Hagel, a widely respected voice on military affairs and recipient of two Purple Hearts. Without hesitating, Republicans filibustered him.[9]

Republicans used the filibuster against Obama's nominees to cripple laws and government agencies that they opposed. They blocked

Congressman Mel Watt, a twenty-year veteran of the House, from leading the Federal Housing Finance Agency in an effort to chip away at the Dodd-Frank Wall Street reform bill that Democrats had passed in 2010. They also blocked the confirmation of Richard Cordray to lead the Consumer Financial Protection Bureau, which was created by Dodd-Frank. After losing their fight against the CFPB itself, Republicans held Cordray hostage to take a second run at defanging the agency, demanding wholesale changes to the structure of the bureau in return for Cordray's confirmation. Democrats were eventually able to confirm Cordray without meeting Republicans' demands, but it took two years. When the CFPB was finally allowed to begin its work, it delivered $12 billion in relief from predatory corporate practices to twenty-nine million Americans—relief that would have come earlier but for Republican obstruction.[10] Republicans also used obstruction to hobble the National Labor Relations Board, which adjudicates workplace disputes and—when properly functioning—provides a counterweight to the heavy bias toward corporations in such situations. For more than a year, Republicans blocked President Obama's highly qualified nominees to the NLRB in an explicit effort to keep the agency understaffed and unable to do its job.[11]

On judicial nominations, the situation was worse. Although Republicans' refusal to confirm Judge Merrick Garland in 2016 was the most notable incident (and will be discussed in detail in Chapter Nine), it was merely the culmination of years of systematic obstruction of Obama's nominees to the federal bench. Usually, nominees move through the confirmation process in a few months at the most.[12] Obama was the only president since Reagan whose nominees had to wait an *average* of six months, at a time when the nation was experiencing a crisis of judicial vacancies.[13]

More often than not, Republicans had a clever rationale for why they were blocking a given nominee, and sometimes daily news coverage strained to capture the scale of the obstruction. But it is clear that by any measure, the level of obstruction Obama faced was historic and unprecedented. All other presidents combined had endured a total of eighty-two filibusters against their nominees. But from 2009 to 2013, President Obama alone faced eighty-six.[14]

It is theoretically possible that Republicans held principled objections to scores of nominees with sterling professional qualifications and spotless ethical records, and were obstructing on the merits. But what makes principled explanations hard to accept is that, in addition to the examples above, Senate Republicans routinely filibustered nominees whom *no one voted against*. Delay is delay, and these nominees were just as useful as any in slowing the Senate down. A study by the nonpartisan Congressional Research Service found that under President Bill Clinton, unanimous judicial nominees—those who ended up having zero votes cast against their nomination—waited an average of 17 days to receive their confirmation votes. Under President George W. Bush, the wait was 29 days. Under President Obama, it was 125 days.[15]

The sheer scale of Republicans' obstruction pushed observers who spent their careers striving to understand both parties' perspectives to conclude that this had become a clear case of right and wrong. Thomas Mann is the W. Averell Harriman Chair and Senior Fellow in Governance Studies at the center-left Brookings Institution, and Norman Ornstein is a resident scholar at the conservative American Enterprise Institute. Together, they track Congress's vital signs in a database that is relied on by reporters, scholars, and professional staff. In 2006, they published a highly regarded book called *The Broken Branch* analyzing Congress's dysfunction, and attributed blame evenly to Democrats and Republicans. By 2012, their view had shifted. "The GOP has become an insurgent outlier in American politics," they wrote. They explained that in the hands of Republicans, the "filibuster, once relegated to a handful of major national issues in a given Congress, became a routine weapon of obstruction, applied even to widely supported bills or presidential nominations." For the two veteran umpires, it was time to make a call. "Let's just say it: the Republicans are the problem."[16]

A CARDINAL RULE OF successful Senate leaders is that when you have the votes, you vote. For Reid, it was time to vote. Placing the blue folder on his podium, he began his remarks. "The American people think the Senate is broken, and I believe the American people are right," he said, his face impassive. "The Senate is a living thing, and to survive it must change, as it has over the history of this great country," he continued. "To remain relevant and effective as an institution, the Senate must evolve to meet the challenges of this modern era."[17] In about an hour, he started the process of going nuclear. He brought up a vote on a nomination and asked the presiding officer, Senator Patrick Leahy, for a ruling on whether it took a supermajority to invoke cloture. Leahy ruled that it did, since that is what Senate rules stated. Reid then called a vote to overturn the ruling of the chair and it passed, 52 to 48. This method of changing Senate rules was dubbed "the Reid Precedent" by longtime Senate staffer William Dauster. The change executed by Reid and Senate Democrats that day meant that from then on, it would take only a majority to invoke cloture and end debate on most presidential nominations, excluding, for the time being, Supreme Court nominees. But the precedent meant that a simple majority of fifty-one senators could restore the right of the majority to end debate, as the Framers had intended.

For the time being, the rule change did not apply to legislation. At the time, that was viewed by many Democrats—including Reid himself—as a step too far. Just as it took time for reformers to see what Rule 22 could become in the hands of visionaries like Russell, in the fall of 2013, it was still hard to decipher the larger forces shaping the political reality around the Senate. To some, it still seemed possible that one day, things would return to normal; that the Tea Party would fade and cross-party participation would resume. Since then, Senator Reid, along with many of his former colleagues, has reached a different conclusion. In 2019, Reid called for eliminating the filibuster on legislation, writing that "the future of our country is sacrificed at the altar of the filibuster."[18] But for the time being, the 2013 rules change was the most consequential reform since the advent of Rule 22 in 1917, and marked the first time a Senate majority had the power to impose cloture since the deletion of the previous question rule in 1806.

With one glaring exception, the nuclear option allowed Democrats to confirm enough judicial nominees to put Obama on par with recent presidents by the time he left office. The lower threshold for confirming nominees allowed Reid to push through a wave of confirmations in 2013 and 2014, before Democrats lost the Senate majority in the 2014 midterms. The judges who were confirmed made up a diverse group: 42 percent of the judges confirmed were female and 36 percent nonwhite.[19] Since then, Trump has pushed through his own judicial nominations and, as we will see, McConnell quickly went nuclear to aid him. Some have argued that if Democrats had not gone nuclear in 2013, McConnell would not have gone nuclear himself under Trump, and instead allowed Democrats to filibuster Trump's judicial nominees. But that argument requires ignoring McConnell's record, which will be discussed in Chapters Eight and Nine. One thing is certain: when Trump took office in 2017, there were many more Obama nominees serving lifetime judicial appointments than there would have been if Democrats had not gone nuclear. Taking stock of the windfall, Jeffrey Toobin, the legal correspondent for *The New Yorker*, called the nuclear option "Harry Reid's enduring gift to Barack Obama."[20]

REPUBLICANS' OBSTRUCTION OF Obama was many things, but it was not irrational. To the contrary, it was a perfectly logical response to the forces shaping our politics and the system of incentives they create. To understand the modern Senate, it is critical to understand how those dynamics shape the decisions senators make.

The most important trend acting on the modern Senate is polarization. In a polarized America, people pick sides and stay there. In a polarized Senate, senators who used to range freely across partisan and ideological lines now toe the party line. The reasons why polarization has become such a dominant force in our daily lives are examined in recent books like Bill Bishop's *The Big Sort* and Ezra Klein's *Why We're Polarized*.[21] But in Congress, the trend is unmistakable. The magazine *Congressional Quarterly* keeps a party-unity "score" for every member, tracking how frequently they side with their party. In the early 1970s, the average score was 60 percent. Today, it is close to 90 percent.[22]

Senators generally follow their states, and while states used to swing back and forth between the parties, most now stay stuck in one column or the other. Landslide elections used to be common: from 1956 to 1972, Eisenhower, Johnson, and Nixon all carried more than forty states.[23] Since they were of different parties, their successive landslides meant many states swung back and forth. Senators could not have aligned themselves with their state's partisan identity if they tried; dozens of senators saw their states go from Republican to Democratic and back to Republican in the span of four elections. By contrast, today, each side generally goes into a presidential election enjoying a large number of "safe" states, and the two sides fight over a handful of swing states.[24] Even the concept of red and blue states is a product of the past two decades. Back in 1980, which party was what color on the map on election night depended on which TV network you watched. But during the recount that followed the 2000 election, the map of red and blue states was plastered across American TV screens for months, and the color assignments stuck.[25]

At the risk of blaming the victim, a big part of the reason senators are toeing the party line is that their voters are, too. Split-ticket

voting used to be common; voters would often vote for a Democratic president but a Republican senator, or vice versa. Now, it
has become almost nonexistent.[26] Senate elections are increasingly
nationalized, with the outcome of Senate races in a given state aligning with the outcome of the presidential race in that state. In 2016,
for the first time in history, there was not a single split-ticket state—
or a state that voted for a presidential candidate of one party, and a
Senate candidate of the other.[27] In every state, voters chose a presidential candidate and a Senate candidate of the same party.

The result of this trend is that the Senate, like much else in American life, is sorted. As recently as the 1990s, there was little correlation between how a state voted in presidential elections and the
partisan identity of its senators. Today, the overwhelming number
of Democratic senators come from blue states, while Republican
senators come from red states. This creates less pressure to work
across the aisle, and more pressure to stick with the party. A Republican senator who comes from a red state, for example, has little to
gain politically from working with a Democratic president whom
the voters of that state oppose.

The second major force critical to understanding the modern
Senate is negative partisanship. If polarization means sorting people
into teams, negative partisanship means that the people on those
teams are motivated to play the game more by a desire to see the
other side lose than by wanting to see their own side win.[28] If this
sounds like merely a semantic distinction, consider how it translates
to the Senate. Politically, today's senators reap far greater rewards
for opposing the other side than for accomplishing things for their
side. Senator Tom Cotton of Arkansas, for instance, has very few
accomplishments to his name. But in the spring of 2015, while President Obama was engaged in high-stakes negotiations with Iran over
its nuclear program, Cotton spearheaded an open letter to Iran's
leaders undermining Obama and trying to scuttle the deal.[29] It was
a mere press stunt, and it sparked outraged cries from the left. But
on the right, Cotton became a hero. Today, he is floated as a leading

contender for the Republican presidential nomination in 2024.[30] Negative partisanship is neatly summed up in the popular phrase "Own the libs," which has become a depressingly accurate three-syllable encapsulation of how politics works today. Around 2016, the phrase went viral because it captured the glee conservatives took in actions and words that "triggered" liberal "snowflakes"—such as wearing, to Whole Foods, a T-shirt featuring Ronald Reagan portrayed in the famous Che Guevara pose.[31] But as the political scientist Lilliana Mason details in her essential book *Uncivil Agreement*, this is more or less how our political system functions today.[32]

Theoretically, neither negative partisanship nor polarization advantages one party over the other. Indeed, in the 2020 election, polls consistently showed that Democratic voters were driven by negative partisanship, with more Democrats reporting that they were motivated to vote against President Trump than for their own nominee, former vice-president Joe Biden; in June, a Pew poll found the number of Democrats who said they were voting against Trump to be twice as large as the number voting for Biden.[33] However, when these forces combine with the rules of the modern Senate, they form a powerful structural advantage for conservatives.

Polarization turned the conservative movement into a conservative party. In 1955, William F. Buckley famously described the conservative movement as the one that "stands athwart history, yelling Stop."[34] At that time, conservatives were spread across the two parties, and the most conservative senators were Democrats. In the years since, polarized sorting has pushed most conservatives into the GOP. As late as 1972, fewer than half of white Republicans self-identified as conservative; today, 68 percent do.[35] What was once an ideological movement standing athwart history yelling "Stop" is now a party.

As the conservative party, Republicans reap far greater rewards from obstruction than Democrats do. To be sure, there are laws conservatives want to pass. But as we will see in Chapter Nine,

Republicans today struggle to pass major legislation because it is difficult to cobble together even a bare majority of votes among senators who are far more united by what they want to stop than what they want to pass. Republicans' incentive to act is weaker, since they can accomplish much of their agenda simply by doing nothing, while waiting for conservative courts to roll back laws and regulations. Liberals, on the other hand, are traditionally the force of social change, and their agenda tends to rely on passing major legislation. Other means of executing liberal priorities are far more limited in what they can do; establishing universal child care, banning assault weapons, or addressing climate change, for example, cannot be accomplished through executive actions, regulatory rollbacks, or court decisions.

The modern Senate creates a structural advantage for conservatives because its rules have evolved to make it incredibly easy to stop legislation. The chapters that follow will explain how, starting in the 1970s but exploding under McConnell, the filibuster became a commonplace feature of everyday Senate life. For now, it is enough to note that it did, and that it is therefore routinely accepted that forty-one senators can (and do) stop most legislation. Under any circumstances, assembling even a simple majority of votes to pass a bill is difficult—let alone the sixty votes needed to pass a bill through the modern Senate. With polarization pushing senators to their corners and negative partisanship rewarding them for making the other side fail, it is virtually impossible. By contrast, finding forty-one votes to block bills is relatively easy. This asymmetry goes beyond the level of checks and balances the Framers intended, since they designed the Senate as a majority-rule institution, and it creates an imbalance that tilts the system dramatically toward conservatives.

When these broad trends combine with the way Senate rules have evolved, they make Republicans' ability to impose their will virtually immune to electoral setbacks. In a polarized era infused with negative partisanship, Republicans are virtually guaranteed to maintain a grip on the forty-one Senate seats they need to block most major legislation—even if they occasionally find themselves on the wrong side of a wave election (or two). In 2020, Senate Republicans can assemble forty-one Senate seats using only states Trump carried in 2016 by an average margin of 24 points.[36] Senators from these deep red states—like Cotton—are the least likely to be vulnerable to political pressure that pushes them toward cooperation. Since their agenda is predominantly focused on stopping legislation and rolling back regulations, and since their voters reward them for any setback they inflict on Democrats, they are the most likely to reap political rewards through obstruction. In purely political terms, it is in these Republican senators' interests to focus more on "owning the libs" than working across the aisle.

It is tempting to think that at some point, Senate Republicans will decide it is in their interests to pursue bipartisanship, or that incentives will somehow align to push them toward cooperation. If a Democratic president wins in a landslide, for example, it is logical to think that it would be in Republicans' political interests to work with them. Unfortunately, the incentive structure of today's politics will consistently produce the answer that it is not, at least over any sustained period of time. Consider the elections of 2006 and 2008. In 2006, public anger at the Bush administration's mishandling of Hurricane Katrina and the Iraq War propelled Democrats to big midterm gains, taking back the House and Senate. In 2008, further propelled by the Great Recession, and with Bush's approval rating hitting a low of 25 percent, Democrats built on their gains, riding Obama's decisive victory to even bigger gains in the House and a sixty-vote supermajority in the Senate.[37] When Obama was inaugurated, his approval rating stood at 69 percent and Democrats controlled the House and Senate by the biggest margins either party had seen in decades.[38] If there was ever a time for Republicans to calculate that it was in their political interests to work with Democrats, this was it. Instead, Republicans responded with the relentless obstruction detailed in this chapter (and further in Chapter Nine). Obama's approval rating quickly declined, and by the end of 2010,

Republicans had retaken the House and cut Democrats' Senate majority by seven seats.

It has been suggested that Republicans were especially motivated to obstruct Obama because he is black, and it is indeed possible that a white president would not have provoked such an unprecedented experiment in obstruction. But whatever the motivation, the experiment was carried out, and for conservatives, it is impossible to argue with the results. Obstruction simply worked. Today, there is no reason for the new generation of eager obstructionists who rose to prominence through this system, like Senators Ted Cruz, Cotton, and Josh Hawley, to conclude that the results will be any less advantageous for them against the next president.

Unprecedented though it was, Republican senators' obstruction of Obama was a rational response to political incentives. But voters are the ones providing those incentives. If we are going to understand the modern Senate and the minority rule it imposes, we have to get to know the voters who power it.

THE VOTERS WHO fuel Senate Republicans' minority rule are themselves a minority of the U.S. population. In the twenty-first century, Senate Republicans have represented a minority of the population every year, despite holding as many as fifty-five seats, as they did from 2005 to 2006. At their low point this century, in 2009, Senate Republicans represented just 35 percent of the population.[39]

To some extent, this is a function of the original minority protection built into the Senate: the Great Compromise, which gave all states two senators regardless of population size. The problem is, in a word, California. At thirty-nine million people, California's population is as big as the twenty-two least populous states combined. Its population is as large as Canada's, and its economy is the size of Great Britain's.[40] When the Compromise was struck, the imbalances between the states were of a much smaller scale. The biggest state, Virginia, was about fourteen times larger than the smallest state,

Delaware. Today, California is seventy times larger than the smallest state, Wyoming.[41] The injustice Madison fumed about at the convention has been borne out. As the political scientists Frances E. Lee and Bruce Oppenheimer concluded, "By reference to the one person, one vote standard, the Senate is the most malapportioned legislature in the world."[42]

But while California helps explain Republicans' deficit, it neither excuses it nor fully accounts for it. The fact that Republicans appear to be effectively locked out of California's Senate seats for the foreseeable future is part of the larger problem facing their party, and a result of choices they have made in recent years. Republicans used to regularly win statewide office in California—think Ronald Reagan and Richard Nixon. They held the governor's mansion as recently as 2011. But as a party, the GOP has decided to focus its appeal on an ever-narrowing slice of the white population rather than seeking ways to compete in diverse states like California, often against the advice of many in their party who have urged a different approach.

But California is not the only problem; nor is the small-state bias in general. Looking at the Senate broadly, the small-state bias does not benefit Republicans nearly as much as the California problem implies. Yale political scientist David Mayhew has made this case for years, arguing that the Senate's small-state tilt toward Republicans is "quite small as well as quite stable."[43] The distribution of seats in today's Senate supports his case. In 2020, the Senate was closely divided between the parties: Republicans controlled fifty-three seats and Democrats forty-seven. Looking at seats by state population, there is no significant small-state bias toward Republicans. To the contrary, it's dead even. The twenty Senate seats representing the ten smallest states are evenly split between Democrats and Republicans, with each party holding ten. Wyoming, the smallest state, is deep red, but if you zoom out a little on the list of smallest states, a bunch of blue states are among them, including Vermont, Delaware, Rhode Island, and Hawaii. If you expand the group to the fifteen smallest states, the pattern is the same, with their thirty Senate seats evenly divided between the parties at fifteen each. The same pattern holds at the other end of the spectrum: among the ten most populous states, their twenty Senate seats are evenly split between the parties at ten each. In the mix behind California are Texas, Florida, and Ohio, big states where Republicans are competitive. New York is the third-most populous state, but other Democratic strongholds like Massachusetts fall outside the top ten.[44] Rounding out the ten most populous states are Georgia and North Carolina, which point to the explanation: the big bulge toward Republicans in the Senate comes in the Sunbelt states, which are not small; Georgia and North Carolina are bigger than New Jersey and Virginia.[45] Sunbelt states are also growing fast: in 2019, the South was the fastest-growing region in the country, while the Northeast's population fell.[46] Driven by the Sunbelt, Republicans' strength in the Senate does not represent a small-state bias, but rather a regional trend that has nothing to do with the fundamental structure of the Senate.

The fact that small and big states are evenly represented by Democrats and Republicans shows that the dysfunction in the modern Senate does not lie in its built-in bias toward small states. Instead, as this half of the book will show, it lies in the way its rules have evolved to give certain groups of people—as opposed to states—more power. (There is a silver lining here, since it would be much easier to change the Senate's rules than to break California into multiple states or carry out other proposals currently circulating—more on that in the Conclusion.) In the Sunbelt, for example, the populations that are driving the region's growth are at odds with their representatives in the Senate; the growth is being driven primarily by nonwhite residents who, on balance, are not casting ballots for the mostly white, conservative Republican senators who dominate the region.[47]

The minority of voters putting Republican senators in office are not representative of a rapidly diversifying America riven by income inequality and stagnant wages. They are predominantly white, anti-choice conservatives serving wealthy interests, whom I will call

WWACs for efficiency's sake. They are out of step with the direction of the country, and they spend year after year watching their status and power erode. But because the modern Senate empowers them far beyond their numbers, they are consistently able to impose their will on the majority.

White. In a country on track to be majority-minority by 2045, the voters who put white Republican senators in office are overwhelmingly white themselves. The Senate isn't exactly a bastion of diversity, but what little there is in the institution exists mostly on the Democratic side. As of this writing, ninety-one of the hundred senators are white, but only two—Tim Scott and Marco Rubio—of the nine nonwhite senators are Republican. The bloc of voters that elects Democrats is 42 percent nonwhite. By contrast, 88 percent of the voters who put Republicans in office are white.[48] While racial and ethnic minorities do not vote for conservative senators in significant numbers, they do live disproportionately in the states they represent. Proportionally, Mississippi has the highest black population in the country, but it has not elected a black senator since Reconstruction. One factor in the discrepancy between the large nonwhite populations in these states and their predominantly white, conservative representation in the Senate is that states represented by Senate Republicans tend to rank high on measures of voter suppression: Tennessee, Texas, Wyoming, Kansas, and Georgia make up five of the six worst offenders in a 2018 study of voter-suppression efforts, with Florida and Alabama also high on the list.[49] In his 2018 book *The Turnout Gap*, political scientist Bernard Fraga found that if turnout rates had been the same across racial and ethnic groups, "the Democratic Party would have held the presidency and Senate from 2008 through at least 2018."[50]

Wealthy interests. Senate Republicans represent plutocratic interests, and many of them are plutocrats themselves. With the country facing levels of income inequality not seen since the Great

Depression, senators are growing richer than ever before. In 2018, the total wealth of all members of Congress was $2.43 billion, a 20 percent increase from the previous Congress. Republican senators are the wealthiest of the wealthy, averaging a personal net worth of $1.4 million, 48 percent more than their Democratic colleagues.[51] Recent studies have shown that politicians of both parties are more responsive to the concerns of the rich than to those of poor or middle-class Americans, but Republicans are far more likely than Democrats to represent the interests of the wealthy.[52] Their voters are wealthier, too. Contrary to the countless navel-gazing portrayals of working-class white men in diners that followed the 2016 election, a 2017 study by the Public Religion Research Institute conducted for *The Atlantic* found that "being in fair or poor financial shape actually predicted support for Hillary Clinton among white working-class Americans, rather than support for Donald Trump," in an election that saw the tightest correlation in history between the votes for presidential and Senate candidates.[53]

Anti-choice. The voters who elect Republican senators are overwhelmingly anti-choice, but this was not always the case. In 1975, Gallup found that Americans who believed that abortion should be "legal under any circumstances" were spread evenly across the parties: 19 percent were Democrats, 18 percent were Republicans, and 24 percent were independents.[54] As governor of California, Ronald Reagan signed one of the most liberal abortion laws in the country, and Senator Barry Goldwater, a hard-line conservative on many issues, was prochoice.[55] Today, 75 percent of Republicans identify as "pro-life," but this puts them at odds with the rest of the country.[56] In a 2019 NPR/Marist poll, 77 percent of Americans said they wanted to see *Roe v. Wade* upheld.[57] In Gallup's polling, 78 percent of Americans believe abortion should be legal in all or certain circumstances.[58]

Conservative. As conservatives, WWACs are at odds with the general direction of the country, with America's current mood "the most liberal ever recorded," according to political scientist James Stimson's highly regarded "Public Mood Estimate," which goes back sixty-eight years.[59] So far, we have discussed how the alignment of conservative ideology with the Republican Party that strikes us as obvious today is a development of the past few decades. But we have not discussed why that alignment occurred: in a word, race. Nixon traces the line. From 1957 to 1960, as we have seen, Nixon was advocating for strong civil rights bills and leading a largely successful effort to expand GOP outreach to black voters. But in 1968, Nixon returned to American political life with a very different approach, using Democrats' support for the civil rights bills Johnson passed as president to draw racist white voters—those for whom studies showed that maintaining racial hierarchy was an acute motivating factor in their political choices—away from Democrats and into the GOP.[60] Nixon's strategy worked, and the conservatism Republican senators represent today, laced with racist undertones (and under Trump, overtones), is its legacy. As the Yale political scientist Alan I. Abramowitz writes in *The Great Alignment*, the ideological alignment of conservatives with the Republican Party that we today take for granted was driven predominantly by racism. During the period of realignment, Abramowitz finds, "the increase in Republican identification among white voters . . . was heavily concentrated among racial and economic conservatives—those whites most likely to be disturbed by the growing liberalism of the Democratic national party and by the growing visibility and influence of African Americans and other nonwhites within the party."[61]

Anti-black racism was just one element of the shift. The influx of nonwhite immigration that followed the 1965 Immigration Act inflamed whites' fears that their status and power were threatened.[62] As Duke University political scientist Ashley Jardina writes in *White Identity Politics*, demographic shifts "have led a sizeable proportion of whites to believe that their racial group, and the benefits that group enjoys, are endangered."[63] The belief that racial and ethnic diversification hurts America is not a fringe view; it is widely held among white Americans today. In 2019, a Pew poll found that nearly half of white Americans believed that growing diversity would "weaken American culture."[64] White fears that their power and status were endangered were not politically neutral. They had a clear direction, pushing those that held them to the right. As the political scientists Maureen Craig and Jennifer Richeson found in 2014, "making the changing national racial demographics salient" led whites "to endorse both race-related and relatively race-neutral conservative policy positions more strongly."[65] In 2016, people with a strong sense of white identity were far more likely to vote for Trump.[66] Racism was not just one factor driving partisan alignment; a substantial body of research shows that it was the *most important* factor. As the political scientists John Sides, Michael Tesler, and Lynn Vavreck write in their analysis of the 2016 election, *Identity Crisis*, "No other factor predicted changes in white partisanship during Obama's presidency as powerfully and consistently as racial attitudes."[67]

TOGETHER, these trends have brought together a far-right, reactionary population and put it in control over one of the two major parties in the United States. According to a 2019 *New York Times* analysis of data collected by the Manifesto Project, a group that tracks party-policy positions around the globe, the modern Republican Party is more extreme than Britain's Independence Party and France's National Rally party, both of which are far-right populist parties that verge on neofascism. Ideological polarization has been asymmetric, with the Republican Party moving much farther to the right than the Democratic Party has moved to the left; the same study found that the Democratic Party still aligns closely with mainstream liberal parties.[68]

According to an enormous body of peer-reviewed research from the leading nonpartisan analysts and political scientists in the country, the WWAC voters and interests on whose behalf Republican senators wield power represent a reactionary faction far to the right of the American mainstream; indeed, they are one of the farthest-right factions in any modern democracy worldwide. For the past twenty years, they have represented a minority of the U.S. population as the nonwhite share of the population continues its rapid rise. Because of the way the modern Senate has evolved, combined with the trends of polarization and negative partisanship that have shaped America, this faction is able to wield power far out of proportion to its numbers. The modern Senate gives it the power to exercise a veto over policies backed by a majority of the population and makes likely that it will have the power to do so in perpetuity. This is not just a minority. This is a superminority.

Over the past decade, Senate Republican leaders tried to feed the superminority's insatiable appetite for conflict by relentlessly obstructing Obama. But they quickly found the superminority resisting their control. It did not want to be controlled by Republican leaders. The superminority wanted Republican leaders to answer to them.

Chapter Six

OUTSIDE IN

IN 2013, NONE OF THE elected leaders of either party wanted to shut down the government. President Obama and the top four congressional leaders, who were evenly split between Democrats and Republicans, all wanted to find a way to avoid a shutdown. But the superminority wanted one. And while they were still badly outnumbered in the Senate, they found that they had enough power to bend Republican leaders to their will.

One of their champions was Senator David Vitter of Louisiana. In the summer of 2013, Vitter crafted an amendment aimed at causing financial pain to the people who worked for him and all members of Congress in order to manufacture a political point against Democrats. An ardent social conservative and staunch defender of "family values," Vitter had survived the 2007 revelation that he was on a client list kept by Deborah Jeane Palfrey, otherwise known as the DC Madam, who ran a high-end prostitution ring.[1] Now, he had cooked up a plan to take away the employer contributions to all Hill staffers' health care plans. There was nothing special about the nature of the employer contributions Hill staffers received—they were just like those all Americans receive if their employer offers them, as employers commonly do. But Vitter argued that unless Hill staffers were kicked off their plans and forced to shop for health care on their own, minus the contributions, they would be the beneficiaries of an "exemption" under Obamacare. It was an absurd theory, and it would amount to a financial hit of thousands of dollars for the average person.[2]

Privately, Republicans agreed it was senseless, while supporting it publicly. Quietly, Reid's staff began working with their counterparts in Speaker John Boehner's office to find a way around the problem. For months, Reid's chief of staff, David Krone, and Boehner's chief, Mike Sommers, worked to craft a solution. The White House was involved, and the talks were productive. In a July meeting with Reid, Boehner suggested that he and Reid quietly slip a fix into a must-pass bill. "When I was in the state legislature, we used to stick things in and no one would notice," Boehner said.[3] Reid didn't care if it was noticed and would have been fine with that approach. But given the hundreds of lobbyists and interest groups who comb through every bill, Boehner's hope that it would slip through was unrealistic and the idea was dropped. At one point, Boehner and Reid tried to arrange a meeting with President Obama on the issue. They could not let the topic of the meeting be known publicly, and the president's schedule is public, so Krone and Sommers discussed cover stories. "On next week's meeting—we need a different explanation for the purpose of the meeting," Sommers wrote to Krone in an email. "We can't let it get out there that this is for the Spkr and Ldr to ask the President to carve us out of the requirements of Obamacare." Krone replied, suggesting that the White House tell reporters that the meeting was about immigration. Sommers wrote back, "I really don't care what it is about—it just can't be about what we know it is about!"[4]

The meeting didn't happen. Like most Republicans, Boehner caved to Vitter. In the fall of 2013, Boehner attached the House version of the Vitter amendment to a funding bill. Krone was furious. Fiercely protective of the people who worked for him, he could not believe Republicans would hurt their own staff for something they acknowledged was purely a political ploy. Message bills had become a routine part of politics, but this was a different level of nastiness.

Krone's patience exhausted and sense of fair play violated, he called me into his office and handed me a manila folder with printouts of the emails between him and Sommers. Somehow, they wound up in *Politico*.[5]

Vitter was not the only one starting to bend the Senate to the superminority's will. By the fall of 2013, the fight over his amendment had become part of a larger push to defund Obamacare. The fight was led by Senator Ted Cruz of Texas. Congress controls the power of the purse, so all the funding needed to implement Obamacare passed through the Senate. Cruz urged Republicans to block all funding bills related to Obamacare. There was one problem with his strategy: it had no chance of success. Congressional Democrats were not going to defund the most significant accomplishment of the Obama administration. And if they took leave of their senses and did so, there was no chance Obama would sign a bill undoing his greatest achievement. Cruz's answer to this conundrum was to let the entire government shut down when its existing funds ran out at the end of the fiscal year on September 30.

The Republican establishment deemed Cruz's approach to be politically suicidal. Mike Murphy, a leading Republican strategist, channeled the establishment's angst when he told the Associated Press that the shutdown threat came from "the stupid wing of the Republican Party."[6] Senator Richard Burr of North Carolina told reporters, "I think it's the dumbest idea I've ever heard of."[7] Burr and Boehner were close, and at times like this, reporters took Burr's comments as a proxy for how Boehner felt. Indeed, in private, Boehner fumed. "These people are crazy, crazy," he told a confidant. "They just want a fight."[8] But in public, Boehner deferred to Cruz and his allies.

Boehner and the other Republican leaders were caught between two forces. Establishment Republicans of the ilk represented by Murphy and Burr were calling on them to do the responsible thing, and the leaders knew full well that Vitter's amendment, Cruz's push to defund Obamacare, and the ante-upping drive to shut down the government were all pathologically irresponsible. But on the other hand, they were scared to publicly oppose any of them because of a force they had once celebrated but now feared.

THE TEA PARTY became a household name in the summer of 2009, as white men in tricornered hats launched protests across the country. They claimed to be outraged about government spending despite not protesting against President George W. Bush, who spent more than any president since Lyndon Johnson.[9] For the most part, the media took the Tea Party's claim of profound fiscal concern at face value, even as signs at their rallies carried slogans such as "A Village in Kenya Is Missing Its Idiot: Deport Obama!" and "We Don't Want Socialism, You Arrogant Kenyan!" While Tea Party protests took place all over the country, the South—eleven states—accounted for 56 percent of the Tea Party's membership.[10] Whiter and wealthier than the overall population, anti-choice and extremely conservative, the Tea Party was the superminority base of WWACs in action.[11]

The threat posed to the Republican establishment became clear in Republican primary elections, as Tea Party candidates began knocking off establishment darlings. In the 2010 race for an open Senate seat in Florida, the Republican Party establishment had coalesced behind former governor Charlie Crist, a popular moderate and a finalist to be John McCain's vice-president in 2008. But the Tea Party backed a challenger named Marco Rubio instead. Rubio got the cold shoulder from the Washington establishment, but he did get one important endorsement: Republican senator Jim DeMint, an iconoclastic conservative and constant thorn in the side of Republican leaders. Washington cocked an eyebrow; *Politico* noted with bemusement that DeMint was "convinced the upstart [Rubio] can actually win."[12] Not only did Rubio win, he drove Crist from the Republican Party. Within months, Rubio's lead had grown so commanding that Crist abandoned the GOP primary and ran as an independent instead.[13] Rubio beat him by 19 points.[14] Today, Crist is a Democratic congressman representing St. Petersburg. To the horror of the GOP establishment, this pattern recurred across the map. In Utah, Tea Partier Mike Lee upset Senator Bob Bennett, a pillar of the GOP Senate establishment. In Kentucky, DeMint endorsed Rand Paul over McConnell's hand-picked protégé, Trey Grayson, and Paul won. In the 2012 race, DeMint endorsed Ted Cruz over the establishment favorite, Texas lieutenant governor David Dewhurst, and Cruz won.[15]

The Tea Party was showing strength in the terms that mattered most to politicians: winning elections. Through 2012, DeMint had been mostly freelancing. But in 2013, he sent chills down the establishment's spine by taking over the Heritage Foundation, the bespoke conservative think tank founded under Reagan.[16] Now, the Tea Party had the establishment surrounded. It had candidates inside the Senate, where they could influence the action and act as spies, feeding information to the movement about what Republican leaders were planning. And from the outside, DeMint, Heritage (and its partner organization, Heritage Action), and other Tea Party groups could threaten to wage primary challenges against Republicans who sided with establishment Republican leaders over the base. Republican senators started constantly looking over their shoulders, terrified of becoming the Tea Party's next target.

In 2013, this constellation of forces took up the fight to defund Obamacare and shut down the government. Heritage provided Cruz with a platform to make his case. At a Heritage-sponsored speech in August, Cruz delivered a call for defunding that brought the audience to its feet.[17] They reveled in defying the establishment. "We're not 'good Republicans,'" said Heritage Foundation vice-president Phillip Truluck. "We're conservatives." During the defunding push, Heritage Action would score certain votes as "key votes," and go after Republicans who voted against their recommendation. It put large sums of money behind its pressure campaigns, spending half a million dollars in ads targeting Republicans. Through their own shadowy network of organizations, the billionaire industrialists

Charles and David Koch poured more than $200 million into the effort.[18] "It's tremendous pressure," said Kansas congressman Tim Huelskamp, of the collective influence on lawmakers.[19]

The plan to shut down the government was so politically dangerous that most Senate Republicans tried to work around Cruz. By now, they were used to obstruction, but this seemed like *stupid* obstruction. But the superminority would not be denied. Cruz and his allies shifted their pressure to the House, where they worked closely with a group of Tea Party conservatives. They huddled in the windowless eateries in the basement of the Capitol and across the street at a Mexican restaurant called Tortilla Coast, where interns flock for buckets of Corona and free chips and salsa. Later, the House conservatives who plotted with Cruz would go on to form the House Freedom Caucus, which today remains the power center of the far right in the House. But in 2013, they were known as the "Tortilla Coast caucus."[20]

For weeks the House and Senate volleyed bills back and forth. But it was for naught. Just before midnight on September 30, the White House Office of Management and Budget sent out a memo. "Agencies should now execute plans for an orderly shutdown due to the absence of appropriations," the guidance read.[21] It was official: the government was shutting down. Reflecting on the role of the Tea Party and its network of outside groups, Congressman Matt Salmon enthused, "Without their help we probably wouldn't have gotten it done."[22]

WHILE TED CRUZ, David Vitter, and Jim DeMint were all innovators in their own right, they were building on a model that had been created forty years ago, by a single, visionary senator. Jesse Helms was a tall man who peered out at the world from behind the lenses of his trademark chunky-framed glasses. His owlish visage is not on any of the many marble busts that stand on pedestals throughout the Capitol, nor does he stare out from any of the oil paintings that adorn meeting rooms. Helms was an unrepentant racist, but that is not a disqualifying factor; the Dixiecrat Strom Thurmond has a room named after him. It's as though Helms never set foot in the place. Senate culture prizes institutionalists, and Helms was the furthest thing. Even though he shaped American politics more profoundly than all but a handful of senators in recent history, Helms has been wiped from the Senate's institutional memory.

Born in Monroe, North Carolina, the son of the chief of police, Helms was a devout Baptist and a doctrinaire conservative.[23] For the first half of his life, that meant being a Democrat. A fan of Richard Russell, Helms had served as a press staffer on Russell's ill-fated 1952 presidential run; when Russell lost, Helms urged him to run again (Russell demurred). Helms's first taste of success in politics came when he assisted the senatorial campaign of Willis Smith, a segregationist who was running against Franklin Porter Graham (no relation to the evangelical Grahams), the president of the University of North Carolina. Graham had a reputation as a progressive on civil rights. The Smith campaign used that against him, distributing flyers that said "White People Wake Up" and asked, "Do you want Negroes riding beside you, your wife and your daughters in buses, cabs and trains?"[24] Someone on the Smith campaign, widely rumored to be Helms, started calling UNC the "University of Negroes and Communists."[25] (The Jesse Helms Center contends that Helms's coinage of the phrase is "unproven."[26]) Smith won, and Helms, as an administrative assistant, got his first taste of Washington with him before heading back to Raleigh.

In North Carolina, Helms made a name for himself as a television commentator. In 1960 he became the vice-president of WRAL, one of the largest television stations in the state. He gave himself a segment on the nightly news broadcast, calling it "Viewpoint." His commentary reached about a million people per day.[27] In a tone of what Helms biographer Bryan Hardin Thrift calls "pious incitement," Helms's commentaries decried the moral rot of America brought on by liberal elites. He touched on many subjects, but he was fixated on race. "Dr. King's outfit is heavily laden at the top with leaders of proven records of Communism, socialism and sex perversion," he said in one. In another, he said he had obtained "evidence that the negroes and whites participating in the march to Montgomery engaged in sex orgies of the rawest sort." In another, he complained, "Negroes have been prompted by their agitating leaders to flout the law at every turn, to invade the rights of others, to thumb their noses at personal dignity and moral behavior."[28]

In 1970 Helms switched parties, putting him in the vanguard of racist southerners who were marching out of the Democratic party and into the GOP. In 1972 he ran for Senate against a Democratic congressman named Nick Galifianakis. With polls showing Galifianakis holding a double-digit lead, Helms pounded him with television ads. First the ads hit him for missing votes. "Where was Nick?" one asked. Then they tied Galifianakis to the Democratic presidential nominee, liberal senator George McGovern. Finally, with the race tightening, Helms took out a full-page newspaper ad with the unsubtle slogan, "Jesse Helms: He's One of Us." Helms won by 4 points.[29]

When he got to Washington, Helms had no intention of taking the Senate's slow track to seniority and influence. A week after taking office, he made his first speech. "I knew that tradition was one more way of maintaining the status quo, so I rose to the Senate floor to make my first speech on January 11, just eight days after being sworn in," Helms recalled in his memoir.[30] Looking for ways to make an impact, he became fascinated by the tactics of one of the Senate's least prominent members, Senator James Allen, a segregationist Democrat from Alabama. A "colorless" senator who "had little interest in the Washington social whirl," Allen was a master of Senate procedure who forged new uses for the filibuster.[31] Allen's filibusters were different from the coordinated group efforts launched by Russell and the South. His filibusters were lonely efforts, one man using the rules to make life difficult for his colleagues, with no goal other than to secure a concession on one of his pet issues.

Lacking much institutional power, Allen used the filibuster to make his colleagues pay attention to him and give him whatever he wanted so that he would stop throwing monkey wrenches in their plans. A loner, he operated outside the clubbishness of the party and was not susceptible to peer pressure. He obstructed because he could.

Helms appreciated Allen's tactics but had bigger plans for them. By the time Allen passed away in 1978, Helms had surpassed him as the chamber's master of the filibuster. But unlike Allen, he used it to drive broader messages and advance a larger mission: purifying the Republican Party by pulling it further to the right. At the time, it was common for senators to bring up votes on all sorts of issues, many of which could be politically damaging to their colleagues. And sometimes one party or the other might hold a "message vote" to draw a contrast on a major issue. But such votes were rarely initiated by a single senator, operating on his own, outside of the party.[32] Helms changed that by using Allen's tactics to make everyone in the Senate—Republicans as well as Democrats—take tough votes on whatever issue he felt like elevating. Allen may have innovated the tactic, but Helms made it hurt. As Helms recalled in his autobiography, "I knew when and how to make the call for a voice vote so Senators would have to attach their name to the issues they supported or chose not to support."[33]

Observers scoffed at Helms's tactics because his votes almost always failed, often by overwhelming margins. But these sophisticates were missing the point. The point was not to pass legislation; it was to demonstrate to his conservative base that he, Jesse Helms, was the only man in Washington who cared about the issues they cared about. He was, as Helms biographer Ernest B. Furgurson characterized him, their Horatius at the Bridge, holding back the liberal hordes. "Each of his amendments was like another WRAL editorial, drawn up to make a point," Furgurson writes.[34] When the votes failed, Helms's critics would chuckle at their futility. "My detractors, including newspaper editors, assumed that such losses were failures," Helms wrote. But in fact, "they were small victories on the way to big ones."[35]

What his critics didn't see, at least not for years, was that Helms turned these failed votes into big victories by feeding them into a grassroots fundraising machine, pioneering techniques widely used today. At the time, the political world had not seen anything like what Helms created. To cover a debt from his 1972 campaign, Helms had hired an enterprising conservative consultant named Richard Viguerie, who used a new method of fundraising that he called "direct mail." It was exactly what it sounded like: you sent people mail and asked them for money, the precursor to the fundraising emails that clog our inboxes today. Viguerie found that the more sensational the message, the more money it raised. When he fed Helms's message votes into his direct-mail system, the results were spectacular. Working within Helms's gothic worldview, Viguerie used his votes to craft alarmist messages about the decline of American society. "Your tax dollars are being used to pay for grade school classes that teach our children CANNIBALISM, WIFE-SWAPPING and the MURDER of infants and the elderly are acceptable behavior," one letter read.[36] Another featured pictures of civil rights activist Jesse Jackson and Julian Bond, president of the Southern Poverty Law Center, an antihate group; Bond was labeled a "black radical activist."[37] Enclosed in every mailer was a gentle but clear plea for funds. One read, "By sending $10, you can help expose the voting record of one or more liberal Senators to forty-seven American voters."[38]

It was massively successful, raising millions of dollars. Helms, a rank-and-file senator with no institutional power, now had one of the biggest fundraising machines in American politics. His colleagues begged him to let them use his mailing list. "Needless to say, there are a great many political figures around the country who are salivating over it," he told journalist Elizabeth Drew in 1981.[39] Helms's system was not powered by rich elites writing big checks, as political fundraising had been until then. It was powered by grass-roots donors giving five or ten or twenty-five dollars at a time, stuffing the bills in envelopes and putting them in the mail.[40]

The system thrived on resentment at elites, including the Republican establishment. Much as the Tea Party would decades later, Helms was reaching people who felt condescended to by a Republican Party that seemed more concerned with pleasing editorial boards and remaining in the good graces of the Georgetown cocktail circuit than standing up for rock-ribbed American values. This was, after all, a party that had recently come close to nominating the adulterous, liberal Republican governor of New York, Nelson Rockefeller, for president. Helms courted elites' scorn. Once, a young aide had been ready to dash off a letter in response to a nasty editorial about Helms in the *New York Times*. Helms stopped him. "Son, just so you understand: I don't care what *The New York Times* says about me," he said. "And nobody I care about cares what *The New York Times* says about me."[41] Helms's defiance of the establishment made him a hero to grassroots conservatives. "Many of the donors were in their 70s and 80s, the anti-communist, John Birch Society people," recalled Bob Hall, a liberal activist in North Carolina who worked against Helms in the 1970s. The same "donors who fought child labor laws in the 1930s were still around to bankroll his campaign."[42] As one of Helms's top aides, James Lucier, explained, "What Helms has been doing is appealing to people by going around the leadership structures. The direct mail short circuits the media and goes right into people's mailboxes. . . . What Helms has done is use technology to reach people directly."[43]

With the money he raised, Helms built an empire of pressure groups that, for tax reasons, claimed to be focused on policy issues, but were in fact focused on raising money and exerting political clout on his behalf. Helms's top aide, Tom Ellis, asked the white-shoe law firm Covington and Burling to find ways Helms could create organizations that would help him expand his reach while avoiding as many campaign finance and sunshine laws as possible.

The firm came back with an ingenious plan that would allow Helms to use the groups to pressure candidates while shielding the names of his donors from scrutiny.[44] Driven by his own ambition and ingenuity, Helms had just invented the model that the Tea Party would use to create its network of pressure groups years later and facilitate the 2013 government shutdown.

Helms's empire came to rival the Republican Party itself in its clout and fundraising capacity. He created groups across a range of issues: the Institute of American Relations (foreign policy), the American Family Institute (against abortion), the Institute on Money and Inflation (monetary policy), and so on. Above them all loomed the Congressional Club, his all-purpose hub, which raised $7 million for Helms's 1978 reelection race, a staggering sum at the time for a single Senate race. Helms's only rival for fundraising capacity, aside from the national party itself, was the National Conservative Political Action Committee—but Helms had helped establish it. At one point, Helms was asked to explain why he had created his latest group, and he explained that it was mainly for fundraising. "I think they figured they could be more effective in raising money if they didn't have a letter every week from the Congressional Club," he said.[45] More groups meant more causes he could ask his followers to fund, and they continued to do so eagerly.[46]

Helms used his clout to make and break senators. It was utterly unheard of for a senator to support challenges to other senators, but that did not deter Helms. "The Helms organization was so powerful that he could hand-pick senators," longtime North Carolina political reporters Rob Christensen and Jim Morrill recalled in the *Raleigh News and Observer*.[47] He picked John East of North Carolina and Jeremiah Denton of Alabama, two senators who were not the establishment's choices. Senator Robert Morgan, who was defeated by East, was so disturbed by his experience facing the Helms machine—of seeing what he thought were meaningless votes turned into fodder for a relentless political assault waged from out of state—that he submitted a report to the Senate to describe it. "I found myself faced with a constant barrage of distortions and mis-statements regarding my voting record," he said, seemingly still try-ing to get his head around it. "Procedural votes were taken to be substantive votes on issues, even though in the final analysis I cast my vote directly opposite the intent of the procedural vote."[48]

Senators were shocked at Helms's violation of norms. "He's brought a sort of mean mood to the Senate by taking on senators directly in a campaign—which is not done," said Helms's contem-porary, Senator Alan Cranston of California, at the time. "There hasn't been this kind of direct take-on since Joe McCarthy: the raising of money, the putting up of amendments he knows won't pass just to put Democrats to the test and then have mailings sent out against them," Cranston went on. But Helms's colleagues could whine about norms all they wanted. Every new victory expanded his influence, increasing his coterie of Senate allies and his ability to intimidate his colleagues, who feared they might be next.[49]

Consciously or not, Helms was rebuilding Russell's bloc of con-servative senators within the Republican Party. In 1981, the *New York Times* marveled at the coalition Helms commanded. "At least five of the freshman Republican senators are natural recruits to the Helms-McClure faction; many others, such as Alfonse D'Amato of New York and Dan Quayle of Indiana, are much closer to Helms than to such Republican liberals as Charles Percy of Illinois or Charles Mathias of Maryland," reporter Peter Ross Range wrote. "They will often join the right wing in issue-oriented coalitions, also supported by such incumbent Republicans as Strom Thur-mond of South Carolina and John Tower of Texas, who have now assumed powerful committee chairmanships. On many votes, the Helms faction can also count on sympathetic Southern Democrats, who have always felt more comfortable voting with Republicans on military and social issues than with the liberal leadership of their own party."[50]

In a time of flux, Helms was barraging his colleagues with mes-sage votes and using grassroots pressure to drive the GOP to the right. For his efforts, he was a hero to the conservative base. "You can be the leader who will save America," conservative activist Phyllis Schlafly told him.[51] Terry Dolan, another prominent conservative activist, gushed to Elizabeth Drew, "I don't think there's a more important person to the conservative movement in America than Jesse Helms—except, maybe, Ronald Reagan."[52]

BUT THERE MIGHT NEVER have been a President Reagan if it wasn't for Jesse Helms. Reagan's ascension to the nomination in 1980 was the culmination of a civil war within the Republican Party, touched off by incumbent Lyndon Johnson's landslide victory over Senator Barry Goldwater in the 1964 presidential election. Goldwater's book *Conscience of a Conservative* was a manifesto of the metastasizing movement called the New Right, and Goldwater campaigned as a proud extremist. In his 1964 convention speech, Goldwater famously declared that "extremism in defense of liberty is no vice," a phrase that thrilled conservative activists but horrified the establishment, prompting moderate senator Kenneth Keating to walk out of the convention and New York governor Nelson Rockefeller to call Goldwater's speech "dangerous, irresponsible and frightening."[53] They were right to fear: Goldwater won only six states, five southern states plus his native Arizona. In 1968 and 1972, Nixon won by straddling the warring wings of the party, appeasing conservatives with "law and order" rhetoric while pursuing more moderate policies like establishing relations with Communist China, which infuriated conservatives like Helms. When Watergate forced Nixon to resign in 1974, it left a void at the top of the party, and the moderates warred with the hardliners for supremacy. Nixon's successor, Gerald Ford, was squarely in the moderate camp, giving them the upper hand. But the New Right conservatives recruited Reagan, the charismatic governor of California, to run against Ford for the nomination in 1976.[54] The first senator to endorse Reagan was Helms.[55]

Reagan's 1976 campaign started off terribly. By the spring, he had lost the first five primary contests, he was in debt, and he was hounded by demands to drop out so the party could unify behind Ford. He was not just facing the end of a campaign; he was facing exile. Furious at him for challenging Ford, the moderate Republican establishment was ready to chase him and his Bircherite followers from the party. The next primary looked likely to be Reagan's last stand. But it was in North Carolina—Helms country.

Days before North Carolinians went to the polls, the state's Republican governor, James E. Holshouser, called for Reagan to drop out of the race. "With a deep appreciation for the past services which he has rendered to the Republican party," Holshouser said at a televised press conference, on behalf of a group of Republican governors, "we the undersigned Republican governors now call on Ronald Reagan to withdraw from the presidential race and to, with us and all other Republicans, work for the election of President Ford."[56] Luckily for Reagan, Helms had the real clout in the state. Helms's top adviser, Tom Ellis, seized control of Reagan's campaign. He drew staff for it from the Congressional Club, and pressured a local TV station to run a tape of a recent Reagan speech for five straight days before the election. Helms traveled the state as a surrogate. Under the control of the Helms machine, "Reagan's campaign in North Carolina was hard-hitting, aggressive, and heavily dependent on media exposure," Helms biographer William Link writes.[57] Reagan won the primary by 6 points, saving his political life.[58] His newfound momentum propelled him to a string of victories that were still not enough to win the nomination but gave him clout going into the convention. He won a number of concessions, the most important of which was a prime-time speaking slot. He seized the opportunity, using it to deliver a speech that electrified the convention and overshadowed Ford. As veteran political journalist and Reagan biographer Lou Cannon observed, "North Carolina was the turning point of Reagan's political career."[59]

When Ford went on to lose to Carter, the hard-liners were vindicated. The strength of Reagan's speech at the 1976 convention, along with the backing of the New Right, made Reagan the odds-on favorite to win the Republican nomination in 1980. He rolled to the convention, winning forty-four primary contests. In the general election, Helms's Congressional Club spent $4.6 million on Reagan's campaign as he marched to victory over Carter.[60] "Jesse Helms and Tom Ellis saved Ronald Reagan's career," recalled Reagan adviser Charlie Black; "without them, he wouldn't have been president."[61] Veteran political analyst Mark Shields concurs, writing that "without Jesse Helms's all-out support in Ronald Reagan's losing 1976 presidential primary fight with President Gerald Ford, the Gipper would never have won the White House in 1980 and 1984."[62] Reagan seemed to agree, too. On Helms's seventieth birthday, in 1991, the president wrote him a letter. "I'll never forget what you did for me in 1976," he wrote. "I shudder to think how things would have turned out had North Carolina not gambled on this guy."[63]

HELMS WAS NOT content with Reagan's victory, since it was just one part of his broader mission to drag the party as far to the right as possible. On the day of Reagan's inauguration, Helms made clear he was going to push the president, when necessary, from the right, by voting against Reagan's nominee for secretary of defense, Caspar Weinberger. Helms was one of only two senators to vote against Weinberger, who was confirmed by a vote of 97 to 2.[64]

The issue Helms had the greatest influence on was abortion. In the Senate, Helms was the most forceful opponent of abortion, by far. In a speech on the Senate floor, he called abortion "a few steps away from the reasoning that Hitler used to exterminate people."[65] Shortly after the *Roe v. Wade* decision in 1973, Helms introduced a constitutional amendment banning abortion.[66] He went after his colleagues, Democrats and Republicans alike, with message votes on abortion, slipping antiabortion amendments into legislation again and again.[67] Heading into 1980, the GOP was still relatively liberal on issues of women's equality and abortion, supporting both the

Equal Rights Amendment and abortion rights. But with his influence strengthened by Reagan's ascendance as the party's standard-bearer, Helms moved to remake the issue for Republicans. At the 1980 convention, he eliminated the GOP's support of the ERA from the party platform and replaced it with a call for his constitutional amendment banning abortion.[68]

Helms's efforts on abortion were backed by a new group that he helped bring into the Republican fold: conservative evangelicals. Helms realized that evangelicals were an untapped source of volunteers, donors, and voters for his conservative counterrevolution. In 1979 he helped facilitate the Reverend Jerry Falwell's efforts to create the Moral Majority, the organization that became the main vehicle for Falwell's political influence and a cornerstone of the Christian Right. "By 1980, Jesse had become the Christian Right's most important advocate in the Senate," Link writes.[69] Falwell returned the favor, leading registration drives that created thousands of new voters for Helms. "A voter registration drive by the Rev. Jerry Falwell added thousands of conservative whites to the rolls this year," the *New York Times* reported during Helms's reelection race in 1984.[70] Falwell's Liberty University would later name its school of government after Jesse Helms.[71] "I've had two heroes in my life: Jesse Helms and Ronald Reagan," Falwell said.[72]

At a moment in history when the GOP was still relatively liberal on social issues, Helms pushed it to become the culture-warring party we know today. "When he began to push the issues that we started with when we opened the door in 1973—abortion, a balanced budget, family issues, sound money, a strong foreign policy—he was derided as a hopeless reactionary," Helms's aide, James Lucier, said in 1981. "Now those issues have become the mainstream issues that senators rise and fall on."[73]

WHEN MIKE MURPHY, the GOP strategist, called the Tea Party the "stupid wing" of the party for shutting down the government

in 2013, he was voicing a widely held sense of consternation at conservative activists' determination to torpedo the party's broader
appeal simply to motivate the base. Decades earlier, and provoking
the same revulsion among establishment Republicans, Helms had
showed how to practice this base-centric appeal, putting his own
party on the spot and alienating moderates by using the Senate floor
to rail against Martin Luther King Jr.

In 1983, most Democrats and Republicans in Washington backed
a bill creating a federal holiday honoring the Reverend Dr. Martin Luther King Jr. But facing a tough reelection and knowing that
his voters in North Carolina would rally to his side, Helms filibustered the bill, sparking widespread coverage and making the entire
Republican Party look like a bunch of troglodytes. On the floor, he
argued that King did not deserve to be honored because his legacy
was really one of "action-oriented Marxism" that "is not compatible
with the concepts of this country."[74] King was a divider, not a uniter,
Helms contended, since his "very name itself remains a source of
tension, a deeply troubling symbol of divided society."[75]

Republican leaders were aghast. The Republican majority leader,
Howard Baker, reached for Rule 22 to cut off Helms's filibuster.
Trying to cordon off Helms from the rest of the party, Republican
aides assured reporters that even President Reagan supported the
bill (he signed it, after Helms's filibuster was broken). One Republican aide told the *New York Times*, "You've got a bunch of people
out there who are scared to death. They don't need this hanging
around their necks." Helms laughed off reporters who didn't understand that his display would motivate his base and help him win
reelection. "I'm not going to get any black votes, period," he told a
reporter.[76] Helms needed to raise money, and stunts like his opposition to the King holiday were exactly the kind of thing that brought
in the cash-stuffed envelopes and kept his empire funded. His race
that year, against the popular Democratic governor Jim Hunt, was
the most expensive Senate race in history to date, with the two
sides spending a record-shattering $22 million combined.[77] It was

close, but Helms knew who his voters were, and what they wanted. He prevailed.

In 1990, Helms faced another stiff challenge, this time from former Charlotte mayor Harvey Gantt, who was black. Helms used the same playbook, running an ad that would go down as one of the most racist in recent American history. Titled "Hands," it showed a pair of white hands holding, then crumpling up, a letter. "You needed that job, and you were the best qualified," the narrator explains. "But they had to give it to a minority, because of a racial quota." In another tight race, the ad helped put Helms over the top.[78]

On October 16, 2013, the government shutdown ended with a whimper, and the establishment breathed a sigh of relief. For sixteen days, Reid and House minority leader Nancy Pelosi, working closely with President Obama, held firm and gave Republicans nothing. Under pressure from an outraged public, Republicans caved, allowing the government to reopen with nothing to show for their effort. Obamacare remained untouched. "Goose egg, nothing, we got nothing," said GOP representative Thomas H. Massie. The Tea Party's strategy had been a disaster, it seemed. They had succeeded only in making their entire party look incompetent.[79] At a Heritage-sponsored lecture earlier that fall—part of its Jesse Helms Lecture Series—Cruz had enthused, "We need 100 more like Jesse Helms in the U.S. Senate."[80] Among his Senate Republican colleagues, it was probably an unpopular opinion.

But outside the Senate, the system Cruz had used to shut down the government was undiminished by the failure. Modeled, consciously or not, on the structure, messaging, and tactics that Helms had pioneered, and powered by a grassroots base of far-right conservatives and evangelicals he had helped bring into the Republican fold, the superminority was immune to Beltway opinion. Operating in a political environment defined by polarization and negative partisanship, it didn't matter to the superminority if its side lost, so long as it kept attacking the other team.

If establishment Republican leaders hoped the failure would teach the Tea Party a lesson, they would be disappointed. The superminority did not draw its strength from the support of savvy Beltway strategists, or even Republican leaders, and it scoffed at antiquated notions like broadening the party's appeal. It drew its strength, as Helms had, from conflict. After the 2013 shutdown the superminority would only grow in strength, and Republican leaders would face a choice: they could stand against, and inevitably fall to, this force pounding them from the outside. Or they could choose to invite this outside force in, as one Senate Republican leader soon would.

Chapter Seven

MEANS OF CONTROL

THE 2010 WAVE THAT MARKED the arrival of the Tea Party was a grievous setback for Democrats. The losses up and down the ballot were crushing and could not have come at a worse time. Seats in the House of Representatives are redistricted at the start of each new decade to reflect the new census, and the Republican wave flooded statehouses across the country, in addition to congressional races. Republicans' newfound power at the state level put them in control of the redistricting process, allowing them to gerrymander districts and entrench their power. But as the red wave washed away Democrats from coast to coast, there was one politician, widely expected to fall, who did not: Senator Harry Reid of Nevada.

As the 2010 election cycle began, Republican Party leaders made clear that beating Reid was their top priority in the Senate, and they felt bullish about their chances. Reid was the easiest man in politics to underestimate. Stiff on camera and unskilled at rhetoric, Reid often left people wondering how he had managed to rise to the rank of Senate majority leader. But those who knew his story did not wonder. Reid was born to a penniless family in the mining town of Searchlight, which to this day is miles from anything but desert. His mother did laundry for the town brothels and he learned to swim in one of their pools. His childhood home can only be described as a shack ("I thought it was nice," he said when I asked him about a picture of it).

Determined to make it out of Searchlight, Reid grew up fighting. "I was raised where you settled your differences physically," he explained to an interviewer.[1] A slender man, he became an amateur boxer and learned that while he would never be the biggest or strongest guy in the ring, he could win if he threw the hardest punch. One punch he landed was against a man named Doc Gould. The father of Reid's high school sweetheart, Landra, Doc stood in the doorway of the Gould family home one day when Reid came to pick up his date, demanding that the youngsters break off the relationship because Reid was not Jewish, as the Goulds were. Pushing and shoving ensued, and the two men spilled out into the front yard, where Reid slugged Doc. He and Landra eloped and they are still married today. Later, Reid and Doc reconciled, and Reid wears Doc's ring in his memory. "It's hard to say what goes through your mind as you start a fistfight with your future father-in-law," Reid recalled in his memoir. But, he shrugged, "life must be lived."[2]

Now, in 2010, as the top target of the Republican Party and facing what would be the worst political year for Democrats in decades, Reid fought back from every angle. At a time when other Democrats were running scared on immigration and tacking to the right, Reid's senior strategist, José Parra, advised him to do the opposite and emphasize his support for immigrants. Reid listened, and followed Parra's recommendation. He also recruited Nevada's top Republican operative, Sig Rogich, to help run "Republicans for Reid." Most importantly, Reid picked his opponent. The eventual Republican nominee, former state assemblywoman Sharron Angle, was so erratic that many pundits assumed Reid was the luckiest man in Las Vegas; "You look a little more Asian to me," she told a group of Latino students at one campaign stop.[3] But what pundits wrote off as luck was the result of years of painstaking work. There had been no shortage of strong Republican challengers eager to face Reid in this high-profile race, and from the beginning, the national GOP made clear that whoever ran against him would have all the resources they needed. Yet in the lead-up to the race, all of the potential A-list challengers discovered alternative futures.

One of the first Republicans to signal his intention to run against Reid was Lieutenant Governor Brian Krolicki. Less than three weeks after saying he was considering a run, Krolicki was indicted for misappropriation of public funds by then attorney general Catherine Cortez Masto. Forced to focus on beating the charges against him instead of challenging Reid, Krolicki fell out of the picture. (A federal judge later dismissed the charges.)[4] Another rising Republican star named Joe Heck, a doctor and Iraq War veteran, was eyeing a run, too. But first, he had to win reelection to his state senate seat, and he found himself up against a surprisingly well-funded neophyte named Shirley Breeden, who beat him by one percentage point; now Heck was out of the picture, too.[5] Congressman Dean Heller was eager to run, but Reid raised so much money so fast for his own campaign that he convinced Heller to wait and run for the state's other senate seat, which looked like it might open up soon; it did. Then there was Brian Sandoval, Nevada's former attorney general. A charismatic moderate and a Latino leader in a state with a large Latino population, Sandoval was widely seen as one of the GOP's brightest talents and would have been a daunting opponent against Reid. But Reid had already helped Sandoval secure a federal judgeship, recommending him to President George W. Bush in 2004. In 2010, Sandoval resigned his seat on the bench to run for office— but not against Reid.[6]

At least, not against Reid the elder. One person who resisted the future Reid had picked for him was his son, Rory. The executive of Clark County, the state's most populous, Rory was eager to run for governor. Reid advised him not to. In a year like 2010, facing major headwinds, there was probably only room for one Reid on the ballot in Nevada, he figured. But Rory ran anyway. While his dad built a juggernaut of a campaign, Rory got no help from it. At the same time, he drew Sandoval as an opponent (and away from his father). As the campaign wore on, it became clear that Harry's focus on turning out Latino voters was helping Sandoval and hurting Rory. Though ticket splitting was rare by this point, in this unique situation Latino voters, at least, were splitting their votes. The elder Reid knew he was helping Sandoval but did not shift his priorities, as his campaign continued to aggressively turn out voters who were voting for him but against his son.[7]

That November, Reid's election-night party at the Aria Resort and Casino was one of the few happy ones for Democrats anywhere in the country, as race after race went to Republicans. In Reid's race, the final poll from the *Las Vegas Sun* had him losing by 5 points; instead, he won by 5.[8] (Rory lost.) I had joined Reid's office earlier that year, assuming the job was just a brief foot in the door to Senate leadership, given the universal expectation that Reid was going to lose. I had applied to law school to keep my options open and was planning to enroll. But as I stood in the crowd of supporters watching Reid give his victory speech, I realized that this might not be a short-term gig after all.

THE ARIA CASINO was a fitting venue for Reid's election-night party. He had personally intervened to save the financing for it and other immense casinos on the Las Vegas Strip that were under construction when the financial crash of 2008 hit. But his career was intertwined with the casinos of the Strip going much further back.

Reid first made his mark in the late 1970s by squeezing the mob out of their control of the big casinos. The Martin Scorsese movie *Casino*, which Reid has never watched, revolves around a key moment in his career. The setting was a 1978 meeting of the Nevada Gaming Commission, which controls all gaming licenses. The passage of the Racketeer Influenced and Corrupt Organizations Act, better known as the RICO Act, had weakened the mob. In Las Vegas, corporations were pushing out the Teamsters pension fund and other sources of mob capital to secure control of the highly profitable casinos for themselves. Reid was chair of the Gaming Commission, and under his leadership, it voted to deny the license of Frank "Lefty" Rosenthal, who in addition to being tied to the mob was widely considered to be the greatest oddsmaker in America. (In the movie, Robert De Niro's character is based on Rosenthal.) In Las Vegas, having your license denied was a professional death sentence since it exiled you from the city's dominant industry. When the commission's decision came down, Rosenthal was apoplectic.

Watching old news footage one night, I noticed that what took place at that Gaming Commission meeting was portrayed almost shot for shot in the movie—except Scorsese seemed to tone it down to make it more believable. When the vote to deny Rosenthal's license was gaveled down, the real-life Rosenthal stood up, furious, and began stalking around the room, shouting at Reid as the news cameras rolled. Wearing sunglasses (though the meeting occurred, of course, indoors), a tan leisure suit, and a fedora, he accused Reid of accepting a comped lunch and other favors from him prior to denying him his license. "Kangaroo court," Rosenthal spat, and lit a cigarette. While Rosenthal fumed, a camera zoomed in on Reid, who seemed to be thinking about whether to engage. The vote was over. The knife was in. There was nothing Rosenthal could do. Reid engaged, speaking in a calm, soft voice, as he gave answers that didn't *exactly* refute all of Rosenthal's accusations. It didn't matter. Rosenthal's career was over. And the quiet-voiced man, whom one mobster would call "cleanface" in a phone call picked up by an FBI wiretap, had ended it.

Two years later, Reid's wife, Landra, was running errands in their station wagon when the car started to lurch and misfire. She pulled into their driveway, opened the hood, and found a wire leading from a spark plug to the gas tank. The police report found that the device was rigged "in an apparent attempt to ignite the fuel."[9] In other words, it was a car bomb. But the tip of the spark plug had broken off, likely saving Landra's life.[10] "Lefty Rosenthal was the only person I was ever afraid of," Reid would recall decades later. "He was the kind of guy who wouldn't hurt you himself. He'd hire somebody to do it."[11]

Lefty Rosenthal, the American mob, Sharron Angle, and the Republican Party all lost to Reid for the same reason. He instantly recognizes power imbalances, as he did in that Gaming Commission meeting with Rosenthal, and then uses everything at his disposal to exploit the weak spot and achieve his goal. In the Senate, in 2005, Reid saw a weak spot amid the glow of President George W. Bush's reelection, and built a political structure capable of taking full advantage, a system of top-down control more powerful than anything the institution had ever seen. A theme of this book is that building and wielding power in the Senate is a bipartisan pursuit. As we'll see, Reid has been accused of centralizing too much power in the leader's role, and wielding it to the detriment of the institution. But to understand how he built that power in the first place, we need to return to Lyndon Johnson.

IN THE BEGINNING, there were no leaders. The first Senate, designated by the election of America's first two senators in 1788, was tiny, made up of just twenty-six senators.[12] In stark contrast to the empty floor that defines the chamber today, the Senate would meet as a body and the agenda would be set by members who sat together and decided what to do among themselves. For more than a century, when contemporaries referred to Senate "leaders," they were referring to those who had distinguished themselves through skill or accomplishment, not party leaders. Through the nineteenth century, prominence in the Senate rested on things like oratorical skills, as with Webster, or an ability to command the support of a regional bloc, as with Calhoun, or an ability to forge compromises, as with Clay. While senators grouped themselves by party from its earliest days, they did not start organizing the chamber by party on decisions such as committee leadership until the middle of the nineteenth century. Even then, it would be several decades before they created a formal role for party leaders.[13] Bills, votes, and the senators themselves ranged across political boundaries, a dynamic that remained the norm for nearly a century to come.

As the nation grew and the federal government assumed more powers, the Senate expanded, as did its workload. To accommodate the additional responsibilities, the number of committees grew, and in the 1880s the Senate authorized its members to employ clerks; for the first time, senators had professional staff. In 1909, to accommodate senators who now had staffs to run and found the dilapidated Maltby Building insufficient to their needs, the first new Senate office building was opened, the grand beaux arts structure along Constitution Avenue that today is named after Richard Russell.

As the Senate grew and changed, one constant remained: the role of party leader was at best a figurehead. In 1878, the *New York Times* noted that the Senate had no "distinctly recognized leaders." In 1885, Woodrow Wilson, then a political science professor, wrote that in the Senate, "no one may speak for his party as well as for himself; no one exercises the special trust of acknowledged leadership."[14] Finally, to deal with the challenges of memberships and workloads that continued to grow, Senate Democrats created the formal position of leader in 1920 and Republicans followed in 1925. Still, the position remained far more of a secretarial job than one with real power and continued to be dismissed as insignificant through the first half of the twentieth century.[15]

This was true until 1952, when Richard Russell anointed Lyndon Johnson as the Democratic leader. Spurred, as we have seen, by ambition and a fear of ending up like his hapless predecessors as leader, Johnson moved to endow the position with real power. His mission began with the thing senators cared most about: committee assignments. Before Johnson, the leader had virtually no influence over committee assignments. The system was on autopilot according to seniority. When a vacancy opened up, the senator with the most seniority who wanted it, got it. But Johnson saw an opening.

Starting in the 1930s, Democrats had dominated both chambers of Congress and begun taking their control for granted. But they lost their Senate majority in Eisenhower's 1952 landslide, leaving them reeling. Johnson exploited Democrats' insecurity to break the seniority system, convincing the old bulls that the only way they could counter Eisenhower's popularity and avoid being relegated to permanent minority status was to elevate some of their young stars, like Hubert Humphrey and Mike Mansfield, onto the key committees, where they could gain a national platform and serve as compelling spokespeople for the party. Russell backed the move, and the combination of his support and Johnson's persuasive powers convinced the committee chairs to let Johnson play a role in doling out committee assignments. For the first time, a Senate leader had real power over his caucus.[16]

Next, Johnson moved to control the floor.[17] Prior to Johnson, the process of bringing bills to the floor was dominated by the committees, and the idea of the leader exerting control or making policy recommendations was virtually unheard of. For their part, senators decided how to vote on the bills that came to the floor based on a mix of factors, including the information they received from the chairs of the relevant committees and from constituents and interest groups, public opinion, and their own views; the wishes of the leader did not rank. Early in his tenure as leader, Johnson moved to assert control over the floor schedule and inject himself into senators' decision-making process. His vehicle was the Democratic Policy Committee, a sleepy backwater that Johnson reimagined as a way to centralize information in the leader's office—and information was power. In a Senate where issues were siloed by committee, the DPC began ranging across all issues, with the new staff Johnson had hired politely keeping tabs on all committee business. Having a window into the committees enabled Johnson to map out what bills would be coming out of which committees when, and to develop a schedule for the floor. It also gave him a pretense to offer competing recommendations when he wanted to, and constantly check in with chairmen and the members of their committees—ostensibly to inquire about the committees' business, but also to canvass for any other piece of information that might come up in conversation and prove useful down the road. "The Senate Democratic Policy Committee is in need of regular information upon the activities of various Legislative Committees of the Senate," Johnson wrote to each of the fifteen standing committees, asking them to designate a staff member who could provide the DPC with weekly updates. The leader, he made clear, sought "a report upon the status of legislation pending in your committee" along with updates on the "probable timeline for action." The second word in the name of the committee making the request was "policy," but "Bill analyses are not requested," Johnson noted.[18]

With all this information in hand, Johnson was positioned to make his wishes known to his colleagues as only he could. A series of 1957 photographs by *New York Times* photographer George Tames capture what became known as the "Johnson treatment." Squared up to Senator Theodore F. Green, who as the chairman of the powerful Foreign Relations Committee would have been accustomed to deference, Johnson stands belly to belly, prods Green with his left hand, and grabs him with his right before getting nose to nose.[19] As one aide described a conversation between Johnson and Kefauver, the Tennessee senator "couldn't have gotten away without leaving his lapel behind."[20] Unlike previous leaders, Johnson took control of an office steps from the Senate floor so he could be close to the action at all possible times—and to have a nearby sanctuary for conversations that were better held in private than on the Senate floor. It was this space that, once Johnson refurbished it to his liking, became known as the "Taj Mahal" and was where I would later spend years watching Reid use the tools Johnson fashioned to exert control in his own quieter way.[21]

Today, it is taken for granted that the Senate leader controls the Senate floor. But that was not true until Johnson used his sheer ingenuity and ambition to make it so.[22] It got to the point that he controlled the chamber with his hands—literally. As the historian Doris Kearns Goodwin described in her classic account, *Lyndon Johnson and the American Dream*, "If things were moving well, and the votes were in place, he would twirl his finger rapidly in a circular motion, and the roll call would proceed at a fast clip. If his aides were still out looking for a Senator whose vote was essential, Johnson would push the palm of his hand downward, and the names would be called at a slow pace."[23] For most of its existence, the Senate floor had been a wide-open playing field. But now, as Caro writes, "Lyndon Johnson was in charge of that floor."[24]

THERE WAS ONE MORE tool of control that Johnson wielded unlike any other leader before him: money. With his connections to Texas oil barons, Johnson had an enormous reservoir of funds he could distribute at will, at a time when there were few restrictions on political donations. Johnson would dispatch staffers around the country to pick up deliveries of cash, or money would make its way to him in envelopes handed over from lobbyists like Tommy Corcoran, also known as Tommy the Cork. Johnson would then apportion it to senators as he saw fit.[25]

The bagman was often a young Senate aide named Bobby Baker. Baker had a special talent for uncovering skeletons and taking the measure of a senator, assessing what would convince them to move in the direction Johnson wanted. He became an extension of Johnson, trolling the floor for any tidbit that might help the leader work one angle or another. Often, that amounted to calculating a senator's price and delivering it. "On one occasion, I was asked to transmit $5,000 from Lyndon B. Johnson" to another senator, Baker writes in his memoir, *Wheeling and Dealing*. "As was the Washington practice, Johnson handed me the boodle in cash. 'Bobby,' he said, 'Styles Bridges is throwing an "appreciation dinner" for himself up in New Hampshire sometime next week. Fly up there and drop this in the kitty and be damn sure that Styles knows it came from me.' "[26] Baker became so powerful in his own right that he began referring to himself, with some credence, as the "101st senator." In 1963, he faced a federal corruption investigation, an explosive scandal that threatened to consume Johnson and the entire Kennedy administration, until Kennedy's assassination that November shoved it from the news. In 1967, Baker was convicted of tax evasion, conspiracy to defraud the government, and theft. After losing his appeals, he spent fifteen months in prison.[27]

Baker may have been the conduit, but the desire for the cash came from Johnson himself. It was a drive that spanned both his personal and political life, but only the political is relevant here. Under Johnson, money distributed by leadership became a powerful means of control. And he kept it flowing. "It was never enough for Johnson—never," Ed Clark, one of the top fundraisers in Texas, told Caro. "How much did he want?—he *wanted*," said another associate, Claude Wild. "He wanted all you could give and more."[28]

Remarkably, even after Johnson finished remaking the role of Senate leader into a position worthy of the name, it still had little *formal* power. In the House, the Speaker controls the all-powerful Rules Committee, which sets the terms for every bill that comes to the floor, from how long debate will last to when and under exactly what conditions the vote will take place. To this day, the Senate majority leader enjoys no such structural control. Using nothing but scraps, Johnson stitched together an enveloping system of influence. In the blink of an eye in Senate time, the role of leader went from a figurehead to one that could punish or reward senators with the currency they valued most, committee assignments. It could shape and direct the Senate's agenda, and influence what went on in its decentralized nodes of power, the committees themselves. Through Baker, and through his own constant probing and reading of his colleagues, it became a central repository of intelligence about what senators wanted and where their vulnerabilities lay; and through the spigot of cash that he alone could turn on and direct, it became a source of financial gifts that he could use to reward senators—or punish in the withholding—on his whim.

In 1937, the Senate gave the leader the right of first recognition, or the ability to speak first when multiple senators were vying for control of the floor at the same time. At the time it didn't mean much, since whatever the leader had to say tended to have little impact on the chamber. Sometimes, trying to lead the chamber would backfire badly on a leader, as in 1949, when then majority leader Scott Lucas had tried to change Rule 22 over Russell's opposition, only to find himself roundly humiliated by the Georgia senator—who held no formal leadership role but directed the chamber's action more than any of his peers.[29] But starting under Johnson, when the leader spoke, senators listened.

JOHNSON'S SEIZURE OF control was a shock to the institution. At first, the Democratic caucus went along with it, in part because he delivered results, and in part because he imposed his system of control piecemeal, making it hard for others to see how all the parts fit together.[30] There had been no single decision to give him power; even the decision to give him power over committee assignments had been blindered, as senators did not foresee how it would be used in Johnson's hands. Before long, the backlash came.

In 1959, a first-term Democratic senator from Wisconsin, William Proxmire, rebelled. In a television interview in his home state, he complained, "If you want to be treated well in the Senate under the present system, you have to be in good standing with the Senator from Texas," referring to Johnson.[31] He brought his fight to the floor, rising on February 23 to deliver what he said would be the first in a series of speeches criticizing Johnson's iron-fisted rule. "There has never been a time when power has been as sharply concentrated as it is today in the Senate," Proxmire declared.[32] He didn't get very far before Senator Richard Neuberger of Oregon rose to speak and asked Proxmire when he had arrived at his conclusions. Proxmire said he had come to them "over a substantial period of time." Neuberger went in for the kill. "Unless my memory fails me, the Senator from Wisconsin, during that portion of his career before his election to a 6-year term, probably 'buttered up' the majority leader more than any other Senator of the then 96 Members of this body," Neuberger said. Interjecting, Proxmire objected to the use of "buttered up." As Republican senators sat back and smiled at the open conflict among Democrats, Neuberger replied sarcastically, "Let me say 'lavishly praised,' and 'glowingly lauded.' "[33] Then he read a series of quotes of Proxmire praising Johnson. He added an admonition to the more junior senator. "You are biting the hand that feeds you," Neuberger said. "Everything you've got in the Senate was given to you by Lyndon Johnson."[34] Johnson had imposed his will on the Senate, but now senators were divided over whether they wanted to be led.

When Johnson left for the vice-presidency, his deputy, Senator Mike Mansfield of Montana, ascended to the leader's job. But it was not a smooth transition. Johnson was miserable in the Kennedy administration, openly despised by the president's brother Bobby, and finding his Hill Country style an awkward fit in Camelot. "Power is where power goes," Johnson liked to say, but that was not proving to be true.[35] To find a place for himself, he tried maintaining control of the Senate. He asked Mansfield to change the traditional rules governing the Democratic Party caucus to allow him, a member of the executive branch, to preside over the caucus, including sitting in on their closed-door strategy sessions. The deferential Mansfield agreed. When the caucus convened in its private session to elect new leaders, Johnson presided over the election of Mansfield as majority leader. And then he simply didn't leave. Nor did he cede the leader's chair to Mansfield. The members of the caucus were shocked, and a polite senatorial revolt ensued. It quickly became clear that Johnson's position was untenable; he may have been a great leader once, but now he was out of the club. Mansfield was forced to walk back his accommodation and Johnson slunk out of the Capitol, embarrassed.[36]

Though Mansfield recovered, deference to other senators was the signature of his era as leader, and the key to its success. He presided over a series of major accomplishments through the 1960s and into the 1970s, overseeing the passage of Johnson's Great Society programs. The anti-Johnson, Mansfield rarely gave marching orders and encouraged senators to act independently. "Nobody is telling anybody else what to do," he told an interviewer.[37] Mansfield is not a subject of historical fascination like Johnson, but his deference should not be construed as weakness, because he delivered one major law after another. Nor was it a return to the days prior to Johnson, when the leader was a figurehead. Mansfield struck a delicate balance between leading and allowing himself to be led during a period of Senate history defined by what historians and political scientists have dubbed "individualism."[38] It was the right fit for the time and it made him a caucus favorite. Today, whenever leaders of either party are asked who their role models are, Mansfield is a popular answer; whether or not it's true, it's what their members want to hear. Mansfield's popularity and record of success helped make him the longest-tenured leader in Senate history.

The Mansfield model proved so enduring that well into the twenty-first century the keenest Senate watchers concluded that Johnson had been an aberration. In his excellent 2005 history of the Senate, *The Most Exclusive Club*, historian Lewis L. Gould writes, "Lyndon Johnson did not change the Senate or create an enduring new role for the majority leader. . . . The leaders, Republican and Democrat, who have followed Mansfield have not sought a return to the Johnson technique of governing the Senate."[39] At the time, Gould was absolutely correct. But the Mansfield model practiced by subsequent leaders like Robert Byrd and Howard Baker was possible at a time of relatively weak partisanship and low polarization. And times were changing.

UNTIL 1980, Democratic control of Congress seemed like a fact of life. Starting in 1955, Democrats held unbroken control of the Senate for twenty-six years. The story was similar in the House, but more extreme: between 1933 and 1995 Democrats controlled the House for all but four years. With control of the majority out of sight, and plenty of points of ideological connection across the aisle, Republican senators also tended to assume Democratic control was impossible to dislodge, and focused more on exerting their influence on policy than trying to take back the majority.[40] That changed in 1980, when Democrats lost control of the Senate amid the Reagan landslide. That loss inaugurated a new era where the majority frequently changes hands. Between 1980 and 2018, control of the Senate majority has changed hands nine times.

This period, which we are still in today, is defined by what the political scientist Frances E. Lee terms "insecure majorities": the majority is always vulnerable to being reclaimed by the other side. With the exception of Democrats' six-month sojourn with a sixty-vote supermajority from late 2009 to January 2010, since 1980, both sides' majorities have usually numbered in the mid- to low fifties. If reclaiming control is not possible in one two-year election cycle, it is usually possible within two cycles. These small margins of control decrease the incentive to help the other side secure accomplishments and dramatically increase the incentive to block them—or "draw contrasts," in the common euphemism.[41] It also gives leaders a way to keep members in line. Whenever a senator on one side is tempted to cross the aisle and help the other side, a leader can play the trump card: be a team player, they argue. Don't be selfish and put your desire for a career-making policy accomplishment first—be selfless, think of your colleagues, and prioritize our ability to take back the majority, a leader might say. This appeal can be couched in noble terms, urging the wavering senator to think about how much greater an impact they could have on policy if they were in the majority. Committee control goes to the majority, so a senator who cares about energy policy, for instance, would have a lot more influence over it as the chair of the Energy Committee. Or they might be urged to think about how the leader, who is asking them for a favor, would have much more power to advance the bills the wavering senator cares about if they were to ascend from minority leader to majority leader. In the era of insecure majorities, versions of these arguments have been made countless times, in pull-asides, phone calls, and candid conversations in the offices of the leaders of both parties.

As taking back the majority started to become the driving ambition, the parties started to operate more like campaigns. The Democratic Senate leader in 1981, Robert Byrd of West Virginia, began to revive some of the tools of control Johnson had used. At that point, press staffers were relatively rare, and Byrd hired his first full-time press staffer for the leader's office. He also pioneered the practice of holding retreats at the beginning of each session—a practice still in place today. Byrd brought the caucus to West Virginia, inviting pollster Peter Hart to help them strategize about how to draw clear contrasts with Republicans.[42] And though they didn't call it this at the time, they released the first formal opposition-research document generated by Senate leadership of either party. In politics, opposition research usually refers to the practice of unearthing ethical and financial secrets on candidates, like whether they cheated on their taxes or spouse. The tamer Senate template established by Byrd draws contrasts on policies. Entitled "Democratic Alternatives: A Look at the Record," the Senate's first "oppo doc" ran to more than one hundred pages and cataloged more than 112 votes. The message, the document stated, was "that for each major policy question facing the Senate, Democrats had alternatives. . . . These votes create a record which speaks for itself."[43]

At a time when Jesse Helms was sending out alarmist mailers decrying the decline of civilization, this was mild stuff. But it marked a cultural shift. Never before had the leadership of one party in the Senate sought to systematically draw a contrast with the other party. Democrats released a new version of the "Democratic Alternatives" report every year until they took back the majority in 1986. At the bottom of every cover page were words suggesting that Johnson's style, though dormant, might one day be revived: "Prepared by the Staff of the Senate Democratic Policy Committee."[44]

THE SHIFT TO a campaign footing coincided with a new fund-raising race, as Bobby Baker's distribution of Johnson's "boodles" became a formalized and more respectable practice. In 1980, a congressman named Tony Coelho assumed control of the House Democrats' campaign committee. Campaign committees (like the DNC and RNC) are repositories of money, staff, and strategy, along with other resources like voter files and mailing lists, that can be directed to preferred candidates. Back in 1980, they were small, weak, and poorly funded. At the time, Democrats typically raised money from labor unions while Republicans raised from corporations, but Coelho saw no reason why Democrats could not raise from both. In his view, Democrats' support for policies that corporations opposed, like consumer regulation, should not stop them from pointing out the many other ways they could still be helpful. In *So Damn Much Money*, former *Washington Post* correspondent Robert G. Kaiser's chronicle of the rise of corporate influence in Washington, he writes, "To the exasperation of many Republicans who thought *they* were the natural allies of big business, Coelho raised millions of dollars for House Democrats from business interests."[45] Under Coelho's leadership, the DCCC went from raising just $2 million in the 1980 cycle to $12 million in the 1986 cycle. As *The Atlantic* reported at the time, Coelho "tirelessly canvassed the country, spending 150 days a year on the road, many of them devoted to extracting contributions from businessmen and political-action-committee (PAC) managers."[46] It didn't take long for the Senate to take notice. Embracing Coelho's model, the Senate campaign committee (the DSCC) went from raising $1.7 million in the 1980 cycle to $13 million in 1986. Today, the numbers are exponentially higher. In the lead-up to the 2018 midterms, the DSCC raised $148 million.[47]

Backed by these enormous sums, the DSCC exerts cradle-to-grave influence over senators' political careers, directed at every turn by the Senate Democratic leader. It picks what kind of candidates run for office and then shapes those candidates once they run. It is an incumbent-protection operation, discouraging Democrats who contemplate primary challenges to sitting senators. Running a statewide race is hugely expensive: the average winning Senate race cost $10.6 million in 2016, according to the Center for Responsive Politics.[48] Election law places limits on how much committees like the DSCC can direct to candidates; in 2020, these limits ranged from $49,600 to over $3 million. But in addition to those sums, the DSCC can spend an unlimited amount on so-called independent expenditures (known as IEs) on behalf of a candidate, as long as it doesn't coordinate with the candidate's campaign. The ban on coordination is tissue-thin (more on this in Chapter Nine) and IEs are basically shadow campaigns, free to run ads supporting preferred candidates and do everything else a campaign does. The DSCC also helps its candidates tap into donor networks, where the credential of its endorsement goes a long way. It recommends consultants and staff from an informal but closed network. First-time candidates usually follow these recommendations and the relationships often last, as the same consultants guide them throughout their careers. While the DSCC is usually chaired by a different senator each cycle, the leader recruits the chair and exercises informal veto power over all the committee's decisions, down to its staffing. First-time candidates have to quickly get up to speed on every policy issue imaginable since they never know what reporters might ask and cameras are ever present. To help, the DSCC has policy staff who can brief candidates on any issue. The staff are hired from talent pools acceptable to the leader and tend to reflect the mainstream of party thought.[49]

Having sat through many of these meetings, the net result is a group of candidates and staffers who share many assumptions and operate within the boundaries of a political culture controlled by the leader. There are no mechanisms in place to seek sustained input, new ideas, or strategic perspectives from voices outside the leader's preexisting networks. Fueled by money, the process of deciding who runs for the Senate, how they run their campaigns, and how they approach the mix of issues and politics once they get there has become a system of control that flows from the leader down. And the Senate is worse off for it.

REID BECAME THE Senate Democratic leader after two election cycles that dealt major blows to the prevailing political norms. Democratic senator Max Cleland of Georgia was a triple-amputee veteran of the Vietnam War. Yet in his 2002 reelection race, in the wake of 9/11, Republicans ran an ad questioning his commitment to fighting terrorists. Cleland was defeated. In 2004, the Democratic presidential nominee, Senator John Kerry of Massachusetts—a veteran and Purple Heart recipient—saw his military service dragged through the mud by a group called Swift Boat Veterans for Truth. Kerry was defeated. The same year, Senate Republican leader Bill Frist of Tennessee took an unheard-of step and campaigned in the home state of his counterpart, and Reid's predecessor as leader, Tom Daschle of South Dakota. Daschle was defeated as well—by one percentage point.[50]

From the start of his time as leader, Reid knew the gloves were off, and the GOP would be coming for him. So he built a structure in the Senate to fight back. On the advice of Senator Hillary Clinton of New York, Senator Reid created a campaign-style "war room" that he used to make his caucus march in line behind messages and tactics that he devised. "No more Swift Boats," Reid wrote in his memoir.[51] Where Byrd had hired a single press staffer, Reid shifted large sums in his leadership budget to hire an entire team of press, research, and policy staffers who could spend every day pushing back against the Bush administration and keeping the caucus on message with talking points, research documents, and polling presentations.

The first fight the war room faced had ramifications for all Americans. The day after he won reelection, President Bush held a press conference. "Let me put it to you this way: I earned capital in the campaign, political capital, and now I intend to spend it," he said.[52] The first thing he used that capital on was privatizing Social Security. Top Bush strategist Karl Rove "thought it would be the defining domestic legacy of his second term," *New York Times* reporter Peter Baker writes in his chronicle of the Bush years, *Days of Fire*.[53] Bush made the privatization push a focus of his State of the Union address and traveled the country holding town halls in states calculated to exert pressure on congressional Democrats.

As Bush tried to flood news coverage with stories sympathetic to his cause, Reid's war room fought back with counterprogramming. They used the Senate to hold hearings of their own. At one point, they called a hearing while Republicans were off campus at a retreat, precluding any opposing voices and packing the hearing room with their own staffers to make it look well attended.[54] In a crucial move, Reid handed down a decision for the caucus. In a chamber where senators were supposed to roam freely across policy issues, Democrats would not be releasing their own alternative to Bush's plan.[55] It was the Senate version of "Don't fire until you see the whites of their eyes."[56] Centrist voices condemned Reid's approach as irresponsible. The *Washington Post* editorial board asked, "Where, exactly, is his responsible alternative for making Social Security solvent?"[57] Bush cast Democrats as obstructionist and tried seizing the high road, saying, "Now is the time to put aside our political differences and focus on solving this problem for generations of Americans to come."[58] But with Reid and his war room exerting daily pressure, Democrats held the line.

They won. By March, a *Washington Post* poll showed that 56 percent of Americans disapproved of Bush's handling of Social Security.[59] Senate Republicans, warily eyeing the polls, declined to introduce a bill. The air went out of the issue. Bush stopped touring the country and his plans were quietly shelved.[60] Remarkably, Senate Democrats beat Bush's Social Security plan without a filibuster because no bill ever made it to the floor. Soon, his second term would be overtaken by the Iraq War and Hurricane Katrina. But in March 2005, at the height of the Social Security fight, his approval rating slipped below 50 percent and would never break it again.[61]

In the 2006 midterms, the Social Security battle made frequent appearances in political ads and the issue helped power Democrats to majorities in the House and Senate.[62] After the election, observers credited the Social Security fight as playing a key role in Democrats' success. In a post-election analysis headlined "Social Security at Roots of Shift," *Boston Globe* political correspondent Rick Klein wrote that Democrats' midterm victory "had its roots in that early and successful battle against Social Security reform, which gave Democrats crucial unity and momentum at a time when many pundits were predicting a permanent Republican majority."[63] Buoyed by success, the war room was in the Senate to stay.

WITH THE DEMOCRATS' new majority, Reid rose to majority leader in 2007. As the 2008 presidential campaign kicked into gear, six Democratic senators launched campaigns or exploratory committees: Barack Obama, Hillary Clinton, Evan Bayh, John Edwards, Joe Biden, and Chris Dodd. In public, Reid maintained a stance of strict neutrality. Endorsing in the presidential race while also trying to manage this boisterous group in the Senate would have been hopelessly complicated. But in private, he let his feelings be known.

He invited Obama into his office, ostensibly to talk policy, and surprised him by encouraging him to run. "If you want to be president, you can be president now," Reid said.[64] Obama was already planning a run and the first senator to endorse him was Dick Durbin of Illinois. But Reid's early vote of confidence was the beginning of a historic partnership that would shape the lives of both men, and the nation.

However, their accomplishments are familiar history and not the focus of this book. More pertinent to how the modern Senate evolved is not *what* Reid did, but *how* he did it. A key to understanding how he operated as leader—and how he changed the Senate—is the way he ran the floor.

Reid ran the floor as Johnson had, but with far more control. Not only did he know which bills were coming when, but he also prevented any bills or amendments from coming up for a vote without his approval. The reasons are a mix—a desire for control, and the need to play defense against Republicans offering amendments for the sole purpose of attacking their colleagues, like the Vitter amendment. A big part of the job of leader is accommodating requests by senators to bring up this or that vote on the floor. But as frequently as senators ask leaders to arrange votes on certain bills, they just as frequently beg leaders to make sure they do *not* have to vote on certain bills. Lurking constantly are "bad votes," which their opponents, using the method Helms pioneered, immediately turn into attack ads, often backed by millions of dollars in dark money to ensure that these are plastered across the airwaves and internet.

To exert this control, Reid used a process called "filling the tree," which blocked all senators from offering any bills or amendments that he did not approve of. The process gets its name from the chart that keeps track of what amendments are pending. It's a piece of paper kept by clerks in the cloakroom, and the chart looks like a tree; the branches are the lines where the amendments are written in. There are a limited number of branches available on any given bill (about eleven). Filling the tree means putting the bill the leader wants the Senate to consider in one slot and placeholders in all the others. The cloakroom keeps these shell amendments close at hand for the leader to slot in when needed. Because leaders have the right of first recognition and get to speak first on any bill, it's very difficult to stop them from filling the tree, and once it's filled, it is extremely hard to undo. In his time as leader, Reid shattered the record for filling the tree, using the tool far more than any other leader.[65]

Reid's constant use of this tactic outraged Republicans. "I'm just kind of fed up," said Senator Lisa Murkowski of Alaska, in response to one of many moves by Reid to deny Republicans the amendment votes they were seeking. "Why is he bringing down the institution of the Senate?"[66] The tree could be filled on all bills, even the biggest and most important that came before the Senate. Under Reid, it was. "I can't remember," complained Senator John McCain, who was the manager of the bill that sets the nation's defense priorities, "when there was a bill the size of the Defense authorization bill up, and nobody gets to offer amendments."[67] Republicans got so desperate that they tried to use a procedural maneuver to overcome Reid's tactics, or "chop down the tree." It didn't work, as Reid headed them off.[68]

But the sources of criticism were not limited to Republicans. It came from Democrats, too. The fact that Reid was playing defense did not change the end result, which was to limit the total number of votes and, in many cases, deny his fellow Democrats votes on bills that they cared about and that were important to their constituents. The explanation that his goal was to prevent bad votes did not always fly. "Does it mean increased risks? Sure. That's what voting is about," said Senator Mark Begich of Alaska, a Democrat. "Why not take the vote so people know where you stand?" In 2014, a group of dissatisfied Democrats, led by Senator Heidi Heitkamp of North Dakota, opened negotiations with Republicans to try to find a solution. In one news story about their group, I was quoted reminding them that while Senator Reid was "pleased" they were engaging in the effort, "step one is finding a group of Republicans willing to work with us and so far that has not happened." The criticism from Democrats kept coming. "Harry Reid has a new dilemma on his hands: restless Senate Democrats who are frustrated they aren't casting enough votes," *Politico* reported.[69]

Under Reid, there were far fewer votes than under previous leaders—and far more control by the leader. In 2013, senators cast the second-lowest number of votes of any first year of a Senate since 2000. In 2007, Reid's first year as leader, there were 218 votes. From there, the number declined steadily, to 175 in 2009, to 123 in 2012, and to just 67 in 2013. In one six-month stretch in 2013, Republicans received just 4 amendment votes.

Reid took control far beyond where even Johnson had been able to push it, and it changed the institution. What had once been a wide-open floor where senators could usually secure whatever votes they sought had become a place where every single vote ran through the leader. As the *New York Times* reported, in his time as leader, Reid had "engaged in the greatest consolidation of congressional power since Newt Gingrich ruled the House."[70]

AFTER BAD ELECTIONS, senators seek change and 2010 was no exception. After getting pummeled for two years and then beaten badly at the polls, Democratic senators argued that the war room had become outdated and ineffective. It needed to be revamped to drive a more effective message for the caucus. At the same time, they contended that leadership exerted too much control, and wished that things could go back to the way they were under Mansfield. There was too much control from leadership, and not enough control— everything was bad, and there were many ideas about how to fix it. I had started my job in Reid's office earlier that year, and from our perch in the war room, my colleagues and I followed every rumor and speculated about every hallway conversation we observed— Why was that senator talking to that *Politico* reporter, and was he the anonymous source? It was a tense few weeks. But soon, Reid resolved the conflicting demands of his caucus into more power for himself. And he did it by promoting the man many viewed as his most likely rival for the throne: Senator Chuck Schumer of New York. Reid deputized Schumer to run the war room and turned it into a jointly owned subsidiary of Democratic leadership.

Widely liked and highly energetic, Schumer was regarded as Senate Democrats' top messaging and political strategist. Schumer had credibility with the caucus because he delivered results, chairing the DSCC during Democrats' highly successful 2006 election cycle. A big, brash Brooklynite with a voice like a Borscht Belt comedian, Schumer is in constant motion and always on the phone—a flip phone, his constant companion. Off the top of his head, he can tell you the cell phone number of every member of the Democratic caucus. A *yenta*, he prides himself on the many marriages he has helped arrange among his staff. By 2012, *The Atlantic* had already counted twelve such "Schumer marriages."[71] For years my desk was between those of Schumer's top two war room staffers, Katie and Brian Fallon, who married in 2012. Schumer attends as many of these weddings as he can. At theirs, he led a tipsy crowd in a rousing rendition of Frank Sinatra's "New York, New York."

The main pastime that Reid and Schumer shared was conversation. They did it in their polar-opposite ways: Reid in his whisper of a voice, so quiet you had to strain to hear it, and Schumer in a voice so loud you could hear every word through closed doors. But together, they held constant conversations with their colleagues, forming an inescapable dragnet that caught every iota of information about every aspect of life in the Senate. They exchanged intelligence constantly, about the Senate's business and their colleagues' business, from the political to the deeply personal. Some of it was just idle gossip, but most of it got put to use.

Every week the Senate was in session, there were several standing opportunities for the caucus to tell Reid what was on their minds (they are not a shy bunch). Each gathering was also a chance for Reid to observe the group dynamics: Who was sitting with whom;

who was mad at whom and why. The caucus gathered twice a week for lunches hosted by leadership, one of which was hosted by the war room. We would develop presentations on policy, messaging, and polling according to what Reid wanted to convey to the caucus. A small number of staff were allowed in the lunches on Thursdays, but almost none on Tuesdays to allow senators to speak more candidly. The committee chairs met regularly and Reid made a point of attending every meeting, despite not being a chair himself. As Daschle's second-in-command, Reid had spent endless hours sitting on the floor, listening to his colleagues speak and making himself available to field their requests for help with this or that bill or favor. Now, he opened the leader's suite of offices to senators, inviting them to walk in anytime, or to use his office space for meetings or calls when they didn't feel like walking back to their offices in the buildings across the street (or taking the pint-sized subway that runs underneath the Capitol).[72] Often, Reid's staff would be holding a meeting when a senator walked into the room, on the phone or with someone they wanted to talk to in private, and we would scurry out of the room so they could use it. As with Johnson, there was no formal process for collecting intelligence—just many pretexts for checking in, probing questions, and sharp ears. Schumer reported back to Reid about his own conversations so frequently that Reid had to ask him to please stop calling him after 9 p.m.

This information filtered down to staff, who fanned out to help steer the caucus in the direction Reid wanted and fed information back to him. On the communications side, we led weekly meetings with the press staff of every Democratic office to coordinate messaging. Our counterparts in policy offices did the equivalent on their end, coordinating and collecting information down to the most minute detail on their policy issues. At least once a week, if not more, we would meet with Reid as a staff, and he would quiz us on the latest developments on issues—sometimes the ones that were on the floor and sometimes obscure ones, seemingly picked at random, that did not face any imminent action. At least, not to our knowledge.

With Schumer's staff, the other Reid press staff and I worked out of an office on the third floor of the Capitol building, above Senator Reid's suite and about a dozen steps away from the Senate press gallery, where reporters have workstations and doors open into the press viewing gallery overlooking the Senate floor. When we wanted to talk to a reporter we would walk down the hall, and when they wanted to talk to us they would do the same. For reporters, we were a one-stop shop for everything that was going on in the Senate, from floor schedules to votes to the status of bills. We could tell them what the schedule on the floor would be, down to the minute, and what the fates of bills would be, down to the vote. Four decades after Mansfield said that under his leadership "nobody is telling anybody else what to do," we knew exactly what everybody was going to do. As in Johnson's day, painted in gilt lettering above the door to our office was the name of the group he had first imagined as means of control: "Democratic Policy Committee."

REID DECLINED TO run for reelection in 2016 and retired in January 2017, a few weeks before Trump's inauguration. His seat was filled when his hand-picked candidate, Catherine Cortez Masto, won a close election to become the first Latina to serve in the Senate.[73] In the leadership elections months earlier, Schumer ran for leader unopposed and won. Taking a page from Mansfield, Schumer pledged to return the Senate to a more open chamber by working more closely with Republicans. But if anything, it got worse. The forces shaping the Senate were too powerful and the institution too far gone. Beneath the surface, the power of the minority in the Senate had been growing for centuries. In 2016, it would erupt into full view. Now, America was going to see what happened when the tools of control Johnson and Reid had built were wielded by the leader of the superminority.

Chapter Eight

WHAT IT TAKES

*"Do you want to look nice, or do you want to take out
your opponent and win this thing?"*
*"I want to do what it takes," I said. "I want to win
this thing."*[1]

—*A conversation between*
Roger Ailes and Mitch McConnell

ON THE MORNING OF March 16, 2016, I was rushing around my
apartment getting myself and my son out the door, running through
a mental checklist of the things I had to do to prepare for a speech
Senator Reid was scheduled to give that morning at the Center for
American Progress, a progressive think tank whose offices sit blocks
from the White House. The night before, Trump had won four of
five contests in the Republican presidential primary, positioning him
as the overwhelming favorite to win the nomination. He had been
leading in the polls for six months and, by that point, had called
Mexicans "rapists," accused Fox News host Megyn Kelly of asking
tough questions because she had "blood coming out of her whatever," and claimed Senator John McCain of Arizona was considered
a war hero only "because he was captured," adding, "I like people
who weren't captured."[2]

In his speech that day, Reid planned to remind Americans of
everything Republican leaders had done to pave the way for Trump.
"Republican leaders created the drought conditions," he would say,
"Donald Trump has simply struck the match." The speech reflected

years of frustration at Republican obstruction. "Republicans spent eight years torching the institutions Americans once relied on to help them face the challenges of their daily lives," he contended. "So what thrived in the wasteland Republican leaders created? Resentment, hatred—which Republican leaders were all too eager to embrace and too cowardly to renounce."[3] We had previewed the speech with reporters, and stories ran the night before with some of the key excerpts. "I hope to tattoo the whole speech on my chest," Democratic strategist Paul Begala tweeted, as the early stories circulated.[4]

Then an email popped up: Obama was naming his Supreme Court pick that morning. Change of plans. I emailed Neera Tanden, the president of the Center for American Progress. We rescheduled the speech and I rushed to the Capitol.

By that time, the field of potential nominees for the high court had been narrowed to three candidates: Sri Srinivasan, Paul Watford, and Merrick Garland. Our office pool thought it would be Srinivasan. Like many liberals, we were rooting for one of the young people of color against the older white guy. For a little while that morning, our predictions seemed to be accurate, as one national news outlet reported that Srinivasan was the pick.[5] I was the last one to make it to Reid's office, and as I walked in I shot glances at my colleagues Kristen Orthman and Faiz Shakir, who like me were rooting for Srinivasan or Watford. Their faces told me it wasn't going to be either of them.

"The President called me," Reid said, as I walked in. "It's Garland."

Letting out a sigh, I dropped into the maroon sofa across from Reid, next to William Dauster, who ran our policy department. Gary Myrick, who ran the Senate floor for Democrats, was chuckling at my reaction. "Well . . . ," I said, thinking out loud about what I was going to tell the reporters waiting in the hallway outside Reid's office. "Well, this could be good . . . ," I started. Reid threw back his head, laughing.

Judge Merrick Garland is a wonderful human being with an impressive record. At the Justice Department, he had overseen the federal investigations into the Oklahoma City bomber, Timothy McVeigh, and the Unabomber, Ted Kaczynski. His credentials as a jurist were unimpeachable, and he had been confirmed to his current job on the U.S. Court of Appeals D.C. Circuit with Republican support. For eighteen years, he tutored children at a public school in a low-income neighborhood of Washington, DC. And his personal demeanor was so kind and wise, White House aides had started referring to him, affectionately, as Dumbledore, the sagacious wizard from the Harry Potter books.[6]

But he had no chance to make it to the Supreme Court, and Reid knew it. It had been a month since Supreme Court Justice Antonin Scalia had passed away, creating the vacancy Obama was nominating Garland to fill. Democrats were in the minority in the Senate, putting the nomination in the hands of majority leader Mitch McConnell. And McConnell had used the intervening month to consolidate his fellow Republicans behind a pledge he had already made not to consider any nominee. The odds against any nominee were already stacked high. To have any shot at confirming someone, we needed a spark. And an older, relatively moderate white guy was not going to do it.

With the benefit of hindsight, it's clear that the odds were not just high but probably overwhelming. Since that day, I've had countless conversations with former colleagues in the Senate and contemporaries in the White House, and spent many hours lying awake at night, turning over the events of 2016, trying to imagine what we could have done differently. But it's hard to envision a scenario where the outcome is different. A better result to the Garland fight would have required McConnell to put the principle of treating a president's nominee fairly—a principle in line with over two hundred years of Senate practice—ahead of his quest to build power for himself and his side of the partisan divide. If he had, it would have been powerful: amid an election that had already witnessed the rise of Trump, the spectacle of McConnell leading Republican elders to give President Obama a fair hearing and a vote on his Supreme

Court nominee, a well-respected centrist, to replace the conservative icon Antonin Scalia, would have been a forceful affirmation of America's democratic norms and traditions. It would also have inflamed the Republican base and likely meant the end of McConnell's career as majority leader, but at age seventy-four he could have retired a hero and secured a shining place in history.

That this is a laughable notion is telling. McConnell had never been known for choosing principle over power, and he was not about to start then. McConnell never seemed to consider whether he *should* block Garland, only whether he could.[7] And the answer came back a resounding yes. That yes was inscrutable to many at the time. Up to that point, there had been nothing but destructive tension between the Republican establishment and the Tea Party superminority. But McConnell saw that he could use the Garland nomination to resolve that tension and unite the superminority with the institutional power of the modern Senate. Many Republicans had tried and failed to resolve the tension between the Tea Party and the establishment—just a few months earlier, a different GOP leader had been chased from power for his inability to navigate these shoals. To perceive that a fight over a judicial nominee could be the point where the establishment and the superminority connected required a gut-level instinct that could only come from someone who had been building toward this moment for his entire career.

IN 1987, President Reagan made a surprising choice to replace the retiring Supreme Court Justice Lewis Powell: a right-wing ideologue named Robert Bork. A darling of conservatives and a bête noire of liberals, Bork had wielded the knife in Nixon's Saturday Night Massacre. After the top two officials in the Justice Department had resigned rather than carry out Nixon's order to fire Archibald Cox, the Watergate Special Prosecutor, Bork obliged. In 1975, White House chief of staff Donald Rumsfeld put Bork on the list of candidates to replace Central Intelligence Agency director William Colby, who had proved too cooperative with the Senate's investigation into abuses by the intelligence community being led by the chair of the Foreign Relations Committee at the time, Senator Frank Church. Rumsfeld contended that Bork's firing of Cox showed him to be a "strong team player."[8] Bork didn't get the job, but in 1982, he was confirmed to the U.S. Court of Appeals D.C. Circuit, the second-highest court in the land, where he handed down a series of doctrinaire conservative decisions, including ones that declared both the Supreme Court's decision in *Roe v. Wade* and the notion of "private, consensual, homosexual conduct" unconstitutional.[9]

Reagan's nomination of Bork was an odd choice. The year before Reagan nominated him, Democrats had gained eight seats in the 1986 midterm elections and retaken control of the Senate. While it was common for the president of one party to ask a Senate controlled by the other party to confirm a Supreme Court nominee, the president usually nodded to political reality by picking a nominee the other party could live with. Asking a Democratic Senate to confirm a radical conservative like Bork was courting trouble, and Reagan got it. On the Senate floor, Senator Ted Kennedy of Massachusetts delivered one of the most consequential speeches of his career. "Robert Bork's America is a land in which women would be forced into back-alley abortions, blacks would sit at segregated lunch counters, rogue police could break down citizens' doors in midnight raids, schoolchildren could not be taught about evolution, writers and artists would be censored at the whim of government, and the doors of the Federal courts would be shut on the fingers of millions of citizens," he declared.[10] The hearings erupted into the most contentious battle over a judicial nominee in recent memory.[11] Despite the furor, Bork's nomination did not face a filibuster when it came to the floor. It was defeated on the final confirmation vote, held at a majority threshold, mustering just 42 yeas against 58 nays, which remains the largest margin of defeat ever suffered by a Supreme Court nominee.[12]

Nevertheless, it became an article of faith among conservatives that Bork was a victim of injustice, rather than a miscalculation by Reagan. Their outrage turned his name into a verb: for a judicial nominee's views to be harshly criticized, or for their nomination to be voted down, was now to be "Borked." But what happened to Bork was not unusual. Thirty-three Supreme Court nominations had failed prior to Bork's: ten were rejected by the Senate in floor votes, nine were withdrawn by the president (often when it became clear they could not be confirmed), and fourteen lapsed when the Senate adjourned without taking any action (also often a sign that they didn't have the votes).[13] It was a stretch to think that a Democratic Senate would confirm Bork. When President Reagan subsequently nominated the moderate Anthony Kennedy to fill the same vacancy, Kennedy was confirmed by a unanimous vote, 97 to 0.[14]

Conservatives' outrage over Bork's defeat led to the emergence of one of the most influential institutions of the last four decades: the Federalist Society. The Society was founded in 1982 at Yale Law School, with Bork as its faculty adviser. The Federalist Society's members saw themselves as "scrappy outsiders who were waging a lonely struggle against the pervasive liberalism of America's law schools," in the words of New Yorker legal analyst Jeffrey Toobin.[15] The group was heavily invested in Bork's confirmation, with several of its members playing key roles in his nomination process, and his defeat confirmed their sense of victimhood. They funneled their anger into action, and "emerged from the Bork battle determined to win the war," according to Linda Greenhouse, who covered the judicial beat for the New York Times during this period. The Federalist Society began expanding and soon became both the central pipeline for future conservative judges and the cultivator of modern conservative legal thought.[16] As Scalia, an early Federalist Society faculty adviser, reflected, "We thought we were just planting a wildflower among the weeds of academic liberalism, and it turned out to be an oak."[17]

If the Federalist Society started as a seedling in the inhospitable terrain of academia, wealthy conservatives provided truckloads of fertilizer. By the time the Society was founded in 1982, a flood of conservative money was funding an explosion of conservative groups dedicated to influencing federal policy. The Federalist Society's earliest and most important major funder was John M. Olin, a chemical and munitions multimillionaire.[18] Steven Calabresi, one of the Society's original three founders, said that the Olin Foundation was the Society's "absolutely number one" early funder, and it remained the Society's top funder until it was dissolved in 2005.[19] Today, the backbone of the Federalist Society's programming is a lecture series named after Olin. Soon enough, Olin was joined by other major conservative funders like the Scaife and Koch families. By 2010, the five largest foundation funders had contributed $17.3 million to what was essentially a job bank for conservative judges.[20] As Jane Mayer writes in *Dark Money*, this level of funding allowed the Society to grow "from a pipe dream shared by three ragtag law students into a professional political network of forty-two thousand right-leaning lawyers."[21]

A major element of the conservative judicial philosophy honed by the Federalist Society was the legal equivalent of the "greed is good" zeitgeist of the time: inflating money into something grander than dollars and cents. If money was just money, using it to influence the political process was tawdry. But if money was speech, efforts to restrict it were unconstitutional violations of Americans' First Amendment rights. As such, virtually all restrictions on the amount of money that could be spent on politics should be abolished, the theory went.

In the 1980s, the efforts to make this radical philosophy the law of the land gained a major ally when a former Kentucky judge named Mitch McConnell was elected to the Senate. McConnell was an unlikely ally. In the aftermath of Watergate, he had been a passionate advocate for campaign finance reform. In 1973, McConnell wrote an op-ed for Louisville's *Courier-Journal* in which he explained that "the going price for public office has continued to escalate in recent years, further emphasizing the need for truly effective campaign finance reform." It was a question of "integrity," he said, since "many qualified and ethical persons are either effectively priced out of the election marketplace or will not subject themselves to questionable, or downright illicit practices that many times accompany the current electoral process." Borrowing from Dirksen's 1964 speech on the Civil Rights Act, McConnell declared that public funding for presidential elections was "an idea whose time has come."[22]

In subsequent years, McConnell's views on money in politics would undergo a dramatic evolution. When he launched his first Senate campaign in 1984, he found that donations were hard to come by. McConnell was challenging a well-regarded Democratic incumbent named Walter "Dee" Huddleston, and no one thought the young Republican stood a chance. That included his own campaign manager, Janet Mullins, who accepted the job only because she had promised her daughter she would not leave Louisville; since McConnell was sure to lose, there'd be no reason to move. The campaign was a parade of humiliations. McConnell held weekly press conferences to dump on his opponent, calling them "Dope on Dee." But few reporters came, and the press conferences were discontinued. McConnell's former boss, Marlow Cook, endorsed his opponent; McConnell learned the news when it appeared in the paper and regarded it as "an act of betrayal." McConnell's speech at Kentucky's marquee political event, Fancy Farm, fell flat. At his campaign events, he came to suspect that the bumper stickers he was handing out were ending up in the trash. To prevent this, he started asking people to raise their hands if they wanted one. A twenty-one-year-old Murray State student named Terry Carmack would then run around with a notepad, getting the license plate number of everyone who had their hand up, before rushing out to the parking lot to affix the bumper sticker on the bottom-left-hand corner of the rear window of their car, where McConnell thought the sticker was most visible. "It's not that I don't trust you to put it on your car," McConnell would tell the crowd, just that "we want to make this as easy as possible for you."[23]

With his prospects looking grim, McConnell decided to put himself in the hands of Roger Ailes. At the time, Ailes was a TV consultant, making ads for Republican candidates. McConnell wanted an ad that would shake up the race, he told Ailes, and suggested positive ones that would introduce him to voters. Ailes shot them down. "Do you want to look nice, or do you want to take out your opponent and win this thing?" Ailes asked. "I want to do what it takes," McConnell replied.[24] McConnell's staff had been working to find instances of Huddleston missing Senate votes. Mullins, McConnell's campaign manager, described the scene to Gabriel Sherman, who included the comment in his biography of Ailes, *The Loudest Voice in the Room*. "There was Roger, sitting in a cloud of pipe smoke," Mullins recalled. "And he said, 'This is Kentucky. I see hunting dogs. I see hound dogs on the scent looking for the lost member of Congress.'"[25] Ailes found a team of bloodhounds to search for the missing Huddleston, and an actor called Snarfy to lead them. Filming outside the Capitol building, Ailes put hamburger meat around the grounds to give the dogs something to sniff for and some in Snarfy's pantlegs to keep them from straying too far. The crew soon found themselves surrounded by Capitol police. "You get the shot?" Ailes asked his cameraman, who nodded yes. "Okay, we're done here," Ailes said.[26] In the resulting ad, Snarfy and the bloodhounds run around while the narrator declares, "My job was to find Dee Huddleston and get him back to work." Listing the votes Huddleston had missed to give paid speeches, the narrator intones, "Maybe we oughta let him make speeches and switch to Mitch for senator."[27]

Huddleston had a 94 percent attendance record, but it didn't matter—the ad was a massive hit.[28] Ailes parlayed it into a meeting with Reagan's reelection campaign, where he took over debate prep after Reagan's disastrous first debate against former vice-president Walter Mondale, helping Reagan recover and march to a landslide victory.[29] In Kentucky, McConnell started closing the gap on Huddleston and a late injection of money helped put him over the top. Senate Republicans' national campaign committee had noticed McConnell's momentum and gave his campaign "the resources we needed for one more assault in the media," McConnell recalls.[30] He ran a sequel to the Bloodhounds ad, enlisting a Shakespearean actor to play Huddleston. On election night, McConnell eked out a victory by less than a percentage point, becoming the only Republican to defeat a Democratic incumbent that cycle. The Bloodhounds ad became a classic. In 2012, the industry magazine *Ad Age* ranked it as one of its "Top Ten Game-Changing Political Ads of All Time."[31]

Over this period, McConnell's views on campaign finance changed. Claiming the shift was spurred by a revelation that predated his Senate race, McConnell writes in his memoir that he "began to understand the issue for what it truly is: one of First Amendment rights, particularly the right to free speech."[32] A more permissive view toward money was not only justified, McConnell realized, but in line with the Framers' vision. "For the framers of the Constitution, the highest form of speech—the one most needful of absolute protection—is political speech," he writes.[33] But he can't seem to settle on an argument: principle or expediency. On the next page, he writes, "I never would have been able to win my race if there had been a limit on the amount of money I could raise and spend."[34]

One thing is certain: by the time McConnell entered the Senate, the concerns he had expressed in his 1973 op-ed had dissolved. The "questionable, or downright illicit, practices" involved in raising the large sums needed to run for office did not seem to bother him anymore. McConnell has been described by his allies as "the ultimate pragmatist," in the words of Senator John Cornyn.[35] Another

McConnell ally explained the Kentuckian's shift on campaign finance in these terms: "Pragmatically," said Senator Richard Lugar of Indiana, "he's come to the conclusion that raising money is tremendously important for his own success."[36]

In McConnell's early years in the Senate, his newfound zeal for opposing campaign finance reform taught him how to filibuster. In the late 1980s, efforts to limit the amount of money in politics were making their way through Congress and McConnell leaped into the fray. He led the Republican opposition against a campaign finance reform bill in 1987, forcing Democratic Senate majority leader Robert Byrd to try breaking his filibuster a record seven times. Each time, Byrd secured a majority but failed to reach the supermajority needed to invoke cloture and cut off debate. "We will return next year," Byrd declared. McConnell shot back, "The opponents will return as well."[37] True to his word, McConnell engineered a rolling series of filibusters against campaign finance reform bills throughout the 1980s and 1990s, succeeding every time.

McConnell's opposition to campaign finance reform drove him to devise new ways to filibuster. In 1994 he was prodded by Robert Dove, who was in between stints as the Senate parliamentarian and acting as an adviser to McConnell. Dove, an ardent defender of the filibuster who would go on to coauthor the book *Defending the Filibuster: The Soul of the Senate*, offered McConnell a bit of advice. "Bob said something that astonished us," McConnell wrote in his memoir: Dove advised McConnell that a previously unexploited loophole would allow him to filibuster a campaign finance bill that was on the floor at the time.[38] When McConnell moved to put Dove's advice into action, Senator Bob Dole of Kansas, the minority leader, told McConnell it would not work. "We can't win this," McConnell recalled him saying. But Dole was wrong. McConnell won, and "a real esprit de corps developed," McConnell recalled.

"The experience was exhilarating." As a result of this filibuster, "the American people, and my colleagues in the Senate, were finally beginning to know who I was."[39]

For his efforts, McConnell was hammered with criticism from the media. This taught him another lesson: there is power in being hated by elite opinion, as long as it means being loved by your fellow Republicans. His dream was to be majority leader, not president. His target audience was not the broader American public, but the group of around fifty senators who made up the Republican Senate conference in any given year. It was not exactly a diverse group: they were (and are) financially well-off, middle-aged or older, and the overwhelming majority were (are) white and male. Campaign finance reform may have been a popular issue with the broader public and editorial boards, but it was roundly despised among the members of this exclusive club. By publicly opposing reform, McConnell was saying out loud the things senators said in private.[40] He was willing to take the heat on behalf of his colleagues—and he learned to love it. When the good-government group Common Cause dubbed him the "Darth Vader of campaign finance reform," he embraced it, showing up to a press conference and announcing, "Darth Vader has arrived."[41]

But in the 1990s, McConnell encountered a new opponent in the campaign finance reform fight—someone who had undergone his own transformation on the issue, but in the opposite direction of McConnell's. In 1989, a businessman named Charles Keating bankrupted twenty-three thousand seniors and cost taxpayers $3 billion when his company, Lincoln Savings and Loan, imploded after Keating engaged in fraud, spending its capital on risky investments that went south. Thousands of investors lost their life savings. The event was a major contributor to the savings and loan crisis, one of the costliest financial crises in history. Before his company went under, Keating had spread political donations widely among the senators representing states where he had business interests, five of whom pressured federal regulators to back off investigations into Keating.[42]

One of them, Senator Alan Cranston, was reprimanded and accused of "improper and repugnant" behavior. Two others declined to run for reelection. But one of them was not going to let this be the end of his bright political future: a dashing young Arizona senator named John McCain.

The Senate Ethics Committee concluded that McCain "exercised poor judgment in intervening with the regulators," but that was it. McCain would call the incident "my asterisk," and it motivated him to throw himself into the cause of campaign finance reform.[43] In the 1990s, he joined up with progressive iconoclast Senator Russ Feingold of Wisconsin to develop a set of reform proposals that would become known as McCain-Feingold.

Beating McCain-Feingold became McConnell's mission. In 1997, he won the chairmanship of the National Republican Senatorial Committee, which had boosted him to victory in his first Senate race. As chair of the NRSC, McConnell was responsible for raising a huge pot of money, which was then doled out to Republican Senate candidates, giving him an enormous personal stake in bringing in as much money as possible. But he also hinted at a larger vision. At a closed-door meeting of Republican senators that year, McConnell rallied his colleagues against McCain-Feingold by urging, "If we stop this thing, we can control the institution for the next 20 years."[44]

By that time, McConnell knew that there were conservative billionaires itching to find more ways to pour their money into politics. One of them was a flashy Michigan businessman named Richard DeVos. A fan of loud clothes and expensive cars, DeVos had cofounded Amway, a company that sold household products and encouraged its salespeople to spread the gospel of the free market. DeVos had spent huge sums to elect Reagan in 1980 and was appointed finance chair of the Republican National Committee in 1981, before a scandal involving his fundraising tactics forced him out.[45]

In 1997, Richard's daughter-in-law, Betsy DeVos, joined with

McConnell to found the James Madison Center for Free Speech, whose purpose was to end legal restrictions on money in politics by manufacturing lawsuit after lawsuit aimed at knocking down campaign finance laws. To direct the lawsuits, the center hired a Federalist Society member named James Bopp Jr. as counsel.[46] With the Madison Center waging an ongoing legal assault on campaign finance laws and McConnell himself leading the fight against McCain-Feingold in the Senate, McConnell was on his way to realizing his vision.

Meanwhile, McCain was articulating a very different vision for the future of the GOP. In September 1999, he launched his campaign for the 2000 Republican presidential nomination. In a speech in New Hampshire, he told a crowd of one thousand cheering supporters that the fight against corruption in politics was "our new patriotic challenge." For McCain, money in politics was not a side issue; it was "the gateway through which all other policy reforms must pass." He challenged Americans to "join in the fight against the pervasive cynicism that is debilitating our democracy, that cheapens our political debates, that threatens our public institutions, our culture and ultimately, our private happiness," and to "take our Government back from the power brokers and special interests and return it to the people and the noble cause of freedom it was created to serve."[47] His message resonated, and his support in primary polls surged.[48]

While McCain's message was popular with the American people, it provoked a fierce backlash from his fellow Republican senators. McConnell decided to let McCain know how his colleagues felt. Shortly after McCain launched his campaign, McConnell planned an ambush on the Senate floor and the Arizonan walked right into it.

On October 14, 1999, seemingly unprepared for what was to come, McCain opened the latest round of the ongoing Senate debate on McCain-Feingold with a peremptory speech and strode off the floor. A few minutes later, McConnell rose to speak as a staffer behind him propped up an easel. Wearing a tan suit and flashing

the barest hint of a grin, McConnell proceeded to calmly admin-
ister one of the most brutal rhetorical assaults the Senate has ever
witnessed. McConnell started off by taunting McCain, recounting
how in the years since McCain and Feingold first introduced their
trademark bill, McConnell's filibusters had reduced it to a shell of
its former self. "The McCain-Feingold odyssey has arrived at the
point that if it were whittled down any further, only the effective
date would remain," McConnell said, smirking.[49] Then he got to his
main point: McCain had been running around the country calling
the Senate corrupt, McConnell said, so now it was time for him to
say it to their faces. "There have been a lot of charges of corruption both on and off the floor. I think these are very serious charges
and I think they warrant some discussion," McConnell said as the
staffer behind him placed a poster on the easel. The poster featured
a quote from McCain printed in large block letters: "We are all corrupted." Casually glancing over his shoulder to make sure the poster
was in place, McConnell continued. "Based on the Senator's speech
in New Hampshire and his remarks about his legislation, I assume
I am correct in inferring that the Senator from Arizona believes the
legislative process has been corrupted," he said. He wanted McCain
to be present for what was to come. Turning to his right, he sin-
gled out a McCain staffer he recognized. "I see his staffer on the
floor," McConnell said. "I don't want to be talking about your boss
in his absence. I certainly hope he will come back to the floor for
this debate." Then McConnell proceeded to read quote after quote
after quote from McCain accusing the legislative process of being
corrupt, until McCain returned to the floor.

When McCain arrived, McConnell engaged him directly. "The
Senator from Arizona, I see, is on the floor. I am just interested in
engaging in some discussion here about what specifically—which
specific Senators he believes have been engaged in corruption," he
said. "Someone must be corrupt for there to be corruption." McCain
responded by reading a passage from a book about corruption by
veteran political reporter Elizabeth Drew. That was not going to cut

it. When McCain was done, McConnell engaged Senator Bob Bennett of Utah, who appeared to be well prepared to join in the attack. McCain's campaign had made a website highlighting examples of projects it deemed corrupt. One project it held up for criticism was an earmark Bennett had secured for the 2002 Olympics in Salt Lake City. Holding a printout of the webpage that he just happened to have with him, Bennett essentially dared McCain to accuse him of corruption to his face. McCain dodged. Then McConnell turned it over to Senator Slade Gorton of Washington, who also happened to have a printout in hand. Like Bennett, Gorton asked McCain to explain why an earmark he had secured for the 1999 meeting of the World Trade Organization in Seattle was listed as an example of pork-barrel spending. Again, McCain dodged. For nearly three hours, Republicans attacked McCain as McConnell guided the action. At one point, the liberal icon Senator Paul Wellstone of Minnesota, sporting a chinstrap beard and a tie that looked like it had time-traveled from the 1960s, asked McConnell, "How long will you continue with this attack on Senator McCain on the floor?" McConnell laughed him off and, without answering, resumed his assault. He "worked over John McCain like a professional hit man," the columnist Mary McGrory marveled a few days later.[50]

SENATE REPUBLICANS' anger at McCain was rooted in a dispute that would prove consequential in the years to come. The issue at stake was how to define corruption. McCain's argument was that when special interests who benefited from pork-barrel spending donated large sums to help the senators who secured the pork, it created corruption *and* the appearance of corruption, both of which undermined democracy. This argument was squarely in line with how the Framers viewed corruption: in 1785, Benjamin Franklin received the gift of a decorative snuff box from King Louis XVI of France. Franklin returned the box because even though the king had not asked for anything in return, he understood that "at the level of basic human intercourse, Franklin owed something to the king after receiving such a gift," Fordham Law School professor and corruption expert Zephyr Teachout writes in her influential work, *Corruption in America*.[51] This traditional view held that the role of government was to "create structures to curb temptations that lead to exaggerated self-interest," such as rules limiting the amount of soft money special interests could donate, Teachout writes.[52]

McConnell was pushing a far narrower view of corruption. In McConnell's conception, only a direct, quid pro quo exchange should count as corruption. Essentially, a corporation would have to ask a politician for a favor, give the politician money in exchange for the favor, and then have the politician deliver the favor while acknowledging the money as the reason they did it. Under McConnell's definition, it would be permissible for corporate lobbyists to meet with a senator to demand policy changes worth billions of dollars to their bottom line; to give massive contributions to political organizations dedicated to advancing that senator's interests; and to then see their sought-after policy changes enacted. As long as no one, at any point, explicitly stated that the donations were being made in return for the policy change, this sequence of events was not corruption, but coincidence. This was the philosophy that had been honed in conservative legal circles, including the Federalist Society, and, starting in the late 1990s, had begun winding its way through the courts in Madison Center lawsuits.

At first, McCain won this debate over the meaning of corruption. While he lost his presidential bid to then–Texas governor George W. Bush, McCain's campaign had elevated his corruption message, and it stuck. Backed by that momentum, he led Senate reformers to finally break McConnell's filibuster in 2002 and the Senate passed McCain-Feingold, formally known as the Bipartisan Campaign Reform Act, by a vote of 60 to 40.[53] President Bush reluctantly signed it into law. Undaunted, McConnell promptly took the law to court—literally. The lawsuit, *McConnell v. FEC*, went all the way up to the Supreme Court, which ruled for McCain in a

5-to-4 decision, upholding the major aspects of McCain-Feingold and explicitly rebuking the narrow definition of corruption advocated by McConnell. "Plaintiffs conceive of corruption too narrowly," the majority opinion concluded. "Congress' legitimate interest extends beyond preventing simple cash-for-votes corruption to curbing undue influence on an office-holder's judgment, and the appearance of such influence." The Court admitted that proving the details of corruption was sometimes hard. But in keeping with the view that had led Franklin to return the snuff box, the Court stated that the answer to this difficulty was not for the government to give up, but for it to take all reasonable measures to reduce the potential for corruption. "The best means of prevention is to identify and to remove the temptation," the majority wrote.[54]

When the decision came down, McConnell found it "nothing short of depressing," he recalled, and spent "a fair amount of time with my office door closed."[55] But there was a ray of hope. In one of the dissenting opinions, Justice Anthony Kennedy backed McConnell's narrow interpretation of corruption. In his opinion, Kennedy contended that corruption existed only if the *quid* was eventually paired with a *quo*. "The corruption interest only justifies regulating candidates' and officeholders' receipt of what we can call the 'quids' in the quid pro quo formulation," Kennedy wrote.[56]

Kennedy was no hero to conservatives. And his dissent probably offered little immediate comfort to McConnell. But as dark as things may have seemed in the wake of that loss, McConnell's vision would soon become the law of the land.

EIGHT YEARS BEFORE McConnell would lambaste Democrats for triggering the nuclear option, he was busy helping the Bush administration make the case for going nuclear. In January 2005, the Bush administration and its Senate Republican allies were aggressively making the argument that had united Senate reform advocates from Henry Clay to Paul Douglas to Richard Nixon: that the Senate should be able to end debate and cut off filibusters by a simple-majority vote. Democrats had launched what Republicans considered an unfair filibuster against Judge Miguel Estrada in 2003. By 2005, Democrats were blocking about ten of President Bush's appointments to appellate courts, including the staunch abortion opponents William Pryor and Priscilla Owen. Coming off Bush's reelection and in control of the Senate majority, Republicans had decided it was time to give Democrats a choice: back down, or they would go nuclear.

Building on Nixon's 1957 ruling, the intellectual foundation for the Republican case was laid down by two prominent lawyers with unimpeachable conservative credentials: Martin B. Gold, author of one of the foremost books on Senate procedure and former counsel to Republican Senate leader Howard Baker, and Dimple Gupta, a highly respected Justice Department official in the Bush administration. Their case appeared in the *Harvard Journal of Law and Public Policy*. They made arguments familiar to reformers past and present, contending that Senate rules and precedent made clear the chamber could change its rules by majority vote. Since supermajority thresholds are inconsistent with long-standing Senate tradition and practice, they argued, "the constitutional power has been and could again be invoked to allow a majority to establish a new Senate precedent on ending filibusters." Specifically, that meant the "majority could thereby override Rule XXII," restoring the simple-majority threshold the Framers had intended.[57]

Using Gold and Gupta's rationale, Republicans argued that it would be firmly in line with Senate tradition to overturn Rule 22 and end debate with a majority vote—in other words, to go nuclear. Senator Chuck Grassley of Iowa, a senior member of the Judiciary Committee, contended that "filibusters on nominations are an abuse of our function under the Constitution to advise and consent."[58] Senator Orrin Hatch of Utah, one of the longest-tenured senators and another senior member of the Judiciary Committee, explained that the Framers "said 'advice and consent' on judges—no supermajority requirement." By filibustering judicial nominees, Hatch argued, Democrats "have essentially imposed a supermajority requirement, and we are entitled to stop them."[59]

McConnell was the eager floor general for the fight. In 2002, he had ascended to the second-ranking job in Senate Republican leadership; in a profile, the *New York Times* introduced him to the nation as "a political partisan with a zeal for focus" who "has probably been best known for his opposition to legislation overhauling the campaign finance laws."[60] Now McConnell had a new cause, and he prosecuted it with gusto. Despite being second-in-command, McConnell was the Republicans' most experienced leader. The majority leader at the time was Senator Bill Frist of Tennessee, a relative neophyte just starting his second term in the Senate, who had fallen backward into the leader's job after the previous occupant, Senator Trent Lott of Mississippi, was a little too enthusiastic in his celebration of segregationist Senator Strom Thurmond's one hundredth birthday, pontificating that "if the rest of the country had followed our lead, we wouldn't have had all these problems over all these years."[61] This was not the "compassionate conservatism" the Bush administration was advancing. Embarrassed, the administration distanced itself from Lott and helped install the telegenic heart surgeon Frist as leader.

In contrast to the inexperienced Frist, McConnell was entering his twentieth year in the chamber. On the floor, he led the charge for the nuclear option, declaring that "the majority in the Senate is prepared to restore the Senate's traditions and precedents to ensure that regardless of party, any president's judicial nominees, after full and fair debate, receive a simple up-or-down vote on the Senate floor."[62] Reminding Americans that the filibuster was not part of the Framers' vision for the Senate, he explained that by going nuclear, "what Senate Republicans are simply trying to do is get us back to the procedure that operated quite nicely for 214 years."[63] The person in the second-ranking job is called the "whip" because they whip the votes. In the spring, McConnell, the majority whip, reported that Republicans had the votes to go nuclear.[64]

Scuttling his plans, a rogue group of seven Democrats and seven Republicans emerged to strike a deal. They became known as the Gang of Fourteen, and they released a "Memorandum of Understanding" in which they made a pact. Every one of them committed to doing two things: they would oppose all efforts to go nuclear, and support filibusters only under "extraordinary circumstances." They left the definition of "extraordinary circumstances" to the eye of the beholder. The memo bound only the members of the Gang, but there were enough of them to deny Republican leaders the votes they needed to go nuclear, and deny Democratic leaders the votes to filibuster.

In practice, the compromise was a cave by Democrats. While they retained the right to filibuster, it did not help them block any of Bush's nominees. All of the most controversial nominees at the center of the fight, including Pryor and Owen, were confirmed. Republican leaders were furious at the Gang for derailing their efforts to go nuclear and made clear they considered the Gang's memo to be a dead letter. Forcing the issue, they worked with the Bush administration to quickly push through more controversial nominees, daring Democrats to filibuster and give them an excuse to go nuclear after all. "Angered by a bipartisan deal on judicial nominees, many Senate Republicans warned on Tuesday that they were already eager to challenge the agreement by pushing forward contested candidates," veteran *New York Times* correspondent Carl Hulse reported shortly after the Gang of Fourteen deal was cut. Making clear that they did not consider the matter settled, "Republicans threatened to immediately invoke what some have called the nuclear option" if Democrats tried to stop their nominees.[65] In the months after the memo, Republicans confirmed two Supreme Court justices. John Roberts sailed through on a 78-to-22 vote. A few months later, Bush nominated the hard-right Samuel Alito. When Democrats threatened to filibuster, Republicans threatened—again—to go nuclear.[66] Demo-crats backed off, and Alito was confirmed, 58 to 42.[67]

The deal looks even worse zoomed out: all of Bush's far-right nominees were confirmed, but the filibuster was left intact for Republicans to use against President Obama—which they did to devastating effect. That obstruction has already been discussed, but here it is worth noting the enormous political capital that five years of constant obstruction cost Obama before Democrats finally went nuclear in 2013. Hypotheticals are always hard, but this one appears viable: if Democrats had let Republicans follow through on their threats to go nuclear in 2005, there would be the same number of Bush nominees on the bench today because the Gang's deal allowed him to get his nominees confirmed without having to go nuclear. However, many more of Obama nominees would have been confirmed, because by letting Republicans lower the threshold to a majority under Bush, Democrats would have been able to con-firm Obama's nominees with majority votes from the beginning of his first term, instead of facing the five years of relentless obstruc-tion detailed in Chapter Five. Reid was able to make up much lost ground after going nuclear in 2013, but even so, he had only about a year before Republicans retook the Senate majority and slowed the pace of confirmations back to a crawl. If Democrats had had seven years during which they could have confirmed nominees on major-ity votes, instead of just one, there is little question that they would have confirmed more. There are also harder-to-calculate costs like the years-long delay it took to confirm Cordray to the CFPB, or the many qualified nominees who were blocked by Republican filibusters before Democrats went nuclear. Meanwhile, as McCon-nell waged constant filibusters against Obama's nominees, some of the remaining Republican members of the Gang of Fourteen joined many of them, making clear that their definition of "extraordinary circumstances" hinged on which party held the White House, and leaving Democrats looking rather naïve.

One of the controversial Bush nominees the Gang of Fourteen

deal failed to stop was a partisan operative with no judicial experience. His qualifications were primarily political, having been an assistant to Special Investigator Kenneth Starr before becoming staff secretary to President George W. Bush. An active member of the Federalist Society, he had been nominated in 2003, before the Gang's deal was struck, but the Senate declined to confirm him due to his extreme partisanship and lack of qualifications. Daring Democrats to block him again and give Republicans a reason to go nuclear, Bush renominated him in 2005. His hearings were contentious, but he made it through the committee.[68] Intimidated by Republicans' continued threats to go nuclear, Democrats declined to filibuster him when his nomination came to the floor. On May 26, 2006, by a vote of 57 to 36, he was confirmed to the U.S. Court of Appeals D.C. Circuit, the second-highest court in the land and widely viewed as the foremost training ground for the Supreme Court.[69] His name was Brett Kavanaugh.

Chapter Nine

THE UNITER

I think you have to accept the fact that you can't make
everybody happy.

—Senator Mitch McConnell

SENATOR HARRY REID KISSED the TV. It was election night, 2006. Missouri state auditor Claire McCaskill had just been declared the winner of her Senate race, and her victory put Democrats on track to take back the Senate majority. Two days later, it was official, as delayed election results gave Democrats fifty-one seats and control of the Senate.[1] When their majority was official, Reid, along with his top lieutenants Dick Durbin and Chuck Schumer, descended the steps of the Capitol before a cheering crowd. Senate Democrats held the slimmest majority possible, but those fifty-one seats represented 58 percent of the population. In the House, Democrats took back control, too, making Nancy Pelosi the first female Speaker in history and giving the party unified control of Congress for the first time since the Gingrich revolution of 1994 had snatched it away.

Senator Mitch McConnell watched the results with mixed emotions. Earlier in the year, the reigning majority leader, Bill Frist, had announced his retirement. McConnell had spent the months since then quietly whipping votes to secure the top job for himself. By election night, he had it locked up.[2] But as he watched one Republican candidate after another fall to Democrats, it became clear that the job would be downgraded from majority leader to minority leader. "My hopes of being majority leader had been crushed," he recalled, as he watched the returns and contemplated "the disappointment of having to play defense to Harry Reid." As he headed home, he thought, "If there was ever a time I needed a thick hide, it was now."[3]

Two years later, a second blue wave washed across the country. It was even bigger, delivering President Barack Obama to the White House and Senate Democrats to a fifty-eight-seat majority, which would grow to sixty by the summer, as Senator Arlen Specter of Pennsylvania switched parties to become a Democrat and Al Franken was declared the winner of his race after a months-long recount in Minnesota. Representing 65 percent of the population, this was the largest Senate majority either party had enjoyed since 1979. Yet again, McConnell had been downgraded. He found himself stranded in a capital city dominated by Democrats and relegated to leading the smallest Senate minority Washington had seen in nearly thirty years.

Watching Obama's inauguration on January 20, 2009, Republican members of Congress gazed out at the massive crowd and worried that they'd found themselves on the wrong side of a historic political realignment. "I thought we were completely, permanently screwed," Congressman Patrick McHenry of North Carolina said.[4] But that concern did not diminish their defiance. If anything, it seemed to strengthen it. That month, an Indiana congressman named Mike Pence riled up a gathering of his fellow House Republicans with a clip from the movie *Patton*, where George C. Scott declares, "We're going to kick the hell out of him all the time! We're going to go through him like crap through a goose!"[5] On inauguration night, the Republican pollster and message consultant Frank Luntz convened a dinner at the Caucus Room, a stuffy, white-tablecloth restaurant. McConnell was not there, but his second-in-command, Senator Jon Kyl of Arizona, was. Also in attendance was Senator John Ensign of Nevada. Nevada was a bellwether, having given its electoral votes to

Bush in 2004 and then Obama in 2008, so Ensign was a key barometer for Senate leaders. He was also frequently mentioned as a presidential contender (until he was forced to resign a few years later, when it came to light that he was having an affair with the wife of one of his employees).[6] That night, Ensign joined his fellow Republicans in surveying the wreckage of two electoral tsunamis in a row, which had been propelled by the Bush administration's mismanagement of everything from the war in Iraq to Hurricane Katrina to the economy. However, they did not conclude that the remedy was to deliver more effective solutions for the millions of Americans whose lives and livelihoods had been decimated by their party's mismanagement. Instead, they decided that Republicans had become, in Ensign's words, too "obsessed with governing."[7]

Among Senate Republicans, there would be no *Patton* viewings or talk of kicking the crap out of anyone, but McConnell's post-election message to his conference was just as defiant. In the stately Member's Room of the Library of Congress, across First Street from the Capitol building and next to the Supreme Court, Republican senators gathered between century-old mosaics peering out over a pair of Italian marble fireplaces, set off in eleven-foot-high, oak-paneled walls. Ringed by paintings portraying Truth, State, and Excellence, McConnell braced his colleagues for the hard fight ahead.[8] "We're the last line of defense," he said. He established what would become a theme: "Republicans need to stick together as a team," he said. The goal of that teamwork was not to deliver solutions, but to make life as difficult as possible for Obama.[9] As former Republican senator George Voinovich of Ohio would later describe McConnell's message, "All he cared about was making sure Obama could never have a clean victory." But on that dispiriting day, the senators found McConnell's message of defiance uplifting. "We were discouraged, dispirited and divided," said Republican senator Bob Bennett of Utah, according to journalist Michael Grunwald in his book *The New New Deal*. "Some of us were worried whether the party would survive. The one guy who recognized that it need not be so was Mitch McConnell."[10]

McConnell's strategy for reclaiming power rested on the premise that no matter what message the American people sent at the ballot box, Republican senators had equal claim to represent their views. "We got shellacked," McConnell told his fellow senators, "but don't forget, we still represent half the population."[11] He repeated this claim of equal status to a reporter as an explanation for why Obama should defer to Senate Republicans. "It's not just a matter of pride to us," McConnell said that January. "Senate Republicans represent half the population."[12] In fact, the Senate Republican conference at that moment represented just 37 percent of the population, which would drop to 35 percent a few months later after Specter's defection. It was one thing to assert a right to a voice in the process, which the Framers had intended. But McConnell was claiming something different. After two successive elections in which broad, diverse majorities of voters had delivered unmistakable rejections of Republican governance, McConnell was claiming equal standing for the group of forty-one Republicans he led—of whom thirty-six were men and thirty-nine white.[13]

While defiant Senate minorities are nothing new in American history, this one had something no minority before it possessed: the rules and tools to impose their will on the majority, in a political era that would reward them for doing so. In the Federalist Papers, Hamilton and Madison had warned that "impotence, perplexity, and disorder" and "contemptible compromises of the public good" would be the fate of any government that gave a minority veto power over the majority.[14] McConnell was about to prove them right.

McConnell's minority might have been small but, using the unique tools of the modern Senate, it was big enough to block President Obama's most important campaign promise. Obama had risen to national prominence with his 2004 speech at the Democratic National Convention, when he declared, "There is not a liberal America and a conservative America—there is the United States of America."[15] He appeared on the cover of *Newsweek* as "a rising star who wants to get beyond blue versus red."[16] And standing before a crowd of 1.8 million people at his inauguration, the largest to ever gather on the National Mall, he said, "On this day, we come to proclaim an end to the petty grievances and false promises, the recriminations and worn-out dogmas that for far too long have strangled our politics."[17] More than any policy issue, Obama's promise to "fix the broken politics in Washington" was central to his political identity.[18]

McConnell understood that Obama's vision made gridlock his Achilles' heel, and dedicated himself to exploiting it. "The single most important thing we want to achieve is for President Obama to be a one-term president," he told Major Garrett of the *National Journal* in 2010.[19] The unprecedented obstruction McConnell deployed against President Obama's nominees (detailed in Chapter Five) was repeated across everything the Senate did, on every piece of legislation from the major to the routine. McConnell deployed the filibuster at a rate far greater than any minority leader in Senate history. In the twenty-five years before McConnell took over as minority leader, Senate minorities filibustered an average of fifty-two times per two-year session of Congress, regardless of which party was in the minority.[20] In McConnell's first six years as minority leader, he nearly doubled the rate, filibustering an average of ninety-two times per two-year session of Congress.[21]

McConnell's mass obstruction was possible because of a twist in Senate history: after Johnson broke the South's 1964 filibuster against civil rights, changes to the Senate's rules made the filibuster easier than ever to use, while keeping all of its power intact. It may be counterintuitive, but this is the crucial development that gives the minority veto power over everything that passes through the Senate today. After Johnson defeated Russell and the South, the filibuster started to become cleansed of its white supremacist taint. As Roger Mudd, the CBS correspondent whose nightly updates narrated the 1964 filibuster for the nation, recalled, "The filibuster began to lose its mystique, and without its mystique it slowly became just another run-of-the-mill legislative tactic of delay, no longer the exclusive weapon of the South."[22] Like a generic version of a brand-name drug hitting the market, the sanitized filibuster saw a sharp rise in demand. Senators began experimenting with it on their own pet issues and liked the results. In Mansfield's "individualist" Senate that began in the second half of the 1960s, senators found that waging a filibuster was an effective way to force their colleagues to accommodate them, and leaders like Mansfield did not discourage them from doing so.[23]

As demand increased through the 1970s, Senate leaders made a series of reforms that erased most of the downsides of using the filibuster while preserving the benefits. Besides its association with white supremacy, the other drawbacks of the filibuster had historically been that it took a lot of time and energy to use, and generated a lot of attention when you used it. Sometimes attention was the goal, but more often it was ancillary to the core aim of preventing a bill's passage. Plus, attention carried the risk of backlash, especially on a controversial topic. In 1972, Mansfield worked with Senator Byrd of West Virginia, who was emerging as his likely successor, to create a multitrack system that—intentionally or not—helped mitigate both of these downsides. This "tracking" system was supposed to help the leader manage an increasingly complex Senate. As the size of the federal government grew rapidly in the postwar era, so did the Senate's workload, and by the 1970s leaders were overwhelmed. The tracking system allowed the Senate to process other business during a filibuster by creating separate legislative tracks where other business could move along while one track remained blocked by a filibuster. Because the Senate was able to move on to other issues, a filibuster didn't attract as much attention as it used to. However, it still blocked the bill it was aimed at, just as effectively as ever; while the rest of the Senate could move on, the bill being filibustered was still stuck.[24] With this innovation, filibusterers could localize its use, targeting the bill they wanted to block without disrupting the entire Senate, and without becoming the focus of unwanted attention.[25]

In 1975, in response to a marathon series of filibusters by Senator James Allen—the segregationist Democrat who had taught Helms how to filibuster—reformers lowered the cloture threshold from two-thirds to three-fifths, or the sixty votes we know today.[26] But rather than make the filibuster less effective, the change seemed to make it less scary, and more attractive to potential users. After a brief decline at the end of the 1970s, the use of the filibuster resumed its rise in the 1980s. By the middle of the decade, it was being used more than ever (although it was still being used about one-fifth as frequently as McConnell would use it).[27]

As a result of these changes, the silent filibuster we know today began to emerge. The new rules and procedures rendered the old-style talking filibuster antiquated. In part, this was another effect of the tracking system. While there were now multiple tracks, there was still only one Senate floor. When a senator blocked one track with a filibuster, the Senate switched to another track to move forward with other business; the moving track became the main track, and the filibuster got pushed from the floor. (It still continued, just off the floor, while the Senate proceeded with other business.) The silent filibuster is also a result of leaders coming to rely on what are known as "unanimous consent" agreements, or UCs. In the Senate, a UC is an all-encompassing agreement that governs every aspect of the Senate floor: when votes will occur, what amendments will be voted on, how long each vote will last, and so on. They are the Senate's superpower: with a UC, the Senate can do anything it wants. It can hold twenty votes in twenty minutes if it wants to, or set the vote threshold at, say, ten votes to pass a bill. From the leader's perspective, UCs are desirable because once they are in place, the Senate's schedule is set in stone, and events become more manageable. But the downside is the "unanimous" part. Enacting a unanimous consent agreement requires every senator to agree, which makes UCs difficult to secure, since a single objection blocks it. This dynamic increases the leverage of individual senators: leaders and the Senate itself have become reliant on UCs to function, but any senator can block one.

Together, these changes led leaders to start letting senators filibuster in private. Facing enormous workloads and reliant on UCs, leaders got in the habit of canvassing their caucuses ahead of time to see if anyone objected to a bill or nomination they were considering bringing to the floor. Again, this had a benefit to the leader: it was an early-warning system that alerted them to a senator's intent to filibuster. But again, it damaged the institution: to deter a leader from moving forward, all a senator had to do was signal their *intent* to filibuster. This is what is now known as placing a "hold." Due to intractable norms of Senate civility—combined with the fact that a single jilted senator can make a leader's life miserable—leaders have traditionally respected senators' desire to keep their holds anonymous. Holds quickly proliferated to the point where forcing senators to go public was simply not practical for a leader. Leaders rely heavily on personal relationships with their relatively small group of members. If they outed one senator who had a secret hold, there would be pressure to out them all. More importantly, senators would no longer trust the leader to keep their secrets. Since the leader serves at the pleasure of their caucus, a leader who lost their members' trust would not be leader for long.

Today, the leader's canvass for objections is called a "hotline," and Senate staffers' inboxes are clogged with emails hotlining hundreds of bills and nominees. It is, in effect, a canvass for filibusters. When you get a hotline, all you have to do is call the cloakroom, tell them the senator you work for intends to place a hold on the bill, and the bill is filibustered. As we have seen, the only way to overcome a filibuster is by invoking Rule 22 and its supermajority threshold. One phone call, one objection, and the threshold on any bill or nomination goes from a majority to a supermajority.

This series of changes is how the modern Senate ended up giving the minority veto power on every issue, making it more powerful than ever before. Political scientists have dubbed the period before McConnell came along the "trivialization of the filibuster," since the net effect of the changes was to make the filibuster easier to use.[28] But the ease of use is exactly what made it such a powerful tool for McConnell. Even Richard Russell could not have organized 137 filibusters in two years, which is the number McConnell deployed against Obama from 2009 through 2010.[29] But under the rules of the modern Senate, doing so was as easy as making a sign-up sheet. All it took was a phone call or an email from a single Republican senator and the threshold on any bill or nomination would shoot up from a majority to a supermajority, effectively granting the minority veto power. And there is nothing the majority can do about it.

In the first two years of the Obama administration, Democrats controlled between fifty-nine and sixty votes and could sometimes overcome filibusters, although their majority would be reduced to fifty-three by 2011. But even when they had the votes for cloture, the procedure to invoke it takes more than two days. Multiply that by the hundreds of filibusters McConnell waged, and every day became a brutal slog. Obama had promised to fix our broken politics, but the modern Senate made it easy for McConnell to impose gridlock. Far from fixing Washington, to the average voter, it looked like things had only gotten worse.

To take Obama down another peg, McConnell used the tools of control that Johnson and Reid created to deny him bipartisan cooperation on his top domestic priority: health care. With the average American dedicating, at most, a few moments per day to politics, bipartisanship is the Good Housekeeping seal of approval, the signal to voters that a policy is reasonable. For Obama, it would also be a sign that he was delivering on his promise to heal America's partisan divisions. McConnell was not going to let that happen. He had seen the power of bipartisanship up close, having lost his decades-long fight against campaign finance reform to McCain-Feingold, a bill that became a byword for bipartisanship. "When you hang the 'bipartisan' tag on something," McConnell reflected to Joshua Green of *The Atlantic*, as though describing a malady afflicting American politics, "the perception is that differences have been worked out, and there's a broad agreement that that's the way forward."[30]

McConnell outlined his strategy on health care to the *New York Times*, explaining, "It was absolutely critical that everybody be together because if the proponents of the bill were able to say it was bipartisan, it tended to convey to the public that this is O.K., they must have figured it out."[31] There could be no exceptions. "Just one Republican choosing to support it," McConnell explained in his memoir, "threatened to bring others along, and allowed the other side to then label the measure bipartisan."[32] In what was once the "world's greatest deliberative body," a complex policy issue governing 15 percent of America's economy was boiled down to a binary political calculation. "If he was for it," as former Republican senator George Voinovich said, "we had to be against it."[33]

Holding the line was hard. In 2009, more than one-quarter of Republican senators came from states Obama had carried in 2008. But the pressures pulling some key Senate Republicans toward cooperation were not just political. Many of them still genuinely prided themselves on their records of bipartisan accomplishment. Obama was making sustained efforts to reach out to them, through personal contact and by meeting them halfway on the substance of the bill. Two weeks before his inauguration, Obama had met with congressional leaders of both parties in the Capitol. Republicans were stunned to find that Obama's campaign-trail talk of bipartisanship was not just empty rhetoric. In the meeting, they found him to be thoughtful and humble, and were surprised that he engaged seriously with their ideas. Republicans walked away impressed—and a little concerned. "If he governs like that, we are all fucked," said an aide to Republican congressman Eric Cantor.[34]

A number of Senate Republicans, including Olympia Snowe and Susan Collins of Maine and Chuck Grassley of Iowa, had a record of working with Democrats on health care. To court them, Obama and congressional Democrats coalesced around a bill based squarely on Republican ideas. It was a national version of the law enacted by Massachusetts governor Mitt Romney, a Republican.[35] The bills were so similar that Jonathan Gruber, an economist who worked on both, called them "the same fucking bill."[36] The centerpiece was the individual mandate—the requirement that Americans buy health insurance or pay a penalty, like car insurance—which was supported by America's flagship conservative think tank, the Heritage Foundation.[37] The mandate had powerful champions among Senate Republicans, the most important of whom was Grassley, the highest-ranking Republican on the Senate Finance Committee, which would take the lead on drafting the bill. On the committee, Grassley had a trusted negotiating partner in Senator Max Baucus of Montana, the moderate Democrat who was its chair. Under President Bush, Baucus and Grassley had delivered the 2001 tax cuts and the Medicare prescription drug benefit. As an initial draft, Baucus used a plan Grassley had worked on as a Republican alternative to Clinton's health care proposal in 1994, the last time Congress had seriously debated health care reform.[38] The senators and their staffs began meeting regularly to trade ideas. As the negotiations began, there was common ground on policy and good-faith engagement from both sides, among senators experienced at working across the aisle. The conditions seemed primed for bipartisanship.

Then McConnell went to work. Republican leaders had anticipated that Grassley would be tempted to work with Democrats, discussing the prospect at Luntz's dinner on inauguration night where McConnell's lieutenant, Senator Kyl, was in attendance. "We knew guys like Grassley were talking about working with the Dems," Luntz said. "The sense was that we'd let them play along but then come up with the arguments and polling that would get them to drop out."[39] To exert pressure on Grassley, and anyone else thinking of working with Democrats, McConnell used the weekly gatherings of Senate Republicans to explain why voting with Obama would be against the interests of the group, invoking the "team player" trump card that had become more effective in the modern era of insecure majorities. "Mitch did everything he could to keep a Republican from crossing over," said former Republican senator Bob Corker of Tennessee. "We had meetings every Wednesday just to keep discipline."[40] Over the summer, McConnell pointed to declining polls as evidence that Republicans should not work with the president. As one July presentation noted, "We came up with a plan, stuck to it, and now we're starting to see results."[41] As Grassley stubbornly continued to negotiate with Democrats, Kyl went on TV to deliver a message. "Senator Grassley has been given no authority to negotiate anything by all of us Republicans," Kyl said. The interviewer pointed out that several Republicans were negotiating with Democrats, but Kyl rejected any prospect of Republican support on the final product, flatly stating that Obamacare "will not be a bipartisan product."[42] The arm-twisting became an open secret; in July, the *Los Angeles Times* reported that Grassley was "under pressure from GOP lawmakers to break off negotiations."[43]

McConnell did not hesitate to use more aggressive tactics, either. Grassley had his eye on the chairmanship of the Judiciary Committee, which was widely assumed to be his for the taking. But ever since Johnson had broken the seniority system, leaders like McConnell had the power to deny committee assignments. Over the summer, as Grassley continued to work with Democrats, there was much talk in the Capitol that McConnell was planning to deny him his longed-for spot atop Judiciary.[44]

Just before Congress adjourned for its traditional monthlong recess in August, Obama had one of his periodic chats with Grassley. By that point, it was clear that Grassley was having a very hard time getting to yes. "If we give you everything you want," the president asked, "can you guarantee you would support the bill?" Grassley replied, "I can't guarantee I would."[45]

Then Grassley returned to Iowa, where Tea Party protests were erupting as they were across the country. He shocked his Democratic colleagues back in Washington by telling a crowd in Ames, "You have every right to fear" that the plans being discussed would "pull the plug on Grandma."[46] One of the few members of Congress who runs his own Twitter account, Grassley proceeded to get in a Twitter fight with his longtime colleague Senator Arlen Specter over his comments. "Called Senator Grassley to tell him to stop spreading myths about health care reform and imaginary 'death panels,'" Specter tweeted, using the term coined by former vice-presidential candidate Sarah Palin. "Had to leave a message—for now. I will talk to him soon." Grassley replied angrily that he had never used the phrase "death panels" (only "pull the plug"), so "change ur last Tweet Arlen."[47] When an NPR interviewer asked Grassley about his change in tone, he got defensive. "I'm not going to walk away from the table," he said. "If I get away from the table, it's because I'm pushed away from the table."[48] In fact, Baucus was still trying hard to keep Grassley involved. But within weeks, he had come out against the bill, whatever form it might take.

Later, Grassley tried to explain that "the town halls helped me to realize that there were constitutional issues with the [individual] mandate."[49] This is a curious explanation, since Grassley had been championing the mandate for over a decade. Just two months before his Iowa town hall, he had explained to Fox News host Chris Wallace that it was reasonable to require people to purchase health care "because everybody has some health insurance costs, and if you aren't insured, there's no free lunch. Somebody else is paying for it."[50] More likely than a revelation about constitutional law at a Tea Party protest was the simple fact that Obama was for health care reform, so now, after a career spent working on the issue, Grassley was against it—because McConnell had told him to be.

With Grassley back on McConnell's team and Obama's approval rating down 15 points since the beginning of the year, it came down to Senator Olympia Snowe of Maine.[51] In October 2009, Snowe became the lone Republican to vote to advance the health care bill out of the Finance Committee. That vote moved the bill to the Senate floor, where its fate would ultimately be decided. Like Grassley, Snowe had her eye on becoming the top Republican on an influential committee, in her case the Senate Commerce Committee. The same week Snowe joined Democrats to advance the health care bill out of the Finance Committee, an article appeared in *The Hill* by longtime Senate reporter Alexander Bolton. The lede read, "Sen. Olympia Snowe (Maine) is risking a shot at becoming the top Republican on an influential Senate committee by backing Democratic healthcare legislation, according to senators on the panel." A single Republican vote against Snowe could block her from the top spot. The story quoted an anonymous Republican senator on the Commerce Committee, who said, "A vote for healthcare would be something that would weigh on our minds when it came time to vote." If Snowe got in line, however, she needn't worry. "Snowe would otherwise be assured of the ranking member post if not for the healthcare debate," the story concluded.[52]

After the story ran, Snowe told McConnell she'd changed her mind about Obamacare. When the bill came to the floor, Snowe assured him, she would vote against it. She later explained that McConnell "doesn't twist arms so much as he reminds you how unhappy others will be if you go down this path—how hard it'll be—and the importance of sticking together."[53] When Snowe informed him of her decision, McConnell knew that he had succeeded in denying the president any Republican cooperation on an issue affecting millions of Americans. This filled him, he recalled, with "an enormous sense of accomplishment and relief."[54]

As the 2010 midterms approached, McConnell understood that if the elections went poorly for Republicans, his obstruction strategy would be deemed a failure. And since he had presided over big Republican losses in 2008, his only other election as Senate

Republicans' leader, his position in the Republican caucus would be in jeopardy. But before the elections, he got a boost from that other powerful tool of top-down control: money.

Reversing what had been one of the biggest setbacks of McConnell's career, the courts changed gears on campaign finance, taking his side over McCain's in the corruption debate and unleashing a flood of corporate money into American politics. In 2009, the U.S. Court of Appeals D.C. Circuit decided that corporate donations to groups that pretended to be focused on issues but were really focused on politics were not corrupting, unless there was an explicit quid pro quo between the donor and the politician. The decision was authored by Judge Brett Kavanaugh. On the heels of his ruling, the Supreme Court overturned its own 2003 decision in McConnell's case against McCain-Feingold. In 2010, it handed down *Citizens United v. Federal Election Commission*, making McConnell's narrow definition of corruption the law of the land. The majority opinion was written by Justice Anthony Kennedy, whom Reagan had put forward after the failure of Bork's nomination.

Unleashed, corporations and conservative billionaires spent massively in the lead-up to the 2010 midterms, giving Republicans a decisive edge in the money race. Overall, the amount of outside money represented more than a fourfold increase over the previous midterm election, from $70 million to $310 million. The money mainly flowed rightward: in 2010, spending by Republican-leaning outside groups doubled that of their Democratic counterparts.[55] The money "so strengthened the Republican assault across the country that an exasperated Democratic party strategist likened it to 'nuclear Whac-a-Mole,'" the *New York Times* reported.[56]

Many of the groups this money funded were organized on the model created by Jesse Helms. Technically, they were "nonpartisan" and focused on "issues," not political races or candidates. But reasonable people would have trouble telling the difference. "Scandal follows Hillary Clinton like a shadow," an ad from a supposedly nonpartisan, independent group blares, over the hashtag

#NEVERHILLARY.[57] By its new, narrower standard, the Court decided that donations to these groups did not create the potential for corruption because by law they were barred from coordinating with candidates. But that prohibition is almost unenforceable. The "independent" groups are often formed for the sole purpose of supporting or opposing specific candidates. In many states, there is nothing stopping them from coordinating with campaigns until shortly before the election. Staffers can, and often do, leave a candidate's payroll and go directly to work for the groups—and even then, they are free to continue socializing and communicating with the campaign staff and with the candidate. For his or her part, the candidate is allowed to know who is donating to the groups, and what legislative favors the donors (or prospective donors) are seeking. The candidate is also free to court donors to the "independent" group. The only thing the candidate cannot do is *explicitly* ask for money—but the legal standard for what constitutes an explicit ask is extremely high. For example, a candidate can convene a roomful of donors, many of whom might have bills or favors they want from the lawmaker, chat for as long as they want, then tee up the ask before leaving the room, at which point a staff member—who in many cases will be a former aide to the candidate—makes the ask instead. Afterward, the candidate and staff can review who gave how much money and strategize about how to get more. This is not a wacky hypothetical; it is standard operating procedure today. But in the blindered view of McConnell—and fatefully, the Court's *Citizens United* decision—this does not count as corruption.

McConnell's former staff were threaded through these powerful groups, giving him enormous clout in addition to the official Senate Republican campaign committee, which he also informally controlled. One of the largest of the "nonpartisan" groups during this time was called Crossroads GPS. It was run by Steven Law, who oversaw a multimillion-dollar budget. Before Law led Crossroads GPS, he spent a decade fighting "the campaign finance wars," as he put it, as a top aide to McConnell.[58]

But McConnell's contribution goes much deeper. Without the *Citizens United* decision, these groups would not be nearly as powerful today. The plaintiff in that case, the group Citizens United, did not come up with the idea for it on their own. Instead, the idea came from the prominent Federalist Society member and activist lawyer James Bopp Jr., who drafted the lawsuit for them. The case "was really Jim's brainchild," according to Richard Hasen, an election law expert at Loyola Law School.[59] The PBS series *Frontline* described Bopp as the "intellectual architect behind the landmark Citizens United case."[60] For more than a decade, Bopp had been honing his legal theories as the lead counsel of the James Madison Center for Free Speech, which had been founded in 1997 during the Senate debate over McCain-Feingold. One of the founding board members of the Madison Center was the conservative billionaire Betsy DeVos. And the Madison Center had been established under the guidance of the man who was immediately named its honorary chairman, Senator Mitch McConnell. "We had a 10-year plan to take all this down," Bopp said in the wake of *Citizens United*.[61] They had succeeded.

McCONNELL HAD tremendous power, but he still had a problem. The tension between the establishment GOP and the Tea Party superminority was tearing the party apart and endangering his own future as leader. He had to decide what to do with the superminority: beat it or unite it with the establishment. The decision he made would change the country forever.

McConnell was confronted with the power of the Tea Party earlier than most leaders. One of the first major skirmishes between the Tea Party and the GOP establishment occurred in his home state of Kentucky, where McConnell had been grooming an acolyte named Trey Grayson to succeed Senator Jim Bunning in 2010.[62] A handsome, preppy Harvard graduate who returned to Kentucky and was later elected secretary of state, Grayson was on track to Republican stardom. Bunning had not wanted to retire, but McConnell pushed him out to make way for Grayson in an ugly public battle.[63] A cantankerous Hall of Fame pitcher known for beanballs, Bunning called McConnell a "control freak" as he stalked off the mound.[64] McConnell's iron-fisted control of the state and Grayson's eventual victory seemed assured.[65]

Then an ophthalmologist named Rand Paul jumped in the race. In August, he set off alarms by raising a stunning $430,000 in grassroots donations in a single day.[66] As Paul overtook Grayson in the polls, McConnell took the unusual step of recording an ad for Grayson. "I rarely endorse in primaries, but these are critical times," McConnell intoned, looking straight at the camera. "I know Trey Grayson, and trust him."[67] The ad backfired, and Paul crushed Grayson by 23 points.[68] "We closed with ads with Senator McConnell saying, 'I need Trey,'" Grayson recalled. "That was a mistake."[69] When McConnell met with Paul in a hangar at the Louisville airport, he asked if Paul would support him as leader. Paul said he would not, according to reporting by Jason Zengerle of *GQ* magazine.[70]

"There's no education in the second kick of the mule," McConnell likes to say. So when Paul arrived in the Senate, McConnell courted him, helping him secure plum committee spots that set him up for the 2016 presidential run he was openly planning.[71] In his own reelection race in 2014, McConnell staved off a Tea Party primary challenge by hiring Paul's former campaign manager, Jesse Benton. "It is a real honor to join Sen. McConnell's team," Benton said in a statement.[72] But apparently, it wasn't. In August, a recording of a phone call emerged in which Benton told a conservative activist, "between you and me, I'm sort of holding my nose for two years" by working for McConnell.[73] Trying to laugh it off, McConnell's campaign posted a picture on Facebook of McConnell and Benton embracing while Benton held his nose.[74] For McConnell, the embarrassment was worth it. Paul endorsed him early in the race and McConnell's Tea Party challenger never gained traction. While other Republican leaders struggled against the Tea Party,

McConnell, the embodiment of the GOP establishment, had tried inviting them into the GOP's small tent. And it worked. "In 2010, he sensed the world was changing," Grayson later reflected, "and he reacted accordingly."[75]

FOR MCCONNELL, making his peace with the Tea Party in Kentucky was one thing, but making his peace with it in the Senate was another—and much harder—challenge. When Republicans won the majority in 2014, they did it on the promise of a free and open Senate. As majority leader for the first time, McConnell spent a few months struggling to make those promises a reality and to portray himself as someone concerned with the health of the institution. But his commitment was weak, and the superminority was not interested in a functioning Senate. They just wanted to fight, and as usual, he would give them what they wanted.

By 2014, McConnell had been described as many things in his twenty-four years in the Senate, including "Darth Vader," a "hitman," and a hard-core partisan.[76] But being an institutionalist had not been a major part of his identity for most of his career, until it became politically convenient. Democrats' decision to go nuclear in the fall of 2013 gave McConnell an opening. It sparked a cultural shift in the Senate, creating an appetite among reporters and Senate watchers for noble talk of tradition. It also led reporters to rethink who was to blame in the ongoing battle over Senate obstruction. For years, there had been an unspoken understanding that Democrats had the stronger claim to aggrieved status. But Reid had gone off script, and deployed the nuclear option instead of just threatening to use it. This created an opening to shift the blame and McConnell seized it.

When the Senate returned from the winter holidays in January 2014, he delivered what he billed as a "state of the Senate" speech. To ensure that the chamber would not be empty, as it usually was, he requested the attendance of his Republican colleagues, and thirty-six of them showed up. Wearing a banker's shirt, a lavender tie with white polka dots, and a navy suit, he intoned gravely, "I think it's appropriate to step back from all the policy debates that have occupied us over the past few years and focus on another debate we've been having around here, over the state of this institution." He laid out a series of recommendations that were mostly pedestrian, but one major proposal was ending Reid's practice of filling the tree, which the Nevadan had used to block amendment votes and exert control over the floor more than any previous Senate leader. The press ate it up. "McConnell Vows a Senate in Working Order, If He Is Given Control," a *New York Times* headline declared. "McConnell's Lament Stirs Fresh Breeze of Hope," read one in *Roll Call.* Senate Republicans joined in the chorus, calling for changes and decrying the use of the nuclear option. Some of the senators were new to the Senate and less familiar with anything beyond the history of the Obama era. But many of the loudest voices decrying the nuclear option—like Grassley, Hatch, and McConnell himself—had clamored with equal passion to trigger it in 2005, when a president of their own party was in the White House.

McConnell's pledges of a free and open Senate did not survive for long. Republicans romped in the 2014 midterms, winning nine seats and control of the chamber. But within months of assuming control in 2015, McConnell had broken most of the promises he had made, including his biggest. By the end of July, McConnell had filled the tree at the same rate as Reid.[77] In the years since then, he has filled it even more. "Despite McConnell's pledge to increase opportunities for senators to offer amendments, they are offering fewer today than they did back then," a 2019 analysis by James Wallner in the conservative *Washington Examiner* found.[78]

Politically, things were looking grim. Republicans' approval rating had ticked up after the 2014 midterms, but by July 2015 it had taken a nosedive, falling to its lowest level since Obama took office.[79] McConnell's personal approval rating tanked, too, falling to 19 percent.[80] The unrest was coming from inside the party. At the beginning of the year, 86 percent of Republicans had viewed their party favorably. By July, that number was down to 68 percent.

McConnell was finding it hard to maintain the balance Russell had struck between talk of lofty principles and aggressive obstruction. He had started off the year trying to set a moderate tone. "I don't want the American people to think that if they add a Republican president to a Republican Congress, that's going to be a scary outcome," he told veteran congressional correspondent Paul Kane of the *Washington Post*. "I want the American people to be comfortable with the fact that the Republican House and Senate is a responsible, right-of-center, governing majority."[81] But as the 2016 election approached, it became clear that the Republican Party did not want to be a responsible majority—it wanted a scary outcome. On June 15, 2015, Donald Trump descended a golden escalator in Trump Tower to announce his candidacy. By July 20, he had overtaken the front-runner, former Florida governor Jeb Bush, in Real Clear Politics' average of polls. Aside from a few days in September when surgeon Ben Carson briefly took the lead, Trump would never lose it.[82]

The superminority began flexing its muscles in the Senate, too. A few days after Trump surged to the lead in the primary, Senator Ted Cruz of Texas strolled to the Senate floor and dropped a bomb. Contrary to his pledges of running an open Senate, McConnell was denying Cruz votes, and the Texan was furious. In stunning terms, he accused McConnell of hypocrisy and called him a liar. "Not only what he [McConnell] told every Republican senator, but what he told the press over and over and over again, was a simple lie," Cruz declared.[83]

If Cruz calling McConnell a liar on the Senate floor elicited gasps, what happened next caused jaws to drop. The day after an address to Congress by Pope Francis that he had personally arranged, Speaker John Boehner, who was at the pinnacle of his career, announced he was retiring from Congress. He wasn't waiting until the end of his term—he was walking away immediately. For five years, Boehner had battled the Tea Party constantly, often losing. A Tea Party congressman named Mark Meadows had forced a vote of no confidence that would, at a minimum, embarrass Boehner and that might have dethroned him altogether. Instead of enduring that vote, he was walking away. He'd had enough.

Boehner's departure made McConnell the Tea Party's new target. "With their top object of scorn, John Boehner, about to leave the scene, conservatives are already training their ire across the Capitol on Mitch McConnell," reported Burgess Everett and Seung Min Kim of *Politico*.[84] The Tea Partiers made no secret of their aims. "This should be an absolute warning sign to McConnell," said South Carolina congressman Mick Mulvaney, who declared that the focus of the Tea Party "now will invariably and should turn to McConnell in the Senate."[85]

McConnell was in a bind. Trump appeared to be the worst of both worlds: he empowered the Tea Party in the Senate and appeared likely to lose the White House to former secretary of state Hillary Clinton. The only candidate who seemed to have a chance of stopping Trump was the one who had called McConnell a liar on the Senate floor; Cruz had placed first in the Iowa caucuses. McConnell began devising desperate plans for Senate Republican candidates to break with Trump on the campaign trail to save themselves. "We'll drop him like a hot rock," he told his colleagues.[86] It was bold talk, but trying to deny Trump the nomination would have meant nothing short of civil war for Republicans. McConnell could talk a big game, but when it came down to it, he was stuck. Less than two years after achieving his life's dream of becoming majority leader, his party was on track to get crushed in the presidential election and Democrats were poised to take back control of the Senate. Things were not looking good.

And that's when he heard the news.

ON FEBRUARY 13, 2016, McConnell had just arrived in the Virgin Islands on vacation with his wife, former labor secretary Elaine Chao. As he deplaned, he checked his phone and was stunned at what he saw: Supreme Court Justice Antonin Scalia had died.[87] McConnell had known Scalia for decades. One of his earliest jobs in politics had been as a young aide in the Justice Department, where he served under Scalia, awed by the older man's sharp intellect and charismatic presence. The two formed a close relationship, and McConnell's first thought was sorrow for his longtime friend and his family. But his "second thought," McConnell told Carl Hulse of the *New York Times*, "was to immediately turn to the politics of this situation."[88]

He did not have much time. There was a Republican presidential debate that night. McConnell and his advisers quickly concluded that Cruz would use it to call for a blockade of any nominee proposed by Obama, which would put McConnell in the position of having to follow Cruz—a humiliating prospect—or break with him, and likely Trump as well, since Trump would probably also take the hardest-line position. If McConnell wanted to avoid being boxed in, he had a few hours, at most, to make a decision. If he gave Obama's nominee a fair hearing, or even left the door open to one, it could easily precipitate a GOP civil war. Cruz, Trump, and the Tea Party would make McConnell—already the Tea Party's top target—into the weak-kneed villain of the elite Republican establishment, just like Boehner.

On the other hand, denying a president who had nearly a year left in his term a hearing on a Supreme Court nominee would be completely unprecedented. It would damage McConnell's reputation and destroy any pretense of concern for the Senate. For two centuries, from Calhoun to Russell to McConnell, the forces of minority rule had always found it necessary to maintain a facade of respectability in order to carry out their obstruction. Without it, they risked backlash that would empower the forces of reform, which were often rooted in broad, bipartisan coalitions.

But what if that facade was not necessary anymore? In an era of polarization and negative partisanship, blindly blocking Obama's nominee would be the ultimate act of "owning the libs," and Republicans were likely to cheer. Dating back to Bork in 1987, the issue of judges had been uniquely motivating for conservatives. Blocking the nomination would be risky, but the modern Senate put more tools at McConnell's disposal—more control—than ever before. He stood at the top of a leadership structure that gave him control inside the Senate. Since sixty votes were still needed to confirm a Supreme Court nominee, he could afford to lose more than a dozen of his members and still win the fight—a comfortable margin of error. Outside the Senate, he could rely on a network of groups that could spend effectively unlimited amounts of dark money to keep senators in line— with his fight against campaign finance reform, he had helped make sure they were able to do so. If their coffers ran dry, there were conservative billionaires whose bottom lines would benefit from a conservative Supreme Court and who would be eager to replenish them. McConnell did not need a majority or broad appeal, because for the most part, he and his fellow Republican senators needed only the support of the superminority to get elected. For years, establishment Republicans like himself and most of his members had been locked in an uneasy tension with that superminority. But blocking Obama's Supreme Court nominee would, for the first time, bring the goals of the superminority and those of the establishment into perfect alignment. This was the moment—the chance to use the modern Senate to unite the establishment and the superminority.

He made his choice. Before Cruz and Trump could take the debate stage, and just hours after his friend Scalia had been found dead, McConnell sent out an official statement. "The American people should have a voice in the selection of their next Supreme Court Justice," he said of a nomination that would be made by a president elected twice with big, diverse majorities, who had nearly a year left in office. Scalia's seat, McConnell said, "should not be filled until we have a new president."[89]

To keep senators in line, McConnell immediately began deploying the tools of control at the disposal of the Senate leader.

When he returned to Washington, he huddled in the Capitol with the supposedly independent, nonpartisan groups whose budgets were flush with cash in the wake of the *Citizens United* decision. In the meeting, McConnell "urged them to stay vigilant in the weeks and months ahead," according to a report by John Bresnahan of *Politico*.[90] One of the groups in the meeting had originally formed to support the Bush administration's nominees. Back then, the group had been called the Judicial Confirmation Network. Now its mission was opposing nominees, and it had rebranded itself as the Judicial Crisis Network. In the wake of *Citizens United*, it was well funded and more powerful than ever.

The pressure on Republicans to break with McConnell was immense. Down-the-middle commentators were aghast. The condemnations went beyond the usual diatribes from liberal editorial boards, crossing over to the hard-news reporters who prided themselves on strict objectivity. Ron Fournier, the former DC bureau chief of the Associated Press known for driving both sides of the spectrum crazy, tweeted, "Objective as possible, I rarely come across a story where one side deserves 100% of blame. Congrats, GOP. You've stumped me with #scotus."[91] When Obama put a name on the empty seat by nominating Merrick Garland, it was one Republicans had voted for. Seven Republicans had voted for Garland's confirmation to the D.C. Circuit in 2010; former Judiciary Committee chairman Senator Orrin Hatch of Utah had been so effusive about Garland that he volunteered, unprompted, that Garland would be "a consensus nominee" if he were ever nominated to the Supreme Court. Hatch even volunteered to personally whip votes for him. "I will do my best to help him get them," Hatch said in 2010.[92]

McConnell kept close tabs on his members, looking for anyone inclined to break. As he told Hulse, "We were monitoring what anybody might be saying in case I needed to make further calls."[93] In Kansas, Republican senator Jerry Moran broke with McConnell, arguing that Garland should at least get a hearing and a vote. "I would rather have you," he said to a roomful of his constituents, "complaining to me that I voted wrong on nominating somebody, than saying I'm not doing my job." Moran was not just any senator. He had chaired the Republican campaign committee in 2014, when Republicans took back the Senate. Senators respected his judgment on political matters, and for him to break with McConnell on the most contentious issue of the moment required a serious response. The Judicial Crisis Network swung into action. "We are in the process of putting the finishing touches on a robust, multi-faceted TV, digital, and grass-roots campaign designed to remind Senator Moran that he represents the people of Kansas and neither President Obama nor the Democratic Party," said Carrie Severino, JCN's head.[94] A primary challenge to Moran by a Tea Party congressman from Kansas named Mike Pompeo was floated.[95] Spurred on by "independent" groups, local activists railed against Moran in Kansas media. Within a few days, Moran backed down.

After a flurry of furious exchanges, the fight over the Supreme Court seat settled into a kind of sad stasis. Garland dutifully made the rounds on the Hill. After seeing what happened to Moran, Republican senators stayed in line, telling Garland, sometimes to his face, that despite his stellar career and sterling qualifications, they simply would not consider his nomination.

It was heartbreaking, astounding, and deeply frustrating. But in the grand scheme of things, it did not seem like it was going to matter much. By aligning with the Tea Party, McConnell might have succeeded in firming up his job and avoiding Boehner's fate, but it looked like Democrats had him cornered on the Supreme Court seat. By the summer, polls showed Clinton as the overwhelming favorite to beat Trump, and Democrats were favored to take back the Senate.[96] The expectation of just about every pundit and strategist in Washington was that soon, the first female president would be able to renominate Garland, or whomever she wanted, and the nominee would be confirmed by a Democratic Senate, shifting the balance of the Supreme Court to the left for a generation. Even McConnell, by his own admission, went into election night thinking Democrats would win both the White House and the Senate.[97] All the evidence, it seemed, suggested that a Supreme Court seat that should have been filled by a Democratic president eventually would be, just a little behind schedule.

On November 8, 2016, for the second time in sixteen years, a president was elected by a minority of the American people, receiving 2.9 million fewer votes than his opponent. Republican Senate candidates received about 6 million fewer votes than Democratic candidates, but held on to the Senate majority, with their fifty-two seats representing 44 percent of the population.[98] The GOP's margins of victory in Senate races were relatively narrow, and it had taken a fluky series of events for them to win the presidency. But now they had power. And while it might not last, their time in control of two branches of government would be enough to entrench minority rule through the third branch of government: the judiciary.

McConnell immediately coordinated with the White House so that it would feed the Senate a steady stream of nominees. Grassley, the chair of the Judiciary Committee, efficiently marched them through their confirmation hearings before reporting them out for McConnell to confirm on the floor.[99] As of this writing, that pipeline has confirmed more than 50 judges to appeals courts and more than 145 to district courts, putting Trump on track to shape the federal judiciary more than any recent president.

In January 2017, Trump nominated Neil Gorsuch to fill the Supreme Court seat that McConnell had kept open. When Democrats went nuclear in 2013, we had left the supermajority threshold in place for Supreme Court justices because a few Democrats were nervous about giving away this last line of defense against antiabortion nominees. With a flick of the wrist, McConnell got rid of it, going nuclear himself on April 6.[100] Gorsuch was confirmed the following day by a vote of 54 to 45.[101] Only one other Supreme Court justice since the Great Depression, Clarence Thomas, had been confirmed with fewer votes.[102] At a swearing-in ceremony for Gorsuch at the Rose Garden, Trump went out of his way to thank McConnell "for all that he did to make this achievement possible."[103]

The ceremony was presided over by Justice Anthony Kennedy, who wrote the *Citizens United* decision that had made McConnell's narrow view of corruption the law of the land and supercharged the groups that gave Republicans an advantage in the political spending game; that money, and those groups, had been critical to enforcing discipline among Senate Republicans and keeping the Supreme Court seat open. After the ceremony, Kennedy was quietly ushered into Trump's private dining room, a rare one-on-one meeting between a president and a sitting Supreme Court justice. In the meeting, Kennedy took the unusual step of telling Trump that if another seat on the Court should ever open up, Trump should fill it with one of Kennedy's former law clerks: U.S. Appeals Court Judge Brett Kavanaugh.[104] Fourteen months later, Kennedy retired, and Trump nominated Kavanaugh.

McConnell turned Kavanaugh's confirmation into a masterpiece of top-down control. Supreme Court confirmation processes are usually run primarily by the chair of the Judiciary Committee. But not this one. When Christine Blasey Ford came forward to testify that Kavanaugh had sexually assaulted her in high school, and Deborah Ramirez described an alleged sexual assault by Kavanaugh in college, McConnell coordinated the efforts to save his nomination.[105] Before Ford could testify, McConnell told a cheering crowd at the Value Voters Summit, "We're going to plow right through" on Kavanaugh's nomination.[106] And he did. Ahead of Ford's testimony, he held a nearly two-hour-long session in his office with Grassley and Republican senators on the Judiciary Committee to coordinate strategy.[107] Throughout the process, Grassley's investigators on the Judiciary Committee operated not as independent fact finders but partisan operatives carrying out McConnell's plan. As he was deposing witnesses and investigating allegations, Grassley's chief counsel, Mike Davis, tweeted, "Unfazed and determined. We will confirm Judge Kavanaugh."[108] For his part, Kavanaugh felt no need to maintain any pretense of civility or fairness, either. In his testimony, the former aide to Kenneth Starr characterized the sexual assault allegations against him as "revenge on behalf of the Clintons."[109] On October 6, 2018, Kavanaugh was confirmed by a vote of 50 to 48, breaking Thomas's record for the fewest votes to confirm a modern Supreme Court justice.

IN CONTRAST TO McConnell's efficient judicial confirmation machine, his attempts to pass legislation were consistently messy and often futile. Apart from a tax cut bill that delivered its benefits overwhelmingly to the wealthiest Americans, Senate Republicans passed few major bills, despite the fact that their party wielded unified control of Washington for the first two years of the Trump administration.[110] To be sure, Trump caused grievous damage during this period. But from his ban on Muslim immigration to imprisoning children in cages at the border, and from building the border wall to fomenting a revival of white supremacy, he did most of it through executive orders and executive branch actions, not legislation.

The reason McConnell had trouble passing legislation did not have much to do with the filibuster. Indeed, the filibuster proved of little use to Senate Democrats; during the first two years of the Trump administration, they launched the fewest legislative filibusters the Senate had seen from either party since 2009.[111] For the most part, McConnell was able to use end runs around the filibuster to pass the limited number of bills for which he could muster the votes. An early series of regulatory rollbacks was executed using the Congressional Review Act, which established a special category of time-limited legislation that is immune to filibusters (the CRA is not of much use to progressives, since it's only particularly useful for undoing laws and regulations); the CRA bills passed on simple-majority votes.[112] Republicans' tax reform bill passed through another special procedure called budget reconciliation, which is also immune to filibusters (I discuss this more in the Conclusion).[113] But these were relatively modest accomplishments for a party that controlled both chambers of Congress and the White House.

Republicans' failure to pass much major legislation was due more to the structural differences between the parties than to the filibuster or any other defensive tactics by Democrats. While progressives tend to be animated by a desire for sweeping change and require large-scale legislation to accomplish their goals, conservatives—standing athwart history yelling "Stop!"—generally do not. Since much of Republicans' agenda consists of blocking progress while dismantling the regulatory state, it can be accomplished predominantly through filibuster-proof means, such as regulatory rollbacks, executive actions, and simply refusing to take action on pressing issues. Republicans certainly have bills they want to pass, but as McConnell found, finding the votes for them is difficult in a party that is more motivated to stop things than anything else, once taxes are cut. Occasionally, President Trump grew frustrated with the meager accomplishments the Republican Congress was producing for him and demanded that McConnell go nuclear to lower the threshold for passing legislation to a simple majority.[114] But McConnell ignored him. His refusal was not a matter of principle; he had not hesitated to go nuclear to confirm Gorsuch.[115] Instead, McConnell seemed to understand something Trump did not: lowering the threshold for passing legislation to a majority would not have made a major difference because there was not much more that McConnell could have secured even a bare majority of votes to pass. "President Trump might need to hire a vote counter in the West Wing," Paul Kane of the *Washington Post* observed in the spring of 2018. McConnell's refusal was "a recognition that Republicans have passed just about all they can on a simple majority."[116]

Republicans' difficulty in securing a bare majority for major legislation was on full display in their quixotic quest to repeal the Affordable Care Act, otherwise known as Obamacare. Despite campaigning on repeal for seven years, Republicans struggled to follow through once they controlled both chambers of Congress and the White House.[117] In the House, Speaker Paul Ryan's first attempt at repeal in March 2017 ended in embarrassing failure.[118] He succeeded on his second try in May, prompting Trump to invite House Republicans to the White House for a Rose Garden celebration that in retrospect was laughably premature.[119]

In the Senate, McConnell found himself scrambling. Even in our polarized era, and despite all the tools of leadership control at his disposal, taking away popular benefits—such as the ACA's provision barring insurance companies from discriminating against people with preexisting conditions—proved politically toxic.[120] As he would with the tax cut bill, McConnell used reconciliation to bring a slimmed-down version of repeal to the floor for passage at a majority threshold, avoiding the threat of filibusters. But even then he struggled find the votes.

By late July 2017, McConnell had finally managed to piece together forty-nine votes for repeal, leaving its fate hanging on the vote of a single senator: John McCain (Vice President Mike Pence could cast the deciding vote if McConnell delivered fifty). Earlier in the month, McCain had undergone surgery for the brain cancer that would claim his life. When he arrived on the Senate floor around 1:30 am on July 28—the same floor where eighteen years earlier, McConnell had spent nearly three hours humiliating him—Washington was in suspense. In one of his final acts, McCain strode to the well of the Senate as McConnell stood a few feet away, the leader's arms folded expectantly. Looking straight at McConnell, McCain extended his right arm and held it aloft for a few seconds; then he turned his thumb down, signaling a "nay" vote. A gasp went up on the floor. McCain turned his back on McConnell and walked away as the defeated Republican leader stared down at his shoes.[121] A year later, on August 25, 2018, McCain passed away. To honor him, a group of senators pushed to rechristen the Russell Senate office building in his name. The effort seemed a fitting tribute to a man many regard as an American hero, and inarguably an improvement over an avowed white supremacist. But McConnell discouraged the effort, and it petered out.[122]

For all his erstwhile talk of the Senate as a check on the executive,

McConnell presided over a historic erosion of the Senate's oversight role, turning the institution into Trump's Praetorian Guard. The Trump administration spawned such abundant corruption, Bloomberg News launched an interactive guide to keep track of it, sortable by individuals and categories of scandal.[123] But under McConnell, the Senate investigated few of the glaring violations and brought almost none of the officials responsible to account. Most Senate committees have subpoena power, but under their Republican chairs, few subpoenas were issued and the Senate's oversight power withered while Trump administration officials abused the public trust at a shocking rate.

In early 2018, Trump openly contemplated violating Congress' power of the purse by unilaterally diverting federal dollars to build his border wall.[124] Congress's power to appropriate funds is one of the fundamental distinctions the Constitution draws between the legislative and executive branches; presidents can ask Congress for money, but they cannot take it. Some observers predicted that this aggressive violation of the Senate's prerogatives would be the last straw, finally spurring McConnell to break with Trump and assert the Senate's independence. In private, McConnell urged the president against the decision. But when Trump ignored his advice, McConnell meekly acquiesced in the president's power grab.[125]

In September 2019, a whistleblower came forward with damning evidence that Trump had used his office to pressure the Ukrainian government to interfere on his behalf in the upcoming presidential election.[126] In December, the House impeached Trump for this gross abuse of power.[127] The case then went to the Senate for trial. Just as they had before every impeachment trial in the nation's history, senators swore a special oath, administered by the Chief Justice of the United States. "I solemnly swear that in all things appertaining to the trial of the impeachment of President Donald J. Trump, now pending, I will do impartial justice according to the Constitution and laws: so help me God," the oath stated. McConnell swore the oath but made a mockery of it, pledging to Fox News's Sean Hannity that he would be working in "total coordination" with the White House during the Senate's trial.[128] McCain was gone, and McConnell had little trouble holding Republican senators in line on the single biggest test of fealty to Trump. Only Mitt Romney of Utah would break away, declaring Trump guilty of an "appalling abuse of public trust" in a dramatic speech on the Senate floor. But Romney's stance did not impact the result. McConnell had the votes, and on February 5, 2020, the Senate found Trump not guilty and allowed him to remain in office.[129]

VERY LITTLE OF what McConnell did during this period was popular, with polls consistently showing the public opposed to everything from ACA repeal to Republicans' lack of oversight; the tax cut bill they managed to pass was also deeply unpopular.[130] But it did not matter, because Senate Republicans did not need to win over the public to maintain power. To survive, all they needed was the support of the WWAC minority. In the 2018 midterms, Americans overwhelmingly cast their ballots for Democratic Congressional candidates. In the House, the results mostly reflected public opinion, with Democrats gaining forty-one seats to retake control of the chamber. But in the Senate, the votes cast and the seats gained went in opposite directions. Overall, Americans cast 18 million more votes for Democratic Senate candidates than Republican candidates.[131] But one of the ways the Framers protected the Senate against public opinion was by staggering Senate elections so that only a third of the chamber is up for re-election at any given time. In 2018, the seats up for election happened to be clustered in deep red states. When all the results were tallied, Republicans picked up two seats.[132]

Back in 2010, McConnell had declared that the "single most important thing we want to achieve is for President Obama to be a one-term president."[133] He failed at that, but he succeeded at something else: he demonstrated that there is no reason for a conservative Senate minority to ever cooperate with the majority. By deploying the tools of the modern Senate, and by feeding the WWAC minority the obstruction they crave in our polarized era, he showed that conservatives can block the majority with impunity, while reaping a windfall of astounding political gains. Wave elections may happen, but even then Republicans are unlikely to lose their grip on the forty-one seats they need to run McConnell's obstructionist playbook, and the incentives that reward them for doing so are unlikely to change. McConnell will leave the Senate one day, but his playbook is in the public domain and future GOP leaders will use it. Even if the playbook fails occasionally, a radically reshaped federal judiciary and a conservative majority on the Supreme Court are achievements that could stand for a generation, and the impact of the decisions they hand down could reverberate beyond that.

McConnell did not transform the Senate himself. He had the foresight to open the floodgates to corporate cash, and to use the blockade of Garland to unify the Tea Party base with the GOP establishment. He pioneered the blanket deployment of the filibuster, far beyond anything contemplated by previous leaders. But McConnell followed generations of white supremacist southern obstructionists who had come before him. Ever since John Calhoun set foot in the Senate, they had fought against Madison's vision of a majority-rule institution, forging new ways to impose their will on a country where progress threatened their power. Under McConnell, the Senate was finally remade in Calhoun's vision of minority rule. The only question that remains is whether it can be saved.

CONCLUSION

How to Save the Senate

THE SENATE IS SO BROKEN that it is easy to write it off as irredeemable. We are now at the endpoint of a process that started over 150 years ago. In the nineteenth century, obstructionist minorities invented the filibuster to give themselves the power to defy the majority. In the twentieth century, under the banner of "unlimited debate," southerners made the filibuster into a supermajority hurdle. In the postwar period and into the twenty-first century, Lyndon Johnson and Harry Reid created leadership structures capable of making the formerly leaderless institution march in lockstep behind a leader's agenda. And in recent years, Mitch McConnell paired those tools of control with the filibuster to give a reactionary, WWAC minority veto power over everything the majority attempts to accomplish. In our era of polarization and negative partisanship, conservatives can use McConnell's playbook in perpetuity with no fear of political consequences, and every expectation of reward. The outlook for the Senate, and for our democracy, is grim.

But the good news is that while broader developments such as polarization may seem intractable, fixing the Senate itself is actually comparatively easy. It will not require Constitutional amendments, Fox News ceasing to exist, or even a single supermajority vote. All it takes is fifty-one votes, political will, and a reasonable plan. Below I outline a plan that can be enacted at any time, through the same simple-majority procedure that Reid, and later McConnell, used to go nuclear.

As with the Senate's dysfunction, any discussion of how to fix the Senate necessarily centers on the filibuster. But to take the full measure of the stakes involved in the fight over the filibuster, it is worth examining one more episode from the Senate's history.

In 1970, America was on track to eliminate the Electoral College. The messy 1968 election had spooked Republicans and Democrats alike when the strong showing by Alabama governor and open racist George Wallace threatened to deny an Electoral College majority to either Richard Nixon or Hubert Humphrey. Nixon's "southern strategy" of wooing whites with coded racist appeals about "law and order" lifted him to victory, but the margin was exceedingly small; if he had done only slightly worse, he would not have won a majority in the Electoral College, throwing the election to the House of Representatives, where Democrats had long enjoyed a seemingly permanent majority.[1] Meanwhile, Democrats watched Humphrey lose the popular vote by a mere seven-tenths of a percentage point while netting just 191 electoral votes to Nixon's 301.[2] After an ugly campaign that left both sides shaken, America's two major parties were ready to change the method of electing presidents to a direct popular vote.[3]

Since the Electoral College is in the Constitution, eliminating it requires passing a constitutional amendment, one of the handful of actions to which the Framers assigned a supermajority threshold. But in 1970, passing a constitutional amendment wasn't the unfathomable task it seems like today; just a few years earlier, in 1965, Congress had passed the Twenty-Fifth Amendment, clarifying what was to be done if a president were killed or incapacitated, and the states had ratified it in 1967. The amendment to eliminate the Electoral College quickly gained steam. It was overwhelmingly popular with the public, with a Harris poll finding 79 percent of

Americans in support and Gallup putting support at 81 percent.[4] The states were receptive; 38 states were necessary for ratification, and a survey in the fall of 1969 found that 30 were already favorably inclined.[5] In September 1969, the amendment passed in the House by a margin of 339 to 70, well more than the two-thirds needed.[6] Soon after, Nixon—now president—endorsed the amendment and called on the Senate to follow the House's lead.[7] Opponents of the amendment were resigned to its passage. In November of 1969, writing in the *New York Times Magazine*, conservatives Irving Kristol and Paul Weaver lamented that "it now seems very likely" that the Electoral College would be eliminated, since "the amendment seems to have an excellent chance of getting Senate approval."[8]

The Senate effort was led by the same man who had successfully shepherded the Twenty-Fifth Amendment to passage, a rising star from Indiana named Birch Bayh. Bayh was supported by the Democratic majority leader, Mike Mansfield, as well as the Republican president.[9] The House-passed amendment had to make it through the Senate Judiciary Committee, which was still chaired by Mississippi's James Eastland, the white supremacist who had bragged of his "special pockets" for stashing civil rights bills. But even Eastland could not stop it. In August 1970, his Judiciary Committee reported the House-passed amendment, which had passed by a bipartisan vote of 11 to 6, with six Democrats and five Republicans joining together to back it.[10]

For the Senate floor debate, Bayh planned a reliable approach: hold an open process, allow senators to vote on a variety of proposals, and let the best one win.[11] Bayh's amendment—the House-passed version—appeared likely to be the top vote-getter, with Bayh counting 62 votes in his corner as the floor debate approached, just five shy of the 67 needed to pass.[12] There were plenty of gettable votes to make up the margin of victory, with reporters counting between ten and fifteen senators as undecided.[13]

By this time, Richard Russell was a sick man, just months away from death. But the Electoral College was a pillar of the South's structural power, since the winner-take-all system led presidential candidates to cater to the white supremacists who controlled southern states while ignoring their millions of black residents. His powers were diminished, and younger senators like Strom Thurmond took the lead in opposing the amendment. But just as they had been doing since the 1940s, the southern caucus gathered in Russell's office to organize their filibuster—his last, as it would turn out. On September 15, 1970, they emerged pledging to fight Bayh's amendment, along with every other measure to reform the Electoral College.[14]

Bayh now had the same problem reformers had faced for decades: once southern senators began loftily invoking the principle of unlimited debate, votes evaporated on cloture. As the *New York Times* noted, passage would be "harder to achieve with the procedural question of unlimited debate involved."[15] He also faced an unexpected threat on his left flank: Thurmond forged an alliance of convenience with a small but crucial group of liberals, persuading leading advocacy groups that the influence they enjoyed in big cities, which often decided the outcomes in their states in the Electoral College, would be undermined by popular vote elections.[16] Despite his broad bipartisan backing and the support of 81 percent of the American people, Bayh could not break the southern filibuster. The Electoral College survived. Observing this series of events, political scientist Richard MacGregor Burns warned that by keeping the Electoral College intact, America was playing "a game of Russian roulette, and one of these days we are going to blow our brains out."[17]

I raise this episode because it is time to bury, once and for all, the "little harm" thesis I mentioned at the start of this book. Believing that the filibuster has done little harm over the years requires ignoring the incalculable harm the filibuster has done to black Americans, which is reason alone to do away with it; as President Obama said in his eulogy for the congressman and civil rights leader John

Lewis, the filibuster is a "Jim Crow relic." But the harm allowed by the filibuster extends far beyond Jim Crow, and even beyond the many bills it has blocked in the McConnell era. To the present day, it preserves structural imbalances empowering white reactionaries. Without the filibuster, as we have seen, civil rights bills would have passed long before 1957, Obama's agenda would not have been crippled by historic levels of obstruction, Democrats would have passed a raft of progressive legislation—the list goes on and on. But still, we must look beyond these particular matters. If any one of the attempts at reforming the filibuster had succeeded prior to 1970, the only two presidents to lose the popular vote since 1888—George W. Bush and Donald J. Trump—might never have taken office. The filibuster does not just block bills from both sides. It makes white conservatives' structural advantages, and their ability to impose their will on our diverse majority, self-protecting. To fix our democracy, and to rectify the many injustices within our system today, the first step must be to curtail the filibuster. Senate reform—and democracy reform—starts with filibuster reform.

In 1970, the well-intentioned liberals who allied with Strom Thurmond—on the theory that the narrow gains they would reap from preserving the Electoral College outweighed the benefits of eliminating it—clearly miscalculated.[18] But today, some liberals make a similar case for preserving the filibuster: that the narrow benefits to progressives of occasionally being able to block conservative bills outweigh the benefits they will gain from eliminating it.[19] This, too, is a miscalculation. Denying themselves the ability to pass desperately needed legislation, including reforms to our democracy, while trying to protect their gains against conservative-controlled courts at a time when conservatives can (and routinely do) win elections with a minority of the vote—this is a fight progressives will lose, and indeed have been losing for decades.

The filibuster benefits conservatives far more than progressives, and it is not close. For the first few decades after the 1960s, when the filibuster came into frequent use, it is difficult to distinguish which bills were blocked by conservative filibusters and which by liberal ones because ideology did not align neatly with party affiliation; for example, in 1972, a Democratic bill to end busing was blocked by a Republican filibuster.[20] Even so, a distinct conservative tilt is evident. In more recent years, when ideologies aligned more closely with partisanship, the picture is clearer.

Since 2008, Democrats and Republicans have held unified control of Washington for two years each (meaning they controlled both houses of Congress and the White House). This allows us to isolate which bills would have become law had they not been blocked by filibusters in the Senate. Excluding appropriations bills, Republican filibusters blocked fifteen Democratic-sponsored bills from becoming law, while Democratic filibusters blocked six Republican bills from becoming law.[21] But even this does not tell the whole story, because some of the bills made it into legislation in other, if altered, forms, and in a few cases bills sponsored by one party were bipartisan. To sift through this uncertainty, it is best to look at what these bills were. Of the six Republican bills blocked by Democratic filibusters, three were different versions of immigration deals McConnell tried to pass on a single day in 2018 (February 15), one of which was a bipartisan bill supported by a mixture of Democrats and Republicans.[22] Another of the bills blocked by Democrats was a 20-week abortion ban, which secured 51 votes on cloture but included three Democrats among its supporters on what those Democrats knew was a throwaway vote. The remaining two Republican bills blocked by Democratic filibusters since 2009 were a reauthorization of the Coast Guard and a tribal labor bill.

On the other side of the ledger, the Democratic bills blocked by Republican filibusters included: a paycheck-fairness bill to reduce the wage disparity between men and women who perform the same work; the DREAM Act to protect undocumented immigrants who came to America as children from deportation; the DISCLOSE Act to expose the anonymous, superrich donors pumping millions of dollars into our political system; a bill to allow public safety officers to collectively bargain and form unions; a bill to close tax loopholes that reward corporations for sending American jobs overseas; and an expansion of Social Security benefits.[23] Although it never received a floor vote, a public option for health care—giving Americans the choice of a Medicare-type plan alongside private insurance options, without eliminating private insurance—was included in the ACA until the very end, when it had to be removed because it became clear to negotiators that it no longer had the sixty votes needed to pass (even though it still enjoyed majority support).[24] On top of all this, many observers at the time believed the climate change bill known as "cap-and-trade" that passed the House in 2010 would have passed the Senate, if not for the filibuster. As climate journalist David Roberts wrote, "Why did cap-and-trade fail? Because of filibuster abuse. That's the simplest and most directly causal answer."[25]

THE PLAN TO FIX the Senate centers on the filibuster. It is about restoring balance. The institution is tilted dramatically toward the WWAC superminority, who are able to impose their will whether or not they have a majority in the Senate. The point of reforming the filibuster is not to give one side's policies a better chance of passing, but to give both sides' agendas an equal chance. Some reformers would like to see the filibuster reformed without preserving minority protections, such as extended debate; here again, we should look to the Framers, because they got this right. In their vision, majority rule and the minority's right to extended debate—real, persuasive debate—go hand in hand. Their vision was also of a chamber where senators enjoyed independence and operated free from hierarchical control. To preserve the Senate's unique character, and to prevent it from becoming another House, we must restore all of these features. Here is how to do so.

RESTORING DEBATE

Debate is the *sine qua non* of the Senate, yet today real debate is vanishingly rare. In Senate parlance, debate has become synonymous with delay because when senators block a bill by placing a hold on it (i.e., a modern filibuster) they claim they are doing so in the name of debate. Real debate must be revived. Senate rules should adopt a "use it or lose it" standard for debate that restores meaning to the word: if senators are delaying a bill because they claim they want to debate it, they should actually debate it.

The ability for the minority to have its say in a prominent public forum was one thing that distinguished the Senate from the House in the Framers' vision. That ability must be preserved. When a bill is on the floor, senators in the minority should be provided every opportunity to explain their support or opposition, and to persuade the public to take their side. The rules governing debate should go out of their way to make sure the minority is afforded ample opportunity to make their case. Senate rules could establish a minimum period of debate (for example, five calendar days) during which the minority can have its say on the issue with no threat of being overrun by the majority. After the five days are up, a cloture vote will automatically occur, at a majority threshold. If the vote fails, debate continues; if the vote succeeds, debate is brought to an end and the Senate proceeds to vote on final passage of the bill.

For the Senate to reclaim its status as a deliberative body, senators have to be present to take part in the deliberation. In the early days of the Senate, before senators had office buildings to retreat to, a senator's workspace was their desk on the Senate floor. When senators arrived at the Capitol, they sat there, listening to their colleagues. Today, senators spend almost no time together. They use the floor to give scripted speeches and cast votes several times a week. Mostly, they avoid the floor for reasons covered in this book: first and foremost, they need to raise money, which consumes more time in a senator's schedule than any other single activity. They also live in fear of gaffes that can be turned into attacks, and the fewer words they put on the record, the less chance there is that they will commit one. As a result, senators do not linger on the floor or, frankly, listen to each other. The cloakrooms have been reduced from sanctuaries in which senators mingle and exchange views to hallways they pass through in their rush to get on and off the floor.

The daily routines of Senate life are segregated by party, and senators can go weeks at a time without having a meaningful interaction with a member of the other party. Senators lunch together as a group twice a week, but only with members of their party. In an average week, there are various meetings of committee chairs, working groups, and leadership committees, but those are usually split by party. It's so rare for even an informal bipartisan group of senators to get together that when it happens, they're labeled a "gang" and it becomes headline news.

To reestablish a basic norm that senators should interact with their peers in free and open debate, the Senate should establish an American version of the British Parliament's "question time." Senate rules should require a minimum number of senators (perhaps a quorum, or fifty-one) to be present on the Senate floor for a minimum number of hours (say, five) before it is allowed to adjourn for more than sixteen hours (or overnight). In practice, this means that in a given week, before the Senate can go home for the weekend, at least fifty-one senators would have to spend a minimum of five hours on the floor together. It's entirely possible the Senate will find a way to suck the lifeblood out of question time sessions like these. If senators choose to spend this time watching the clock tick down like students in detention, that's their prerogative. But it is more likely that once they're together, on the Senate floor and in full public view, they will actually talk to one another and engage in extemporaneous debate.

RESTORING MAJORITY RULE

Open debate and majority rule go hand in hand. In a more open Senate, senators in the minority will have ample opportunity to persuade their colleagues and the public to switch to their side. If they fail to persuade, they lose. That's how democracy is supposed to work, and that's how Madison intended the Senate to work. If the minority does not like the outcome of a given debate, they can use the next election to try to become the majority. But for our system to function, every decision point in the Senate should be majority rule, aside from those assigned supermajority thresholds by the Constitution. That—combined with a restoration of debate—will help bring the Senate back in line with Madison's vision.

When making tough decisions, consensus is ideal; but by definition, the most controversial issues are the ones where consensus is least achievable. When there are strong opinions on both sides of an issue and reaching a consensus (or a supermajority) proves impossible, the only options become stasis or majority rule. The Framers argued in clear terms that when faced with these options, the majority should rule. Since their era, studies have confirmed that majority rule protects minorities better than any other decision-making process. As the game theorist Anthony McGann concludes in his book *The Logic of Democracy*, "the only social decision rule that treats all people equally is majority rule."[26]

In Federalist 22, Hamilton took note of the flawed assumption that a tactic like the filibuster (which he never knew, of course) would promote compromise, writing of supermajority thresholds that "what at first sight may seem a remedy, is, in reality, a poison."[27] As Hamilton and his fellow Framers understood from their experience under the Articles of Confederation, supermajority requirements might *seem* like they would promote moderation and cooperation, but instead, they exacerbate partisanship and increase gridlock. The filibuster routinely stops our government from addressing problems long after expert solutions, political will, and public support exist to solve them. Nothing good happens when a nation's most pressing problems are left to fester for years and sometimes decades. It is impossible to argue that it was anything but disastrous to wait to pass civil rights bills until decades after broad majorities of Americans, majorities in both houses of Congress, and presidents of both parties were ready for action. Today, the same is true for climate change, gun control, and many other issues where the cost of delay can be measured in human suffering and lost lives, consequences of such gravity that any theoretical benefits of delay pale in comparison.

It is arguably true that the filibuster promoted moderation for the anomalous period between when it came into frequent use and when polarization set in—the Mansfield era of the 1970s, before parties became locked in constant competition for control of the majority.[28] Notably, that was the formative period for many of the Senate's current elders and "traditionalists." During that time, the idea that the filibuster promoted moderation was intuitive: forcing legislation to clear a supermajority threshold forced more people to agree on an issue to move forward. But the assumptions underlying that view have to be updated to reflect the reality of the current age. It is no longer safe to assume that both parties involved in a negotiation want to move forward—to the contrary, the dominance of negative partisanship in today's politics makes it far safer to assume the opposite. Now, if the minority party gains when the majority party fails, the minority party will withhold cooperation to make the majority fail. Under these conditions, expecting the minority to help the majority secure a legislative victory is to expect politicians to act against their interests, which is not something they will do on a regular basis.

Restoring a majority-rule Senate narrows the minority's options to helping the majority achieve a victory or sitting on the sidelines. The minority may still decide they're better off abstaining, but the cost-benefit analysis is not nearly as clear-cut: in an era dominated by polarization and negative partisanship, the minority gains from making the majority fail—but does it gain from standing idly by while the majority notches wins? Maybe, but it's not immediately obvious that it does. More importantly, their decision becomes less consequential for the nation as a whole. In a majority-rule Senate, if the minority decides to sit on its hands, the majority will be able to conduct the nation's business while they pout.

It is often assumed that the broad bipartisan majorities behind the passage of major laws were secured because the filibuster forced compromise. But these arguments deserve skepticism, because they are often not true. Medicare, passed in 1965 by a vote of 66 to 21, is one of the most frequently cited examples.[29] But a filibuster did not forge a compromise that made Medicare possible. Rather, for years, Medicare was bottled up in committee by Congressman Wilbur Mills, the chair of the House Ways and Means Committee, who blocked it at the behest of the American Medical Association and other special interests.[30] It was shaken loose not by a bipartisan compromise brought together by the filibuster, but by Democrats' landslide victory in 1964.[31] The huge majorities Democrats won that year made clear that Medicare was passing with or without Mills' cooperation. Once this became clear, Mills jumped on board, and the bill passed.[32]

A majority-rule Senate cannot guarantee a return to bipartisanship; in our era, it would be a lousy bet that anything will. But it can make a productive, functioning Senate far more likely. That has to be the goal; bipartisanship is perhaps a goal to strive for, but it cannot be the primary consideration. Facing the enormous challenges we have today, the test that matters is whether the Senate can deliver intelligent policy responses, not whether it can do so through bipartisanship. However, despite the long odds against bipartisanship, there is reason for optimism, as the historical record suggests that a more productive Senate is more likely to facilitate bipartisanship than a gridlocked one.

AMENDMENTS

Amendments are the principal method by which senators can influence legislation once it is on the floor. In a given session, most senators will not be the lead sponsors of one of the bills the Senate considers, and very few will be a "manager," the name given to the senator responsible for guiding a bill through the floor process. If rank-and-file senators are unable to offer amendments, then they are mostly powerless to affect the legislation that the Senate is considering. Any senator who has put in the time and effort to write a piece of legislation should have a reasonable shot at getting a vote on it as an amendment. When debate opens on a bill, each side should be guaranteed a minimum number of amendments. A minimum guarantee of ten amendments for each side, or a total of twenty per bill, is a reasonable number.

RECONCILIATION

A popular idea in circulation as of this writing is to expand the use of budget reconciliation to pass certain bills at a majority threshold. But the promise of reconciliation is a mirage. Reconciliation is a fasttrack made available by the Budget Control Act of 1974. To use the track, legislation needs to have a demonstrable fiscal impact, and the Senate Parliamentarian judges whether bills comply with reconciliation's strict rules. The advantage of reconciliation, and its attraction to reformers, is that all provisions that comply with its rules can be brought up for a majority vote. But trying to force more and different kinds of legislation through the reconciliation track is bound to end badly, for at least four reasons.

First, reconciliation is off-limits to many categories of legislation, such as gun control and voting rights, that cannot credibly be shown to have a major fiscal impact (the Parliamentarian is no fool). Second, broad bills that get forced through reconciliation will inevitably turn into legislative "Christmas Trees" laden with unrelated provisions; that is how Alaska's Arctic National Wildlife Refuge was opened up to oil drilling as part of the GOP's 2017 tax cut bill, which was passed through reconciliation. These bills become the stuff of lobbyists' dreams: leadership-driven mega-packages assembled in secret with no oversight and little committee involvement, a shady process that anyone concerned with the health of the Senate should oppose. Third, designing policy to comply with reconciliation's strict rules leads to poorly designed legislation—costs that are passed on to the American people, while making the bills more vulnerable to legal challenges. Finally, the chances that every important provision will survive the strict rules (the test of compliance is called a "Byrd bath" because former Democratic leader Robert Byrd wrote it) are slim. Major provisions are virtually certain to get struck, which will leave supporters with no choice but to go nuclear anyway.

DEMOCRATIZING LEADERSHIP

Senate leaders perform some valuable functions. But the control they wield also prevents senators from thinking for themselves about floor strategy. Leadership convenes the caucus twice a week and lays out the agenda. That in itself is not a problem—but there should be other power centers where members come together and develop alternative agendas to the ones leadership concocts. Leadership has a monopoly on information regarding floor strategy, which enables them to curtail the set of options that members think are available to them. Senators should seek to democratize the flow of information, putting in the time to cultivate alternative sources on parliamentary procedure and floor strategy.

Most importantly, the incumbent-protection racket should be eliminated. The DSCC and NRSC should not participate in primaries. When incumbents are running, the Senate campaign committees should not direct funds to the incumbent senators until they win their primary and become the party's official nominee. New voices within the parties should be given space to make their case and offer competing visions for how to conduct policy and politics.

STATEHOOD AND REPRESENTATION

The injustice created by the Great Compromise and decried by Madison at the Constitutional Convention is unlikely to go away anytime soon. While serious proposals to split up California into multiple states are being discussed, they will have to be decided by Californians. But in the meantime, we can go a long way toward rectifying the problem of representation through other means. One important step is to add states in places where Americans are currently bound by federal laws but lack the representation to shape them, starting with the District of Columbia. In terms of population, the District is bigger than Wyoming and Vermont, and roughly the same size as Alaska and North Dakota.[33] Far from being occupied by lobbyists and Hill staffers, the District is mostly made up of nonwhite working-class Americans, none of whom have voting representation in Congress.[34] The District is afforded one representative in the House—but by rule, this representative is not allowed to vote since the District is not part of a state—and no senators. Statehood should be voluntary and driven by the wishes of the residents. The residents of the District have made clear, over and over again, that they want to be a state. And frankly, there is simply no viable argument against it. Puerto Rico, which has a larger population than twenty states, should also be welcomed to apply for statehood, if it chooses to do so.[35]

The problem of representation in the Senate is not just about potentially adding states. Across the country, state authorities have used a range of voter suppression tactics to prevent certain populations from voting—usually liberal-leaning, nonwhite populations.[36] The Senate should pass a new set of civil rights legislation, including a renewed Voting Rights Act, that guarantees access to the ballot for all voting-age Americans. To effectively represent their states, senators must be sent to Washington by elections where all residents have equal access to the ballot.

MOST OF THE PROBLEMS America faces today are seemingly much broader than the Senate. But because the Senate lies at the heart of our government, the solutions to these problems must pass through it, almost without exception. As long as the Senate remains a kill switch that reactionary white conservatives can hit whenever they choose, it is difficult to see how America can meet the challenges it faces. But with a functional Senate, solutions suddenly appear within reach.

To fix the Senate, we must keep in mind that restoring an institution capable of producing intelligent solutions is the goal—the Framers' vision is a corrective to "traditionalists" today, not the goal itself. We do not elect senators to bask in pundits' praise for upholding Senate tradition; as this book has shown, most of what passes for "tradition" is in fact myth, invented by people seeking to protect their power from the march of change that has so often threatened it. Calhoun and his modern acolytes, from Russell to McConnell, destroyed the best things about the Senate—its deliberative nature, the forum it provided for free and open debate—and replaced them with gridlock, all while telling us it was for the good of the institution. The Senate needs to be rescued from its own self-indulgent myths, saved from the twisted, damaging Calhounian thing that it has become, and restored to Madison's model—a model in which the minority is protected, the majority rules, and the business of the nation moves forward.

ACKNOWLEDGMENTS

This book is an attempt to understand an inscrutable institution. My work in doing so owes much to the support and prior efforts of countless people.

The work of Robert Caro provided a gateway into the Senate before I set foot in the building. In particular, his insight into the interplay between the institution and the personalities molding it influenced the approach of this book. Once I arrived in the Senate and found myself confronted on a daily basis with the discrepancy between my expectations and the reality of the modern Senate, the work of several scholars bridged the gap. Sarah Binder and Steven Smith have defined the field of filibuster scholarship, and the first time the conflict between perception and reality of the Senate began to resolve into understanding was when I picked up *Politics and Principle*. To Binder, especially, I am grateful for years of guidance. Gregory Koger has provided the field with an invaluable resource with his *Filibustering*, translating centuries of obstruction into data and bringing clarity to much cloudy history. Gregory J. Wawro and Eric Schickler's *Filibuster* shows that what is too often regarded as entrenched Senate tradition is, in reality, the product of complicated choices—and as such, subject to change through different choices in the future. Norman Ornstein and Thomas Mann have chronicled the decline of Congress as an institution with an unparalleled combination of detail, insight, and narrative force. The work of Frances E. Lee, both in *Insecure Majorities* and *Sizing Up the Senate*, the latter coauthored with Bruce Oppenheimer, captures the trends defining the political world around the Capitol and the incentives driving the behavior of those within it. The work of many others, including Barbara Sinclair, David Mayhew, and Molly Reynolds, also contributed enormously to this book. The multitude of compelling legal arguments against the filibuster add up to the unavoidable conclusion that it is a misfit within the Madisonian system: Catherine Fisk, Erwin Chemerinsky, Josh Chafetz, Akhil Reed Amar, and Dan Coenen have contributed pathbreaking work in this arena.

Senate historian emeritus Richard Baker has guided generations through the workings of the Senate. His body of work, including *The American Senate*, coauthored with the late Neil MacNeil, constitutes a foundation for anyone seeking to understand the institution. A dog-eared, marked-up copy of Martin Gold's *Senate Procedure and Practice* sat on my desk for years, as it does in offices across the Capitol. I disagree with much of what Robert Dove and Richard Arenberg have written, but in *Defending the Filibuster* they make the best case for its preservation.

Understanding the Framers' approach to the Senate was in many ways a process of forgetting the myths that its members and hagiographers hammer home on a near-daily basis. The works of Jack Rakove, Jill Lepore, Robert Dahl, and Gordon Wood were essential guides. In understanding the historical context of the nineteenth century, the work of Eric Foner was indispensable, along with that of W. E. B. Du Bois, Daniel Walker Howe, Sean Wilentz, and David Potter. Charles Wiltse's seminal three-volume history of Calhoun was rich and rewarding, as were the dissections of Calhoun's philosophy by James Read and other scholars.

Bridging the centuries, the journalism of Nikole Hannah Jones, Jamelle Bouie, and Adam Serwer has been vital in upending false but comforting narratives. For understanding the Johnson era, I am indebted to the work of Caro, Doris Kearns Goodwin, and Gilbert Fite. The evolution of the conservative movement, and in particular the white supremacy that drove it through the centuries, undergirds much of this book. For that, I relied heavily on Rick Perlstein, Carol Anderson, Julian Zelizer, Kevin Kruse, Robert Draper, Michael Grunwald, Geoffrey Kabaservice, and others. The works of Charles Mills, David M. Roediger, and Nell Irvin Painter provided analytical frames that yielded critical insights. The works of Jane Mayer, Robert Kaiser, and Zephyr Teachout lifted the hood on money in politics and the intellectual bankruptcy of the laws governing campaign finance. On applying the influence of wealth and inequality to politics, the work of Larry Bartels proved indispensable, as did contributions by Ganesh Sitaraman, Jacob Hacker, and Paul Pierson. A goal of this book is to place the Senate within the contemporary political world, since it is too often considered a fortress isolated from the world around it. The works of John Sides, Michael Tesler, Lynn Vavreck, Carol M. Swain, Alan I. Abramowitz, Ashley Jardina, Lilliana Mason, Ezra Klein, Steve Phillips, and Lee Drutman all proved essential in parsing the forces at work on American politics today and uncovering connection points to the Senate.

The works of Alec MacGillis, Charles Homans, Carl Hulse, and Jason Zengerle deepened my understanding of what made Mitch McConnell tick. (McConnell's memoir, *The Long Game*, was also profoundly, and perhaps unintentionally, revealing.) Indeed, much of my education about the modern Senate itself came from rolling conversations with reporters about Senate politics, procedure, and history that began when I started working in Harry Reid's press office in 2010 and have not stopped; I will not name them here, since that is probably what they would prefer. And I could not have completed this book during the onset of the COVID-19 pandemic in the spring and summer of 2020 without the invaluable work of digital archivists.

The Senate colleagues who shaped my thinking are too many to name, but a few directly influenced the ideas and understanding that went into this book. William Dauster has been my Senate rabbi for years and his guidance was irreplaceable. Gary Myrick taught me how the Senate really works from the cloakroom and the floor. David Krone provided an education in high-level power dynamics. During my years in Reid's office, I did not make a single decision without the counsel of Kristen Orthman and Faiz Shakir. The guidance of Katie Fallon, Brian Fallon, Dan Yoken, and Matt McNally was critical to my understanding of the politics and mechanics of the Senate.

My undergraduate thesis adviser, Anders Stephanson, taught me the craft of writing and researching history. The research, sophisticated analysis, and insights of Andrew Odgren influenced every page of this book, and it simply would not have happened without him. The book also reflects the invaluable research support of Rachael Brown, Chris Rickert, and Hilary McClellen.

Ultimately, this book is a result of the trust, patience, and access Senator Harry Reid extended to me. The first time we met, he was sitting behind his big desk, across an office that seemed to me to stretch for miles. As I crossed the vast expanse, he looked up from what he was doing, took stock of me, and said, "Your tie is crooked." I still don't totally understand what made him take a chance on me—repeatedly over the years—but I will be forever grateful. This book would not have been possible without the support and patience of Anne Harkavy and Andrianna Dunbar, or the responsibility shouldered by Charisma Troiano and Meg Uzzell. I count myself lucky to have worked for Anne; her intelligence and deeply rooted progressive values are an inspiration.

I am deeply indebted to Heather Schroder at Compass Literary—this whole thing was her idea! Dan Gerstle at Liveright is not just an editor but an educator as well, asking incisive questions and probing weak spots in arguments. Indeed, I have been incredibly lucky in the editor department, and am grateful to those who helped develop some of the ideas and themes of this book, especially John Guida at the *New York Times* and Mari Uyehara and William Welch at *GQ*.

Tory Newmyer has been a friend, confidant, early reader, adviser, and inspiration. Patrick Kiker has kept me thinking (and laughing) for twenty years. Max Bergman and Ken Gude were valuable sounding boards throughout the process. Zachary Carter, Benjy Sarlin, and the Raven made writing a book seem possible. Matt Lambert, Ben Lutkoski, and David Sensenig have been asking the big questions with me since seventh grade. Without the daily support of Cinthia, Marcelo, and Christian de Leaños, this book would not have been possible.

My parents, Bruce and Barbara, have built a wonderful life and family on a marriage of Louisiana and Long Island that gave me a bloodline running from Plaquemines Parish to Baldwin. Among many things, my dad taught me to pair values with rigor and my mom taught me to love history and side with the underdog. My sister, Katherine, inspires me every day with her intelligence and compassion. Wyn Kelley and Dale Peterson have been beloved family long before it was official.

My sons give me joy beyond measure. Danny, I am so proud of you and the mature, thoughtful, and kind person you have always been and always will be. Your poise, intelligence and humor helped us all get through the challenge of writing a book during a global pandemic in ways you may never know ("keep calm and write on"), but which your mom and I will never forget. Felix, hearing your irrepressibly cheery little voice every morning as I toiled in the basement—and your footsteps above as you ran around upstairs in your Batman costume—kept me smiling.

Most of all, it is hard to know what to say about someone who has been a part of you for more than half your life, but here goes. Britt Peterson is my partner in everything, and has been for the last twenty years, starting when she agreed to copilot my parents' minivan from New York City back to Maryland at the beginning of junior year. Once we started talking we forgot to stop, and here we are. The love of my life, Britt is also its editor, making everything in it smarter and better. She guided me through every step of this book and made the writing of it possible, for which I will always be grateful. Her wisdom, warmth, and humor kept me going at times when I was ready to give up. Thank you, Britt, for everything. I love you.

NOTES

Introduction: THE LITTLE HARM THESIS

1. McCarthy, Justin. "Gallup Vault: 72% Support for Anti-Lynching Bill in 1937." May 11, 2018.
2. "First Study of Public Opinion of Poll Tax Issue Completed by Institute in National Survey." Public Opinion News Service. April 2, 1941.
3. Daniels, Maurice C. *Ground Crew: The Fight to End Segregation at Georgia State.* Athens: University of Georgia Press, 2019; Garrett, Major. "Top GOP Priority: Make Obama a One-Term President." *National Journal.* October 23, 2010.
4. Hamilton, Alexander; Madison, James; and Jay, John. *The Federalist Papers.* Mineola, NY: Dover Publications, 2014. 102–3; "James Madison to [Edward Everett], August 28, 1830." National Archives. https://founders.archives.gov/documents/Madison/99-02-02-2138.
5. *Charlie Rose*, interview with Mitch McConnell, aired on PBS June 1, 2016.
6. Higginson, Thomas Wentworth. "The Birth of a Nation." *Harper's New Monthly Magazine* 68, no. 4 (1884): 242.
7. Tausanovitch, Alex; and Root, Danielle. *How Partisan Gerrymandering Limits Voting Rights.* Center for American Progress. July 8, 2020.
8. Since the 2000 elections, Senate Republicans' share of the population has never exceeded 50 percent. From 2005 to 2006, when they held fifty-five Senate seats, it was 49 percent. This data is based on a widely used methodology. To calculate the percentage of the population represented by each party in the Senate, each of a state's two seats is assigned half the state's population. My calculations exclude the populations of the District of Columbia, Puerto Rico, and other nonstates, since they do not have senators and therefore cannot be assigned to a party.

Chapter One: BIRTH OF A NOTION

1. Baker, K. C.; and Carlson, Adam. "It Took Years for Sandy Hook Dad to Take Down Christmas Tree Son Helped Put Up before Massacre." *People.* December 15, 2017.

2. Peralta, Eyder. "Poll: 9 in 10 Americans Support Background Check for All Gun Sales." National Public Radio. February 7, 2013. Note on Senate support for background checks: Fifty-four senators voted for the Manchin-Toomey amendment, but fifty-five supported it. When it was clear the bill was going to fail, Senator Reid switched his vote to a "no" vote for procedural reasons. Senate rules contain a provision allowing the leader to bring a bill or amendment back up for a vote with fewer procedural hurdles if they vote "no." This special process is called a "motion to reconsider." Voting "yes" sacrifices this shortcut. Reid was considering bringing the bill back up using this expedited procedure and wanted to preserve his option to do so. Reid made abundantly clear, on the record and on multiple occasions, that he supported the background-checks amendment, nor was his support in question at the time. He also supported the ban on assault weapons that came to the floor during this time. See, e.g., "Reid's Remarks on Assault Weapons Ban Vote." *New York Times.* April 17, 2013.

3. Hamburger, Tom. "Gun Rights Group Endorses Manchin-Toomey." *Washington Post.* April 14, 2013.

4. Dauster, William G. "The Great Holdup: How the Senate and the Filibuster Thwart Gun Legislation Most Americans Want." *Legislation and Policy Brief* 9, no. 1, art. 4 (2020).

5. Draper, Robert. "Inside the Power of the N.R.A." *New York Times Magazine.* December 12, 2013.

6. Lopez, German. "After Sandy Hook We Said Never Again." *Vox.* April 18, 2020.

7. Tweet by @DanCrenshawTX, verified account of Congressman Dan Crenshaw. Accessed May 27, 2020. https://twitter.com/DanCrenshaw TX/status/1165403952411750401.

8. "Race Summary Report: 2018 General Election." Office of the Texas Secretary of State. November 6, 2018. https://elections.sos.state.tx.us/elchist331_state.htm.

9. Hamilton, Alexander; Madison, James; and Jay, John. *The Federalist Papers.* Mineola, NY: Dover Publications, 2014. 44.

10. Konkle, Burton Alva. *James Wilson and the Constitution.* Lecture delivered before the Law Academy of Philadelphia. November 14, 1906. 26.

11. Franklin, Benjamin; and Franklin, William Temple. *The Works of Dr. Benjamin Franklin: Autobiography.* Vol. 2. Philadelphia: W. Duane, 1808. 473.

12. Locke, John. *The Second Treatise of Government and A Letter Concerning Toleration*. New York: Dover Publications, 2012. 44.

13. Jefferson, Thomas. *The Life and Selected Writings of Thomas Jefferson*. New York: Modern Library, 1998. 227.

14. Jefferson, Thomas. *Thomas Jefferson: Diplomatic Correspondence, Paris, 1784–1789*. Brett F. Woods, ed. New York: Algora Publishing, 2016. 230.

15. Binder, Sarah; and Smith, Steven. *Politics or Principle? Filibustering in the United States Senate*. Washington, DC: Brookings Institution Press, 1997. 32.

16. Farrand, Max, ed. *The Records of the Federal Convention of 1787*. Vol. 2. New Haven, CT: Yale University Press, 1911. 450–53.

17. Hamilton, Madison and Jay, *The Federalist Papers*. 102–3.

18. Farrand, *Records of the Federal Convention of 1787*. 198.

19. Vile, John R. *The Constitutional Convention of 1787: A Comprehensive Encyclopedia of America's Founding*. Vol. 1. Santa Barbara, CA: ABC-CLIO, 2005. lxvi.

20. "Madison Debates, Thursday July 5, 1787." The Avalon Project, Yale Law School. Accessed August 21, 2020. https://avalon.law.yale.edu/18th_century/debates_705.asp.

21. Madison, James. Adrienne Koch, ed. *Notes of Debates in the Federal Convention of 1787*. New York: W. W. Norton, 1987. 238–40.

22. Ibid.

23. Coenen, Dan T. "The Originalist Case against Congressional Supermajority Voting Rules." *Northwestern University Law Review* 1091 (2012): 1148.

24. Ibid.

25. Abel, Albert S. "The Commerce Clause in the Constitutional Convention and in Contemporary Comment." *Minnesota Law Review* (1941): 807.

26. Coenen, "The Originalist Case against Congressional Supermajority Voting Rules." 1141.

27. Ibid.

28. Hamilton, Madison, and Jay, *Federalist Papers*. 102–3.

29. Ibid. 288.

30. Ibid. 41–47.

31. Tsebelis, George. *Veto Players: How Political Institutions Work*. Princeton, NJ: Princeton University Press, 2002.

32. *The Edinburgh Review*. Edinburgh: A. and C. Black, 1838. 192.

33. Hofstadter, Richard. *The American Political Tradition and the Men Who Made It*. New York: Vintage Books, 1989. 91.

34. Capers, Gerald M. "A Reconsideration of John C. Calhoun's Transition from Nationalism to Nullification." *Journal of Southern History* 14, no. 1 (1948): 34–48.

35. Ibid.
36. *Vice Presidents of the United States, 1789–1993.* Washington, DC: U.S. Government Printing Office, 1997. 87.
37. Niven, John. *John C. Calhoun and the Price of Union.* Baton Rouge: Louisiana State University Press, 1988. 154–78.
38. Hart, Charles Henry; and Elson, Henry William. *History of the United States of America.* London: Macmillan, 1908. 109.
39. Parton, James. *Life of Andrew Jackson.* New York: Mason Brothers, 1860. 204.
40. Niven, *John C. Calhoun.* 174.
41. Hart and Elson, *History of the United States.* 110.
42. Harvey, Peter. *Reminiscences and Anecdotes of Daniel Webster.* Boston: Little, Brown, 1878. 49.
43. Ticknor, George, et al. *Life, Letters, and Journals of George Ticknor.* Boston: J. R. Osgood, 1876. 330.
44. Webster, Daniel. *Speeches in Congress.* Boston: Little, Brown, 1877. 258.
45. MacNeil, Neil; and Baker, Richard A. *The American Senate.* Oxford: Oxford University Press, 2013. 279.
46. Webster, Daniel; and Hayne, Robert Young. *Speeches of Messrs. Hayne and Webster in the United States Senate on the Resolution of Mr. Foot, January, 1830.* Boston: Redding, 1852. 18.
47. Brands, H. W. *Heirs of the Founders.* New York: Penguin Random House, 2018. 162.
48. March, Charles Wainwright. *Reminiscences of Congress.* New York: Baker and Scribner, 1850. 124.
49. Johnston, Alexander, ed. *American Orations: Studies in American Political History.* New York: G. P. Putnam's Sons, 1896. 390.
50. Ibid. 388.
51. March, *Reminiscences of Congress.* 146.
52. Webster, Daniel. "Daniel Webster to James Madison, May 24, 1830." National Archives.
53. Madison, James. "James Madison to Daniel Webster, May 27, 1830." National Archives.
54. Bordewich, Fergus M. *America's Great Debate.* New York: Simon & Schuster, 2012. 39.
55. Madison, James. "From James Madison to Thomas Jefferson, December 29, 1798." National Archives.
56. Madison, James. "On Nullification, December 1834." National Archives.
57. Madison, James. "Notes on Nullification, December 1835." National Archives.

58. Madison, James. "Notes on Nullification and the Nature of the Union, December 1831." National Archives.

59. "James Madison to [Edward Everett], August 28, 1830." National Archives.https://founders.archives.gov/documents/Madison/99-02-02-2138.

60. Ibid.

61. Cited in Dahl, Robert A. *How Democratic Is the American Constitution?* New Haven, CT: Yale University Press, 2003.

62. "James Madison to Unknown, re majority governments, December 1834." Founders Online, National Archives, https://founders.archives.gov/documents/Madison/99-02-02-3066.

Chapter Two: "VICTORIOUS IN THE MIDST OF UNBROKEN DEFEATS"

1. Sen. McConnell (KY). "Honoring British Prime Minister Baroness Margaret Thatcher." *Congressional Record* 159, Pt. 4 (April 16, 2013). 5298.

2. S. Res. 100. 113th Congress. "A resolution commending and congratulating the University of Louisville men's basketball team for winning its third Division I National Collegiate Athletic Association championship, and the University of Louisville women's basketball team for being runner up in the 2013 Women's Division I National Collegiate Athletic Association Basketball Tournament." Senator Mitch McConnell, lead sponsor. Introduced April 16, 2013.

3. Sen. McConnell (KY). "Gun Amendments." *Congressional Record* 159, Pt. 4 (April 16, 2013). 5339.

4. Author's calculations based on C-SPAN footage.

5. *Congressional Record* 159, Pt. 4 (April 11–17, 2013). 5007–5381.

6. Hamilton, Alexander; Madison, James; and Jay, John. *The Federalist Papers*. Mineola, NY: Dover Publications, 2014. 304.

7. Ibid.

8. "Thomas Jefferson, 2nd Vice President (1797–1801)." U.S. Senate. Accessed April 18, 2020. www.senate.gov/about/officers-staff/vice-president/VP_Thomas_Jefferson.htm.

9. Gold, Martin B.; and Gupta, Dimple. "The Constitutional Option to Change Senate Rules and Procedures: A Majoritarian Means to Overcome the Filibuster." *Harvard Journal of Law and Public Policy* 28, no. 205 (2004).

10. MacNeil, Neil; and Baker, Richard A. *The American Senate*. Oxford: Oxford University Press, 2013. 304.

11. Todd, Charles Burr. *A General History of the Burr Family in America: With a Genealogical Record from 1570 to 1878.* New York: E. W. Sackett & Bro., 1878. 80.
12. "Indicted Vice President Bids Senate Farewell." U.S. Senate. Senate .gov, accessed August 21, 2020. https://www.senate.gov/artandhistory/history/minute/Indicted_Vice_President_Bids_Senate_Farewell.htm.
13. Todd, *A General History of the Burr Family in America.* 80–82.
14. Binder, Sarah A. "The History of the Filibuster." Testimony before the U.S. Senate Committee on Rules and Administration. Brookings Institution. April 22, 2010.
15. MacNeil and Baker, *American Senate.* 304.
16. Burdette, Franklin. *Filibustering in the Senate.* Princeton, NJ: Princeton University Press, 1940. 15.
17. Byrd, Robert. *Senate, 1789–1989, Vol. 1: Addresses on the History of the United States Senate.* U.S. Government Printing Office. 92.
18. *Vice Presidents of the United States, 1789–1993.* U.S. Government Printing Office, 1997. 89–90.
19. Remini, Robert Vincent. *Henry Clay.* New York: W. W. Norton, 1991. 295.
20. Byrd, *Senate, 1789–1989.* 92.
21. "John C. Calhoun, 7th Vice President (1825–1832)." U.S. Senate. Senate .gov, accessed August 22, 2020. https://www.senate.gov/artand history/history/minute/Indicted_Vice_President_Bids_Senate_Fare well.htm.
22. Ibid.
23. Gold, Martin B. *Senate Procedure and Practice.* 3rd ed. New York: Rowman & Littlefield, 2013. 2.
24. MacNeil and Baker, *American Senate.* 307.
25. Koger, Gregory. *Filibustering.* Chicago: University of Chicago Press, 2010. 63.
26. Dove, Robert; and Arenberg, Richard. *Defending the Filibuster.* Bloomington: Indiana University Press, 2015. 20.
27. "John Tyler, Tenth Vice President (1841)." U.S. Senate. Senate.gov, accessed August 22, 2020. https://www.senate.gov/about/officers-staff/vice-president/VP_John_Tyler.htm.
28. Benton, Thomas Hart. *Thirty Years' View, or a History of the Working of the American Government for Thirty Years: From 1820 to 1850.* New York: Appleton, 1856. 249.
29. Roosevelt, Theodore. *Thomas Hart Benton.* New York: Abrams, 1974. 250.
30. Benton, *Thirty Years' View.* 249.
31. Ibid. 251; Peterson, Merrill D. *The Great Triumvirate: Webster, Clay, and Calhoun.* New York: Oxford University Press, 1988. 305.

32. Benton, *Thirty Years' View*. 251.

33. Ibid. 257.

34. Burdette, *Filibustering in the Senate*. 23.

35. Ibid.

36. MacNeil and Baker, *American Senate*. 309.

37. Benton, *Thirty Years' View*. 257.

38. Baker, Richard A. *The Senate of the United States: A Bicentennial History*. Malabar, FL: Krieger, 1988. 43.

39. Hofstadter, Richard. *The American Political Tradition*. New York: Vintage Books, 1948. 117.

40. Calhoun, John Caldwell. *Speeches of John C. Calhoun: Delivered in the Congress of the United States from 1811 to the Present Time*. Harper & Brothers, 1843. 195.

41. Hofstadter, *The American Political Tradition*. 103.

42. Bailey, George A., et al. *The Congressional Globe: New Series: Containing Sketches of the Debates and Proceedings of the First Session of the Thirtieth Congress*. August 14, 1848. Washington, DC: Blair & Rives, 1848. 1084.

43. Wawro, Gregory J.; and Schickler, Eric. *Filibuster: Obstruction and Lawmaking in the U.S. Senate*. Princeton, NJ: Princeton University Press, 2013. 2.

44. Benton, *Thirty Years' View*. 248.

45. Wawro and Schickler, *Filibuster*. 2.

46. Calhoun, John Caldwell. *The Works of John C. Calhoun: A Disquisition on Government and a Discourse on the Constitution and Government of the United States*. Vol. 1. New York: Appleton, 1853. 35.

47. Hamilton; Madison; and Jay. *The Federalist Papers*. Mineola, NY: Dover Publications, 2014. 368.

48. Calhoun, John C. *A Disquisition on Government*. Indianapolis: Hackett Publishing Company, 1953. 55.

49. Read, James H. *Majority Rule versus Consensus: The Political Thought of John C. Calhoun*. Lawrence: University Press of Kansas, 2009. 203.

50. Koger, *Filibustering*. 67–69.

51. Binder, Sarah A. *Minority Rights, Majority Rule: Partisanship and the Development of Congress*. Cambridge: Cambridge University Press, 1997. 183.

52. MacNeil and Baker, *American Senate*. 313.

53. Binder, Sarah; and Smith, Steven. *Politics or Principle? Filibustering in the United States Senate*. Washington, DC: Brookings Institution Press, 1997. 68–69.

54. "Senate Election, Expulsion and Censure Cases from 1789 to 1960." United States Congress. Library of Congress. Compiled for the Sen-

ate Committee on Rules and Administration. Washiongton, DC: U.S. Government Printing Office, 1962. 55.

55. MacNeil and Baker, *American Senate*. 313.

56. Caro, Robert. *Master of the Senate*. New York: Vintage Books, 2002. 383.

57. Kitzhaber, Albert R. "Mark Twain's Use of the Pomeroy Case in *The Gilded Age*." *Modern Language Quarterly* 15, no. 1 (March 1954): 42–56; "The Senator and His Secretary." United States Senate. Senate .gov, accessed August 22, 2020. https://www.senate.gov/artandhistory/ history/minute/Senator_Secretary.htm.

58. Caro, *Master of the Senate*. 33.

59. Binder and Smith, *Politics or Principle?* 72.

60. Ibid. 80.

61. Wawro and Schickler, *Filibuster*. 70.

62. "Whenever upon such roll call it shall be ascertained that a quorum is not present, a majority of the Senators present may direct the Sergeant at Arms to request, and, when necessary, to compel the attendance of the absent Senators, which order shall be determined without debate; and pending its execution, and until a quorum shall be present, no debate nor motion, except to adjourn, or to recess pursuant to a previous order entered by unanimous consent, shall be in order." *Standing Rules of the Senate*. Rule VI.

63. The other major "Force" acts of the nineteenth century were the four bills passed between 1870 and 1875 to enforce the terms of Reconstruction on the South, and the Jackson-backed 1833 bill to send federal troops to collect tariffs from South Carolina. *Harper's Weekly* 25, no. 1781 (February 7, 1891).

64. "The Gag Law Set Aside." *New York Times*. January 27, 1891. 5.

65. *Congressional Record* 22, Pt. 2 (January 22, 1891). 1666.

66. "The Gag Law Set Aside."

67. "Black Eye to Cloture." *Washington Post*. January 27, 1891. 1.

68. Burdette, *Filibustering in the Senate*. 39.

Chapter Three: DAWN OF THE SUPERMAJORITY

1. Englund, Will. *March 1917: On the Brink of War and Revolution*. New York: W. W. Norton, 2017. In 1933, the Twentieth Amendment changed the constitutionally mandated date of adjournment from March 3 to January 3. The passage of the amendment was motivated in large part by a desire to end obstruction, but it would not have much effect.

2. *New York Times*. March 5, 1917.

3. "Text of the President's Statement to the Public." *New York Times.* March 5, 1917. 1.

4. Binder, Sarah A. "The History of the Filibuster." Testimony before the U.S. Senate Committee on Rules and Administration. Brookings Institution. April 22, 2010.

5. Ibid.

6. Proposed Amendments to Rule XXII of the Standing Rules of the Senate, Relating to Cloture: Hearings Before a Special Subcommittee on Rules and Administration, United States Senate, 85th Congress, 1st Session, on S. Res. 17, S. Res. 19, S. Res. 21, S. Res. 28, S. Res. 29, S. Res. 30, S. Res. 32, S. Res. 171, Resolutions Proposing Amendments to Rule XXII of the Standing Rules of the Senate. June 17, 24, 25, 28, July 2, 9, 16, 1957. Washiongton, DC: U.S. Government Printing Office, 1957. 292.

7. Englund, *March 1917.* 103. The bill never got a vote because Wilson decided to arm the ships via executive order, and the issue was soon mooted by his declaration of war on April 2, 1917.

8. Proposed Amendments to Rule XXII. 292.

9. "Senate Cloture Rule: Limitation of Debate in the Senate of the United States." United States Congress. Congressional Research Service. Report prepared for the Senate Committee on Rules and Administration. 112th Congress, 1st Session. 2011. 190.

10. Burdette, Franklin. *Filibustering in the Senate.* Princeton, NJ: Princeton University Press, 1940. 221.

11. Proposed Amendments to Rule XXII of the Standing Rules of the Senate, Relating to Cloture: Hearings Before a Special Subcommittee on Rules and Administration, United States Senate, 85th Congress, 1st Session. June 17–July 16, 1957. U.S. Government Printing Office, 1957.

12. In 1944, the National Committee to Abolish the Poll Tax released a list of fifty senators pledged to support its abolition (a majority was forty-nine senators at the time). "50 Senators Listed as Against Poll Tax; Majority Pledged to Support Bill for Its Abolition." *New York Times.* April 24, 1944. 17.

13. In 1944 the National Committee to Abolish the Poll tax released a list of fifty senators who supported the 1944 bill to abolish the poll tax. Fifty was more than a majority at the time since the Senate was made up of ninety-six members. The fifty senators were twenty-nine Democrats, twenty Republicans, and one progressive. See, e.g., "50 Senators Listed as Against Poll Tax." 20. On more than sixty senators supporting an anti–poll tax bill, see Burdette, *Filibustering in the Senate.* 222.

14. McCarthy, Justin. "Gallup Vault: 72% Support for Anti-Lynching Bill in 1937." May 11, 2018; "First Study of Public Opinion of Poll Tax Issue

Completed by Institute in National Survey." Public Opinion News Service. April 2, 1941.

15. United States Congress. Senate. *Congressional Record*. August 2, 1948. 9601.

16. De Vore, Robert. "Cloture Defeat Spells Doom of Poll-Tax Foes." *Washington Post*. November 24, 1942.

17. Barkley, Frederick. "Poll Tax Upheld as Senate Defeats Closure, 41 to 37." *New York Times*. November 23, 1942. 1.

18. Ibid.

19. Burdette, *Filibustering in the Senate*. 223; On the Prohibition vote, fifty-five was enough to clear the two-thirds threshold because thirteen senators did not vote. At the time, the threshold was set on a sliding scale according to the number of senators voting, so senators who did not vote lowered the threshold.

20. Ibid. 222.

21. Proposed Amendments to Rule XXII. 292.

22. Caro, Robert. *Master of the Senate*. New York: Vintage Books, 2002. 90.

23. See, e.g., Katznelson, Ira. *When Affirmative Action Was White*. New York: W. W. Norton, 2005.

24. McIntosh, Kriston; Moss, Emily; Nunn, Ryan; and Shambaugh, Jay. "Examining the Black-White Wealth Gap." Brookings Institution. February 27, 2020.

25. Fite, Gilbert C. *Richard B. Russell, Jr., Senator from Georgia*. Chapel Hill: University of North Carolina Press, 2002. 226–31.

26. Lawrence, W. H. "Truman, Barkley Named by Democrats; South Loses on Civil Rights, 35 Walk Out; President Will Recall Congress July 26." *New York Times*. July 15, 1948. 1.

27. Offner, Arnold A. *Hubert Humphrey: The Conscience of the Country*. New Haven, CT: Yale University Press, 2018. 53.

28. Fuller, Helen. "The Funeral Is Called Off." *New Republic*. July 26, 1948.

29. Frederickson, Kari. *The Dixiecrat Revolt and the End of the Solid South, 1932–1968*. Chapel Hill: University of North Carolina Press, 2003.

30. Truman, Harry S. "Address in Philadelphia upon Accepting the Nomination of the Democratic National Convention." July 15, 1948. Harry S. Truman Presidential Library and Museum.

31. White, William. "21 Southern Senators Map a Filibuster on Civil Rights." *New York Times*. July 28, 1948. 1.

32. "'Turnip Day' Session." United States Senate. Accessed June 16, 2020. https://www.senate.gov/artandhistory/history/minute/Turnip_Day_Session.htm.

33. Kiker, Douglas. "Russell of Georgia: The Old Guard at Its Shrewdest." *Harper's Magazine*. September 1966. 101.

34. Caro, *Master of the Senate*. 206.

35. Misra, Tanvi. "The Neighborhood inside a Building." Citylab, *Atlantic*. June 27, 2017. See also: Booker, Brakkton; and Misra, Tanvi. "The Woodner: 65 Years of D.C. History in a Single Building." WAMU 88.5. June 27, 2017.

36. Booker and Misra, "The Woodner."

37. Fite, *Richard B. Russell, Jr.* 203.

38. Ibid. 201.

39. Caro, *Master of the Senate*. 207.

40. Fite, *Richard B. Russell, Jr.* 201–5.

41. Byrd, Robert C. *Senate, 1789–1989, Vol. 2: Addresses on the History of the United States Senate*. U.S. Government Printing Office, 1991. 185.

42. Oberdorfer, Don. "The Filibuster's Best Friend." *Saturday Evening Post*. March 13, 1965. 90.

43. Fite, *Richard B. Russell, Jr.* 496.

44. Sen. Russell (GA). "Journal of Thursday, January 17, 1946." *Congressional Record* 92, Pt. 1 (January 25, 1946). 380.

45. Sen. Russell (GA). "Promotion of National Defense—Increase in Personnel of Armed Forces." *Congressional Record* 94, Pt. 6 (June 8, 1948). 7361.

46. Kenworthy, E. W. "Relocate Negroes Evenly in States, Russell Proposes." *New York Times*. March 17, 1964. 1; Fite, *Richard B. Russell, Jr.* 245.

47. "The Rearguard Commander." *Time*. August 12, 1957.

48. Ward, Jason Morgan. *Defending White Democracy: The Making of a Segregationist Movement and the Remaking of Racial Politics, 1936–1965*. Chapel Hill: University of North Carolina Press, 2011. 16.

49. Ibid.

50. Daniels, Maurice C. *Ground Crew: The Fight to End Segregation at Georgia State*. Athens: University of Georgia Press, 2019. 26.

51. "The Rearguard Commander."

52. McGill, Ralph. "What Can the South Do?" *Atlanta Journal-Constitution*. July 18, 1948. 2D.

53. Fleegler, Robert L. "Theodore G. Bilbo and the Decline of Public Racism, 1938–1947." *Journal of Mississippi History* 68, no. 1 (2006): 1–28.

54. Daily News Bulletin, Jewish Telegraphic Agency. Vol. 12, no. 155. July 9, 1945.

55. Fite, *Richard B. Russell, Jr.* 229.

56. Loevy, Robert. *To End All Segregation: The Politics of the Passage of the Civil Rights Act of 1964*. Albany: SUNY Press, 1997. 156.

57. Martin, Harold. "The Man behind the Brass." *Saturday Evening Post*. June 2, 1951.

58. Sen. Vandenberg (MI). "The Poll Tax." *Congressional Record* 94, Pt. 8 (August 2, 1948). 9602–4.
59. "Senate Cloture Rule." 20.
60. United States Congress. Senate. Committee on Rules and Administration. Hearings on Limitation on Debate in the Senate. January 28, 1949. Washington, DC: U.S. Government Printing Office, 1949. 186.
61. Sen. Russell (GA). "Amendment of Cloture Rule." *Congressional Record* 95, Pt. 2 (February 28, 1949). 1583.
62. Ibid.
63. Sen. Russell (GA). "Amendment of Cloture Rule." 1584.
64. Sen. Lucas (IL). "Amendment of Cloture Rule." *Congressional Record* 95, Pt. 2 (February 28, 1949). 1584.
65. Strout, Richard L. "Truman Drops Grenade into Senate Filibuster." *Christian Science Monitor.* March 4, 1949. 3.
66. Ibid.
67. White, William. "Truman Proposes Ending Filibusters by Majority Vote." *New York Times.* March 5, 1949. 1.
68. Ibid.
69. Ibid.
70. Morris, John D. "Lucas Makes Peace Bid on Closure but Southerners Reject Move." *New York Times.* March 6, 1949. 1.
71. White, "Truman Proposes Ending Filibusters." 1.
72. Sen. Lucas (IL). "Amendment of Cloture Rule." *Congressional Record* 95, Pt. 2 (March 5, 1949). 1922.
73. Morris, "Lucas Makes Peace Bid on Closure." 1.
74. Sen. Lucas (IL). "Amendment of Cloture Rule." *Congressional Record* 95, Pt. 2 (March 5, 1949). 1922.
75. White, William. "Compromise Cloture Rule Adopted by Senate, 63 to 23; Filibuster Battle Is Ended." *New York Times.* March 18, 1949. 1.
76. Ibid.
77. Calhoun, John C. *A Disquisition on Government.* Indianapolis, IN: Hackett Publishing Company, 1953. 55.

Chapter Four: AN IDEA WHOSE TIME HAS COME

1. Caro, Robert. *Master of the Senate.* New York: Vintage Books, 2002. 215.
2. Ibid. 466.
3. Ibid.
4. Fite, Gilbert C. *Richard B. Russell, Jr., Senator from Georgia.* Chapel Hill: University of North Carolina Press, 2002. 272.

5. See, e.g., Hardeman, D. B.; and Bacon, Donald C. *Rayburn: A Biography*. Austin: Texas Monthly Press, 1987; "Speaker of the House Sam Rayburn of Texas." U.S. House of Representatives. House. gov, accessed August 23, 2020. https://history.house.gov/Historical-Highlights/1851-1900/Speaker-of-the-House-Sam-Rayburn-of-Texas/.

6. Caro, Robert. *Means of Ascent*. New York: Vintage, 1991. 124.

7. Caro, *Master of the Senate*. 158.

8. Kearns, Doris. *Lyndon Johnson and the American Dream*. New York: Signet, 1976. 393–98.

9. Balz, Dan. "The Mystery of Ballot Box 13." *Washington Post*. March 4, 1990.

10. Kearns, *Lyndon Johnson and the American Dream*. 107.

11. Caro, *Master of the Senate*. 122.

12. Kearns, *Lyndon Johnson and the American Dream*. 109.

13. Ibid.

14. "Lyndon Johnson, Watchdog in Chief." *Newsweek*. December 3, 1951; Caro, *Master of the Senate*. 154.

15. Kearns, *Lyndon Johnson and the American Dream*. 110.

16. Daniels, Maurice C. *Ground Crew: The Fight to End Segregation at Georgia State*. Athens: University of Georgia Press, 2019. 26.

17. Caro, *Master of the Senate*. 212.

18. Ibid. 219.

19. "Senate Leaders: Ernest McFarland." United States Senate. Senate.gov, https://www.senate.gov/artandhistory/history/common/generic/People _Leaders_McFarland.htm.

20. Caro, *Master of the Senate*. 475.

21. Kearns, *Lyndon Johnson and the American Dream*. 107.

22. Douglas, Paul. *In the Fullness of Time*. New York: Harcourt Brace, 1971. 208–9.

23. Sen. Clark (PA). "The Senate Establishment." *Congressional Record* 109, Pt. 2 (February 20, 1963). 2670.

24. Douglas, *In the Fullness of Time*. 208–9.

25. Zwiers, Maarten. *Senator James Eastland: Mississippi's Jim Crow Democrat*. Baton Rouge: LSU Press, 2015. 1.

26. Ibid. 119.

27. Douglas, *In the Fullness of Time*. 281.

28. Miller, Merle. *Lyndon: An Oral Biography*. New York: Ballantine Books, 1980. 232.

29. Douglas, *In the Fullness of Time*. 282.

30. Caro, *Master of the Senate*. 798.

31. Douglas, *In the Fullness of Time*. 283.

32. See, e.g., Green, Kristen. *Something Must Be Done about Prince Edward County*. New York: Harper Perennial, 2016.

33. Mayer, M. "The Eisenhower Administration and the Desegregation of Washington, D.C." *Journal of Policy History* 3, no. 1 (1991): 24–41; Nichols, David A. *A Matter of Justice: Eisenhower and the Beginning of the Civil Rights Revolution.* New York: Simon & Schuster, 2008; Serwer, Adam. "Why Don't We Remember Ike as a Civil Rights Hero?" MSNBC. May 17, 2014.

34. A compelling account of Brownell's role pushing Eisenhower to the left on civil rights is Anderson, J. W. *Eisenhower, Brownell and the Congress: The Tangled Origins of the Civil Rights Bill of 1956–1957.* Tuscaloosa: University of Alabama Press, 1964.

35. Caro, *Master of the Senate.* 842.

36. Baker, Russell. "Powell, Switching, Backs Eisenhower." *New York Times.* October 12, 1956. A1.

37. Wright Rigueur, Leah. *The Loneliness of the Black Republican: Pragmatic Politics and the Pursuit of Power.* Princeton, NJ: Princeton University Press, 2016. 31.

38. Caro, *Master of the Senate.* 842.

39. Pearson, Drew. "Truman's Political Gloss Is Worn Off." *Indianapolis Star.* August 18, 1956. 10; Caro, *Master of the Senate.* 826–28.

40. Goldfield, David. *The Gifted Generation: When Government Was Good.* New York: Bloomsbury, 2017. 323.

41. Proposed Amendments to Rule XXII of the Standing Rules of the Senate, Relating to Cloture: Hearings Before a Special Subcommittee on Rules and Administration, United States Senate, 85th Congress, 1st Session, on S. Res. 17, S. Res. 19, S. Res. 21, S. Res. 28, S. Res. 29, S. Res. 30, S. Res. 32, S. Res. 171, Resolutions Proposing Amendments to Rule XXII of the Standing Rules of the Senate. June 17, 24, 25, 28, July 2, 9, 16, 1957. Washington, DC: U.S. Government Printing Office, 1957. 64.

42. Sen. Russell (GA). "Rules of the Senate." *Congressional Record* 103, Pt. 1 (January 4, 1964). 154–55.

43. Caro, *Master of the Senate.* 855.

44. "Senate Cloture Rule, Limitation of Debate in the Congress of the United States and Legislative History of Paragraphs 2 and 3 of Rule XXII of the Standing Rules of the United States Senate (Cloture Rule)." United States Congress. Congressional Research Service. Report prepared for the Senate Committee on Rules and Administration. 94th Congress, 1st Session. 1975. 70.

45. Morris, John. "Filibuster Foes Set New Attack Based on Nixon's Decision." *New York Times.* January 6, 1957. 1.

46. Morris, John. "Senators Block Filibuster Curb by 55–38 Vote." *New York Times.* January 5, 1957. 1.

47. Lawrence, W. H. "Democrats Seek Militant Leaders." *New York Times.* January 5, 1957. 1.

48. HR 6127. Civil Rights Act of 1957. June 18, 1957. GovTrack.us.

49. Caro, *Master of the Senate*. 873.

50. Ibid. 873–77.

51. "The Rearguard Commander." *Time*. August 12, 1957.

52. "Thurmond Filibuster a Natural; Senator Right in Character." Associated Press. August 29, 1957.

53. "Thurmond Talks Hours on Rights." *New York Times*. August 29, 1957. A1.

54. White, William S. "Senate Votes Rights Bill and Sends It to President; Thurmond Takes 24 Hours." *New York Times*. August 30, 1957. A1.

55. "Last-Ditch Southerner: James Strom Thurmond." *New York Times*. August 30, 1957. A1. The AP also reported that Thurmond's speech sparked renewed chatter about reforming Rule 22: "Thurmond Filibuster a Natural."

56. "Excerpts from Speech on Civil Rights by Senator Russell." *New York Times*. July 3, 1957. 10.

57. Gittinger, Ted; and Fisher, Allen. "LBJ Champions the Civil Rights Act of 1964." *Prologue Magazine* 36, no. 2 (Summer 2004).

58. "Hells Canyon Dam." *CQ Almanac*. Accessed August 22, 2020. https://library.cqpress.com/cqalmanac/document.php?id=cqal57-1345481.

59. "Senate Roll-Call Vote on the Civil Rights Bill." Associated Press. August 29, 1960.

60. "Denounce King, Wilkins on Rights Stand." *Chicago Defender*. August 31, 1957.

61. *The Papers of Martin Luther King, Jr. Volume IV: Symbol of the Movement, January 1957–December 1958*. Clayborne Carson, Susan Carson, Adrienne Clay, Virginia Shadron, and Kieran Taylor, eds. Oakland: University of California Press, 2000. 263–64.

62. *Congressional Record* 103, Pt. 2 (July 16, 1957). 11832–37.

63. "The Nation: Rights on the Hill." *New York Times*. March 13, 1960. E1.

64. Levingston, Steven. *Kennedy and King: The President, the Pastor, and the Battle over Civil Rights*. New York: Hachette Books, 2017. Chapters 20–21.

65. Levingston, Steven. "John F. Kennedy, Martin Luther King Jr., and the Phone Call That Changed History." *Time*. June 20, 2017.

66. Ibid.

67. Caro, Robert. *The Passage of Power*. New York: Alfred A. Knopf, 2012. xv.

68. O'Donnell, Michael. "How LBJ Saved the Civil Rights Act." *Atlantic*. April 2014.

69. Caro, *The Passage of Power*. 489–90.

70. Mudd, Roger. *The Place to Be: Washington, CBS, and the Glory Days of Television News.* New York: PublicAffairs, 2008. 141.

71. Mansfield filed cloture on June 8, 1964. See United States Congress. Senate. *Congressional Record.* June 8, 1964. 12922.

72. On packed galleries, see "Civil Rights Filibuster Ended." United States Senate. Senate.gov, accessed July 19, 2020; "Whispering Willie": see Mudd, *The Place to Be.* 156–58.

73. Sen. Russell (GA). "Civil Rights Act of 1963." *Congressional Record* 110, Pt. 10 (June 10, 1964). 13329.

74. Fite, *Richard B. Russell, Jr.* 415–16.

75. Ibid.

76. Cited in Zelizer, Julian. *On Capitol Hill.* Cambridge: Cambridge University Press, 2004. 61.

77. "Classic Senate Speeches." United States Senate. Senate.gov, accessed August 23, 2020.

78. The Senate Rules Committee tracks the ultimate fate of bills that face filibusters in what it calls "later action on filibustered measures." See Congressional Research Service. "Limitation of Debate in the Congress of the United States." United States Congress. Senate. Report prepared for the Committee on Rules and Administration. September 1977. 53.

Chapter Five: **THE SUPERMINORITY**

1. Sargent, Greg. "Harry Reid Is Set to Go Nuclear." *Washington Post.* November 19, 2013.

2. Zaveri, Mihir; Gates, Guilbert; and Zraick, Karen. "The Government Shutdown Was the Longest Ever. Here's the History." *New York Times.* January 5, 2019.

3. Tau, Byron. "Obama: Republican 'Fever' Will Break after the Election." *Politico.* June 1, 2012.

4. Safire, William. "Nuclear Options." *New York Times.* March 20, 2005.

5. Memo from Senator Jeff Merkley to Colleagues. November 18, 2013. On file with the author.

6. Email exchange with NBC reporter. November 21, 2013. On file with the author.

7. Among the leading scholars of the Senate, there is general agreement that counting the number of cloture motions is an imperfect method but the best available one of measuring the number of filibusters. This book uses that method. During the 2013 debate over the nuclear option, Republicans disputed this counting method. Their objections, such as

the idea that Senate leaders file cloture on purpose in order to drive up the number of filibusters, have been considered and largely dismissed by the leading scholars on the topic. In a discussion of the objections in *National Journal*, Norm Ornstein, resident scholar at the conservative American Enterprise Institute, concedes that cloture motions "are far from a perfect representation"; nonetheless, he argues, contending that they don't indicate the presence of a filibuster is "naïve at best," since "anything that raises the bar from 50 votes to 60, or that threatens to do so to use up precious time, is a filibuster." In a similar vein, political scientist Steven Smith defines a filibuster as "a refusal to allow a matter to come to a vote." Cloture motions mark such refusals, since leaders reach for cloture when a senator is preventing a matter from coming to a vote. It is an onerous and time-consuming process, and while there are occasional exceptions, it is not regularly used for any other purpose. Brookings Institution scholar Sarah Binder has also considered these issues, and makes the point that, if anything, cloture motions are a conservative estimate because they likely undercount filibusters. For more, see Ornstein, Norm. "Why We Can't Stop Talking about Filibusters." *National Journal*. May 14, 2014; Smith, Steven. *The Senate Syndrome*. Norman: University of Oklahoma Press, 2014. 3; Binder, Sarah. "How We Count Filibusters and Why It Matters." *Washington Post*. May 15, 2014.

8. Jacobson, Louis. "Harry Reid Says 82 Presidential Nominees Have Been Blocked under President Barack Obama, 86 Blocked under All Other Presidents." PolitiFact. November 22, 2013.

9. Matthews, Dylan. "Yes, Chuck Hagel Is Being Filibustered. Yes, That's Unprecedented." *Washington Post*. February 15, 2013.

10. "Factsheet: Consumer Financial Protection Bureau: By the Numbers." United States Government. Consumer Financial Protection Bureau. July 2017.

11. Hicks, Josh. "How Obama's NLRB Nominees Became Central to Senate Filibuster Deal." *Washington Post*. July 17, 2013.

12. McMillion, Barry J. "Length of Time from Nomination to Confirmation for U.S. Circuit and District Court Nominees: Overview and Policy Options to Shorten the Process." Congressional Research Service. November 20, 2013.

13. McMillion, Barry J. "President Obama's First-Term U.S. Circuit and District Court Nominations: An Analysis and Comparison with Presidents since Reagan." United States Congress. Congressional Research Service. May 2, 2013.

14. Graves, Allison. "Did Senate Republicans Filibuster Obama Court Nominees More Than All Others Combined?" PolitiFact. April 9, 2017.

15. Ibid.

16. Mann, Thomas; and Ornstein, Norman. "Let's Just Say It: The Republicans Are the Problem." *Washington Post*. April 27, 2012.

17. Sen. Reid (NV). "Rules Reform." *Congressional Record* 159, Pt. 12 (November 21, 2013). 17821.

18. "Harry Reid: The Filibuster Is Suffocating the Will of the American People." *New York Times*. August 12, 2019.

19. Toobin, Jeffrey. "Harry Reid's Enduring Gift to Barack Obama." *New Yorker*. November 1, 2018.

20. Ibid.

21. Bishop, Bill. *The Big Sort*. Boston: Mariner Books, 2009; Klein, Ezra. *Why We're Polarized*. New York: Simon & Schuster, 2020.

22. Carney, Eliza Newlin. "Standing Together against Any Action." *CQ Weekly*. March 16, 2015. 37–40.

23. Skelley, Geoffrey. "Are Blowout Presidential Elections a Thing of the Past?" FiveThirtyEight. May 28, 2019.

24. Kondik, Kyle. "Why the Number of Swing States Is Dwindling." *The Hill*. July 20, 2016.

25. Battaglio, Stephen. "When Red Meant Democratic and Blue Was Republican. A Brief History of TV Electoral Maps." *Los Angeles Times*. November 3, 2016.

26. Abramowitz, Alan. *The Great Alignment*. New Haven, CT: Yale University Press, 2018. 62.

27. Enten, Harry. "There Were No Purple States on Tuesday." FiveThirtyEight. November 10, 2016.

28. See, e.g., Mason, Lilliana. *Uncivil Agreement*. Chicago: University of Chicago Press, 2018.

29. Fisher, Max. "The Uproar over Sen. Tom Cotton's Letter to Iran, Explained." *Vox*. March 10, 2015.

30. Olsen, Henry. "Trump Looks Down and Out. But the 2024 GOP Field Is Forming." *Washington Post*. June 26, 2020.

31. Winkler, Jeff. " 'Own the Libs' Was a Snide Way to Mock Conservatives, and Is Now a Fun Way to Respond to Liberalism." NBC News. August 4, 2018.

32. Mason, *Uncivil Agreement*.

33. "Public's Mood Turns Grim; Trump Trails Biden on Most Personal Traits, Major Issues." Pew Research Center. June 30, 2020.

34. Buckley, William F. "Our Mission Statement." *National Review*. November 19, 1955.

35. Abramowitz, *The Great Alignment*. 15.

36. Author's calculations based on Senate seats held by Republicans in 2020, ranked by Trump margin of victory in their corresponding states, counting to forty-one seats and averaging the margin of victory. Elec-

tion results via *New York Times.* www.nytimes.com/elections/2016/results/president.

37. Gallup. Presidential Approval Ratings, George W. Bush. Accessed July 21, 2020. https://news.gallup.com/poll/116500/presidential-approval-ratings-george-bush.aspx.

38. Saad, Lydia. "Trump Sets New Low Point for Inaugural Approval Rating." Gallup. January 23, 2017.

39. Author's calculations using common methodology. Using census data, each Senate seat is assigned half the state's population and averaged by party. (Theoretically, each senator represents the entire state, but mathematically, assigning each seat the entire population then dividing by two before averaging would produce the same result.) Nonstate populations like the District of Columbia are not included because they do not have senators and cannot be assigned to one of the parties.

40. "Canada Hits Population Record, California Still Has More People." *Canadian Press.* March 17, 2016; Corcoran, Kieran. "California's Economy Is Now the 5th-Biggest in the World, and Has Overtaken the United Kingdom." *Business Insider.* May 5, 2018.

41. Mihm, Stephen. "How the Senate Gives Wyoming 70 Times More Clout Than California." Bloomberg News. February 11, 2019.

42. Lee, Frances E.; and Oppenheimer, Bruce. *Sizing Up the Senate.* Chicago: University of Chicago Press, 1999. 3.

43. Liptak, Adam. "Smaller States Find Outsize Clout Growing in Senate." *New York Times.* March 11, 2013. For more, see Mayhew, David. *Partisan Balance.* Princeton, NJ: Princeton University Press, 2011.

44. U.S. Census Bureau. 2010 census results by state, cross-referenced to Senate seats.

45. All state population data from U.S. Census Bureau.

46. "2019 U.S. Population Estimates Continue to Show the Nation's Growth Is Slowing." U.S. Census Bureau. December 30, 2019.

47. Schaeffer, Katherine. "In a Rising Number of U.S. Counties, Hispanic and Black Americans Are the Majority." Pew Research Center. November 20, 2019.

48. Abramowitz, *The Great Alignment.* 15.

49. Li, Quan; Pomanante II, Michael J.; and Schraufnagel, Scott. "Cost of Voting in the American States." *Election Law Journal* 17, no. 3 (2018): 234–46.

50. Fraga, Bernard L. *The Turnout Gap.* Cambridge: Cambridge University Press, 2018. 9.

51. Hawkings, David. "Wealth of Congress: Richer Than Ever, but Mostly at the Very Top." *Roll Call.* February 27, 2018.

52. See, e.g., Lax, Jeffrey; Phillips, Justin; and Zelizer, Adam. "The Party or the Purse? Unequal Representation in the US Senate." *American Political Science Review* 113, no. 4 (2019): 917–40. For a discussion of recent research, see Matthews, Dylan. "Studies: Democratic Politicians Represent Middle-Class Voters. GOP Politicians Don't." *Vox.* April 2, 2018.

53. Cox, Daniel; Lienesch, Rachel; and Jones, Robert P. "Beyond Economics: Fears of Cultural Displacement Pushed the White Working Class to Trump." Public Religion Research Institute. May 9, 2017.

54. "Abortion Trends by Party Identification." Gallup. Accessed June 7, 2020. https://news.gallup.com/poll/246278/abortion-trends-party.aspx.

55. Horton, Alex. "Trump Says He's an Antiabortion Champion Like Reagan. History Says: Not Quite." *Washington Post.* May 19, 2019; Halpern, Sue. "How Republicans Became Anti-Choice." *New York Review of Books.* November 8, 2018.

56. "Abortion Trends by Party Identification."

57. Montanaro, Domenico. "Poll: Majority Want to Keep Abortion Legal, but They Also Want Restrictions." National Public Radio. June 7, 2019.

58. "In-Depth Topics: Abortion." Gallup. Accessed June 7, 2020.

59. Levitz, Eric. "America's Political Mood Is Now the 'Most Liberal Ever Recorded.'" *New York Magazine.* June 8, 2019.

60. The classic, contemporaneous account of Nixon's "southern strategy" is Kevin Phillips's *The Emerging Republican Majority.* Geoffrey Kabaservice's compelling historical account is *Rule and Ruin.* Rick Perlstein's engaging account is *Nixonland* (2008). For more, see Phillips, Kevin. *The Emerging Republican Majority.* Princeton, NJ: Princeton University Press, 2014 (first published 1969); Kabaservice, Geoffrey. *Rule and Ruin.* New York: Oxford University Press, 2012. 326–63.

61. Abramowitz, *The Great Alignment.* 50–51.

62. Yang, Jia Lynn. *One Mighty and Irresistible Tide: The Epic Struggle over American Immigration, 1924–1965.* New York: W. W. Norton, 2020.

63. Jardina, Ashley. *White Identity Politics.* Cambridge: Cambridge University Press, 2019. 3.

64. "Looking to the Future, Public Sees an America in Decline on Many Fronts." Pew Research Center. March 2019.

65. Craig, Maureen A.; and Richeson, Jennifer A. "On the Precipice of a 'Majority-Minority' America: Perceived Status Threat from the Racial Demographic Shift Affects White Americans' Political Ideology." *Psychological Science* 25, no. 6 (2014). 1189–97.

66. Tesler, Michael; and Sides, John. "How Political Science Helps Explain the Rise of Trump: The Role of White Identity and Grievances." *Washington Post.* March 3, 2016.

67. Sides, John; Tesler, Michael; and Vavreck, Lynn. *Identity Crisis.* Princeton, NJ: Princeton University Press, 2018. 28.

68. Chinoy, Sahil. "What Happened to America's Political Center of Gravity?" *New York Times.* June 26, 2019.

Chapter Six: OUTSIDE IN

1. Budoff Brown, Carrie. " 'D.C. Madam' List Includes Sen. Vitter." *Politico.* July 10, 2007.

2. Bresnahan, John. "Boehner's Fight for Hill Subsidies." *Politico.* October 1, 2013.

3. Ibid.

4. Email exchange between Reid and Boehner staff. June–September, 2013. On file with the author.

5. Bresnahan, "Boehner's Fight for Hill Subsidies."

6. Peoples, Steve. "Republicans Lash Out at Tea Partiers for Causing 16-Day Crisis That Crushed the Party's Popularity." Associated Press. October 18, 2013.

7. Siddiqui, Sabrina. "Richard Burr: Mike Lee Government Shutdown Threat 'Dumbest Idea I've Ever Heard Of.' " *Huffington Post.* July 26, 2013.

8. Thrush, Glenn. "The Prisoner of Capitol Hill." *Politico.* January 2015.

9. Edwards, Chris. "George W. Bush: Biggest Spender Since LBJ." Report. Cato Institute. December 19, 2009.

10. Maxwell, Angie. "How Southern Racism Found a Home in the Tea Party." *Vox.* July 7, 2016.

11. Montopoli, Brian. "Tea Party Supporters: Who They Are and What They Believe." CBS News poll. December 14, 2012. On income, Gallup found that Tea Partiers have higher-than-average incomes, and observed similar demographics as CBS. "Tea Partiers Are Fairly Mainstream in Their Demographics." Gallup. April 5, 2010.

12. Isenstadt, Alex. "DeMint Rattles GOP with Rubio Nod." *Politico.* June 16, 2009.

13. Shipman, Claire. "Florida Gov. Charlie Crist Announces Senate Run as Independent." ABC News. April 29, 2010.

14. "November 2, 2010 General Election: Official Results." Florida Department of State. November 2, 2010. Accessed June 16, 2020. https://results.elections.myflorida.com/Index.asp?ElectionDate=11/2/2010&DATAMODE=.

15. Toeplitz, Shira. "DeMint Endorses Ted Cruz in Texas Primary." *Roll Call.* July 19, 2011.

16. Steinhauer, Jennifer. "Tea Party Hero Is Leaving the Senate for a New Pulpit." *New York Times*. December 6, 2012. A1.

17. Alberta, Tim. *American Carnage: On the Front Lines of the Republican Civil War and the Rise of President Trump*. New York: HarperCollins, 2019. 167.

18. Ibid. 170.

19. Miller, Zeke J. "Hidden Hand: How Heritage Action Drove DC to Shut Down." *Time*. September 30, 2013.

20. "Tortilla Coast: Congress's Power Restaurant, with Extra Cheese." *Washington Post*. October 16, 2013.

21. Email on file with the author.

22. Miller, "Hidden Hand."

23. Holmes, Steven A. "Jesse Helms Dies at 86; Conservative Force in the Senate." *New York Times*. July 5, 2008.

24. Drew, Elizabeth. "A Reporter At Large: Jesse Helms." *New Yorker*. July 20, 1981.

25. Gura, David. "Jesse Helms." National Public Radio. July 7, 2008.

26. "Fictional vs Factual: The Truth behind the Rumors about Jesse Helms." The Jesse Helms Center Foundation. Accessed June 7, 2020. https://jessehelmscenter.org/fictional-vs-factual.

27. Link, William. *Righteous Warrior*. New York: St. Martin's Press, 2008, 99.

28. Drew, "A Reporter At Large."

29. Morrill, Jim. "A Speech Jesse Helms Never Gave Would Have Changed U.S. Politics." *Charlotte Observer*. November 4, 2017.

30. Helms, Jesse. *Here's Where I Stand*. New York: Random House, 2005. 66.

31. Farber, M. A. "Senator James B. Allen Dies; Alabamian Led Canal Pact Fight." *New York Times*. June 2, 1978. B2.

32. Furgurson, Ernest B. *Hard Right*. New York: W. W. Norton, 1986. 104–6.

33. Helms, *Here's Where I Stand*. 66.

34. Furgurson, *Hard Right*. 106.

35. Helms, *Here's Where I Stand*. 66.

36. Mark, David. *Going Dirty: The Art of Negative Campaigning*. New York: Rowman & Littlefield, 2007. 106.

37. Furgurson, *Hard Right*. 176.

38. Drew, "A Reporter At Large."

39. Ibid.

40. Furgurson, *Hard Right*. 126.

41. Helms, *Here's Where I Stand*. 64.

42. Morgan, Fiona. "Local Leaders Pull No Punches about Jesse Helms' Legacy." *The Indy*. July 9, 2008.

43. Drew, "A Reporter At Large."

44. Furgurson, *Hard Right*. 132–33.

45. Drew, "A Reporter At Large."
46. Furgurson, *Hard Right*. 135.
47. Christensen, Rob; and Morrill, Jim. "Political Kingmaker Tom Ellis Dies." *News and Observer*. July 13, 2018.
48. Drew, "A Reporter At Large."
49. Ibid.
50. Range, Peter Ross. "Thunder from the Right." *New York Times*. February 8, 1981. 23.
51. Thrift, Bryan Hardin. *Conservative Bias*. Gainesville: University Press of Florida, 2014. 195.
52. Drew, "A Reporter At Large."
53. Kabaservice, Geoffrey. *Rule and Ruin*. New York: Oxford University Press, 2012. 116.
54. Perlstein, Rick. *The Invisible Bridge*. New York: Simon & Schuster, 2015. 675.
55. "The Lasting Impact of the 1976 North Carolina Republic Presidential Primary." The Jesse Helms Center Foundation. Accessed July 17, 2020. https://jessehelmscenter.org/1976-nc-republican-presidential-primary; Drew, "A Reporter At Large."
56. "The Lasting Impact of the 1976 North Carolina Republic Presidential Primary."
57. Link, *Righteous Warrior*. 153.
58. Apple, R. W., Jr. "Reagan Tops Ford in N. Carolina for First Triumph in a Primary; Carter Easily Defeats Wallace." *New York Times*. March 24, 1976. A1.
59. Quoted in Hayward, Steven. *The Age of Reagan*. New York: Crown Forum, 2009. 468.
60. Drew, "A Reporter At Large."
61. Morrill, "A Speech Jesse Helms Never Gave."
62. Shields, Mark. "Jesse Helms and the Making of a President." *Washington Post*. August 25, 2001.
63. "Letter from Reagan to Helms, October 18, 1991." The Jesse Helms Center Foundation. Accessed June 8, 2020. https://jessehelmscenter.org/1976-nc-republican-presidential-primary.
64. Roberts, Steven V. "Weinberger Approved, 97–2." *New York Times*. January 21, 1981. B8.
65. Shermer, Elizabeth Tandy. *Barry Goldwater and the Remaking of the American Political Landscape*. Tucson: University of Arizona Press, 2013. 249.
66. Link, *Righteous Warrior*. 177.
67. Furgurson, *Hard Right*. 106; Drew, "A Reporter At Large."
68. Drew, "A Reporter At Large."
69. Link, *Righteous Warrior*. 178.
70. Brinkley, Joel. "The 1984 Elections: Hard-Fought Contests for the Sen-

ate; Helms Beats Hunt to Stay in Senate." *New York Times*. November 7, 1984. A22.

71.   Dunham, Teresa. "Sen. Jesse Helms, Friend of Liberty University, Dies at 86." *Liberty News*. Liberty University. July 7, 2008. Accessed June 16, 2020. https://www.liberty.edu/news/index.cfm?PID=18495&MID=6123.

72.   Bresnahan, John. "Jesse Helms, Former Senator, Dead at 86." *Politico*. July 4, 2008.

73.   Drew, "A Reporter At Large."

74.   Roberts, Steven V. "King Holiday Bill Faces a Filibuster." *New York Times*. October 4, 1983. A17.

75.   Dewar, Helen. "Helms Stalls King's Day in Senate." *Washington Post*. October 4, 1983. A1.

76.   Roberts, "King Holiday Bill Faces a Filibuster."

77.   Brinkley, "The 1984 Elections: Hard-Fought Contests."

78.   Edsall, Thomas B. "Helms Makes Race an Issue." *Washington Post*. November 1, 1990.

79.   Weisman, Jonathan; and Parker, Ashley. "Republicans Back Down, Ending Crisis over Shutdown and Debt Limit." *New York Times*. October 16, 2013.

80.   Bendery, Jennifer. "Ted Cruz: 'We Need 100 More Like Jesse Helms' in the Senate." *Huffington Post*. September 11, 2013.

Chapter Seven: MEANS OF CONTROL

1.   Hickey, Walt. "The Fabulous Life of Senate Majority Leader Harry Reid." *Business Insider*. November 21, 2012.

2.   Reid, Harry; and Warren, Mark. *The Good Fight*. New York: Penguin Random House, 2008.

3.   Afzal, Sara. "The Top 10 Political Quotes of 2010." *Christian Science Monitor*. December 29, 2010.

4.   McCoy, Cara. "Charges Dismissed Against Lt. Gov. Brian Krolicki." *Las Vegas Sun*. December 7, 2009.

5.   Ralston, Jon. "Reid to the End." *Reno Gazette-Journal*. August 30, 2016.

6.   Myers, Dennis. "Citizen Reid." *Reno News & Review*. December 2, 2004.

7.   Ball, Molly. "Comeback: How Did Reid Do It?" *Politico*. November 4, 2010.

8.   Coolican, J. Patrick. "Election Polls under Scrutiny after Missing Mark." *Las Vegas Sun*. November 4, 2010.

9.   "Reid Releases Police Report from '81 Bomb Attempt." Associated Press. October 28, 2009.

10.   Reid and Warren, *The Good Fight*.

11. Hagar, Ray. "Harry Reid Watched 'The Irishman'—It Brought Back Memories of Fighting the Mob in Vegas." *Reno Gazette-Journal.* December 18, 2019.

12. "The First Two Senators." United States Senate. Senate.gov, accessed August 22, 2020. https://www.senate.gov/artandhistory/history/minute/The_First_Two_Senators_-_An_Odd_Couple.htm.

13. MacNeil, Neil; and Baker, Richard. *The American Senate.* Oxford: Oxford University Press, 2013. 173.

14. "Floor Leaders' Right of Priority Recognition." United States Senate. Accessed June 16, 2020. https://www.senate.gov/reference/Sessions/Traditions/Priority_recognition.htm.

15. MacNeil and Baker, *The American Senate.* 175, 197.

16. Caro, Robert. *Master of the Senate.* New York: Vintage Books, 2002. 488–515.

17. Gould, Lewis L. *The Most Exclusive Club.* New York: Basic Books, 2005. 215.

18. Caro, *Master of the Senate.* 512.

19. "The Johnson Treatment." Photographs by George Tames. *New York Times.* 1957. Accessed July 20, 2020. https://store.nytimes.com/products/the-johnson-treatment?variant=36782756360.

20. Caro, *Master of the Senate.* 960.

21. United States Senate. "The Senate's Taj Mahal." Senate.gov, accessed July 20, 2020. https://www.senate.gov/artandhistory/history/minute/The_Senates_Taj_Mahal.htm.

22. MacNeil and Baker, *The American Senate.* 202.

23. Kearns, Doris. *Lyndon Johnson and the American Dream.* New York: Signet, 1976. 136.

24. Caro, *Master of the Senate.* 960.

25. Ibid. 403–13.

26. Baker, Bobby. *Wheeling and Dealing.* New York: W. W. Norton, 1980. 86.

27. Genzlinger, Neil. "Bobby Baker, String-Puller Snared in Senate Scandal, Dies at 89." *New York Times.* November 17, 2017.

28. Caro, *Master of the Senate.* 410.

29. MacNeil and Baker, *The American Senate.* 198–99.

30. Kearns, *Lyndon Johnson and the American Dream.* 144.

31. Potter, Phillip. "Proxmire Charges Johnson with Being Senate Dictator." *Baltimore Sun.* February 24, 1959. 1.

32. "Senate Democrats Feud over Johnson's Powers." Associated Press, February 24, 1959.

33. Ibid.

34. United States Congress. Senate. *Congressional Record.* February 23, 1959. 2817; MacNeil and Baker, *The American Senate.* 207.

35. Caro, *Master of the Senate.* 159.

36. Ibid. 168.
37. "Why Congress Is in the Doghouse." *U.S. News & World Report.* August 16, 1976.
38. See, e.g., Colin Campbell, ed. *Leadership in the U.S. Senate.* New York: Routledge, 2019.
39. Gould, *The Most Exclusive Club.* 214.
40. Lee, Frances E. *Insecure Majorities.* Chicago: University of Chicago Press, 2016. 109.
41. Ibid.
42. Ibid. 85–86.
43. "Democratic Alternatives: A Look at the Record." Washington, DC: U.S. Government Printing Office, 1982.
44. "Democratic Alternatives: A Look at the Record."
45. Kaiser, Robert G. *So Damn Much Money.* New York: Vintage Books, 2009. 114.
46. Easterbrook, Gregg. "The Business of Politics." *Atlantic.* October 1986.
47. All data from the Federal Elections Commission, FEC.gov, accessed July 21, 2020. DCCC 1980: https://www.fec.gov/data/committee/C00000935/?cycle=1980;__DCCC 1986: https://www.fec.gov/data/committee/C00000935/?cycle=1986; DSCC 1980: https://www.fec.gov/data/committee/C00042366/?cycle=1980; DSCC 1986: https://www.fec.gov/data/committee/C00042366/?cycle=1986; DSCC 2018: https://www.fec.gov/data/committee/C00042366/?cycle=2018.
48. Kim, Soo Rin. "The Price of Winning Just Got Higher, Especially in the Senate." Open Secrets. Center for Responsive Politics. November 9, 2016. Accessed June 16, 2020. https://www.opensecrets.org/news/2016/11/the-price-of-winning-just-got-higher-especially-in-the-senate/.
49. Similar dynamics prevail in the House, but unlike the Senate, the House makes no pretense of giving its members much independence, and top-down control is assumed. In the House, campaign committees simply accentuated an existing culture; in the Senate, they played a big role in changing the culture.
50. "2004 General Election Official Returns for U.S. Senate." South Dakota Secretary of State.
51. Bolton, Alexander. "Clinton Was Brain behind the War Room." *The Hill.* May 13, 2008.
52. Stevenson, Richard W. "Confident Bush Outlines Ambitious Plan for 2nd Term." *New York Times.* November 5, 2004.
53. Baker, Peter. *Days of Fire.* New York: Anchor Books, 2013. 381.
54. Stolberg, Sheryl Gay. "For Democrats, Social Security Becomes a Defining Test." *New York Times.* January 30, 2005.
55. Klein, Rick. "Social Security at Roots of Shift." *Boston Globe.* November 12, 2006.

56. Ibid.
57. "Bartleby Democrats." *Washington Post*. February 4, 2005.
58. Baker, Peter; and VandeHei, Jim. "Social Security: On with the Show." *Washington Post*. March 12, 2005.
59. *Washington Post*–ABC News Poll: Social Security/Iraq. March 15, 2005.
60. Simon, Richard. "Overhaul Might Not Happen in 2005, GOP Leaders Suggest." *Los Angeles Times*. March 2, 2005.
61. Gallup. Presidential Approval Ratings, George W. Bush. Accessed July 21, 2020. https://news.gallup.com/poll/116500/presidential-approval-ratings -george-bush.aspx.
62. Nagourney, Adam. "Theme of Campaign Ads: Don't Be Nice." *New York Times*. September 27, 2006.
63. Klein, Rick. "Social Security at Roots of Shift." *Boston Globe*. November 12, 2006.
64. Mascaro, Lisa. "In New Epilogue, Reid Recounts Encouraging Obama to Run." *Las Vegas Sun*. April 26, 2009.
65. Chaturvedi, N. S. "Filling the Amendment Tree: Majority Party Control, Procedures, and Polarization in the U.S. Senate." *American Politics Research* 46, no. 4 (2018): 724–47.
66. Weisman, Jonathan. "Reid's Uncompromising Power Play in Senate Rankles Republicans." *New York Times*. January 9, 2014. A13.
67. Kasperowicz, Pete. "GOP Trying to Chop Down Reid's Amendment Tree." *The Hill*. January 17, 2014.
68. Ibid.
69. Raju, Manu; and Everett, Burgess. "Reid's New Challenge: Fellow Dems." *Politico*. June 23, 2014.
70. Weisman, "Reid's Uncompromising Power Play."
71. Simpson, Conor. "Charles Schumer Is Washington's Best Matchmaker." *Atlantic*. August 18, 2012.
72. "Capitol Subway System." Architect of the Capitol. Accessed July 21, 2020. https://www.aoc.gov/explore-capitol-campus/buildings-grounds/ capitol-building/capitol-subway-system.
73. Phillips, Dave. "Catherine Cortez Masto Wins Nevada to Become First Latina Senator." *New York Times*. November 9, 2016.

Chapter Eight: WHAT IT TAKES

1. McConnell, Mitch. *The Long Game: A Memoir*. New York: Penguin Random House, 2016. 62.
2. Gass, Nick. "The 21 Craziest Quotes from the Campaign Trail." *Politico*. November 25, 2015.

3. Debonis, Mike. "Harry Reid: GOP Leaders Are Responsible for Trump's Rise." *Washington Post.* March 17, 2016.

4. Tweet from @PaulBegala. https://twitter.com/PaulBegala/status/709919 233099100160?s=20.

5. Reuters reported that Srinivasan was the nominee, then later retracted it: "Earlier a source told Reuters that appeals court judge Sri Srinivasan was most likely to be picked, then later said Garland was a stronger possibility." Edwards, Julia. "Obama to Nominate Garland to Supreme Court: Source." Reuters. March 16, 2016.

6. Hulse, Carl. *Confirmation Bias: Inside Washington's War over the Supreme Court, from Scalia's Death to Justice Kavanaugh.* New York: HarperCollins, 2019. 119.

7. Ibid. 12; McConnell, *The Long Game.* 259–61.

8. Wilentz, Sean. *The Age of Reagan: A History, 1974–2008.* New York: HarperCollins, 2008. 51.

9. Ring, Trudy. "Robert Bork's Antigay Record." *Advocate.* December 19, 2012.

10. Sen. Kennedy (MA). "Nomination of Robert Bork." *Congressional Record* 133, Pt. 14 (July 1, 1987). 18519.

11. Marcus, Ruth. *Supreme Ambition.* New York: Simon & Schuster, 2019. 52.

12. Greenhouse, Linda. "Bork's Nomination Is Rejected, 58–42; Reagan Saddened." *New York Times.* October 24, 1987.

13. McMillion, Barry J.; and Rutkus, Denis Steven. "Supreme Court Nominations, 1789 to 2017: Actions by the Senate, the Judiciary Committee, and the President." United States Congress. Congressional Research Service. 13. https://www.senate.gov/legislative/nominations/Supreme CourtNominations1789present.htm.

14. Ibid.

15. Toobin, Jeffrey. "The Conservative Pipeline to the Supreme Court." *New Yorker.* April 10, 2017.

16. Greenhouse, Linda. "Playing the Long Game for the Supreme Court." *New York Times.* October 25, 2018.

17. Toobin, "The Conservative Pipeline to the Supreme Court."

18. Phillips-Fein, Kim. *Invisible Hands: The Businessmen's Crusade against the New Deal.* New York: W. W. Norton, 2010. 162.

19. McLaughlin, Danielle; and Avery, Michael. *The Federalist Society: How Conservatives Took the Law Back from Liberals.* Nashville, TN: Vanderbilt University Press, 2013. 16–17.

20. Ibid. 17.

21. Mayer, Jane. *Dark Money.* New York: Anchor Books, 2016. 134.

22. McConnell, Mitch. "Election Ordinance Is, in Part, Reaction to Past Excesses." *Courier-Journal.* December 10, 1973. A23.

23. McConnell, *The Long Game.* 51–61.

24. Ibid. 62.

25. Sherman, Gabriel. *The Loudest Voice in the Room: How the Brilliant, Bombastic Roger Ailes Built Fox News—and Divided a Country.* New York: Random House, 2017. 117.

26. McConnell, *The Long Game,* 64.

27. "Mitch McConnell 1984 Senate Campaign Ad." WDRB.com. May 18, 2017. Accessed July 21, 2020. https://www.wdrb.com/archive/video/mitch-mcconnell-senate-campaign-ad/video_49aa207e-1103-58b8-916f-80e2f41bbd72.html.

28. Mayer, Jane. "Who Let the Attack-Ad Dogs Out?" *New Yorker.* February 15, 2012.

29. Sherman, *The Loudest Voice in the Room.* 118.

30. McConnell, *The Long Game.* 65.

31. Snyder, Pete. "Forget the Super Bowl: Which Political Ad Was the All-Time MVP?" *Ad Age.* February 7, 2012.

32. McConnell, *The Long Game.* 91.

33. Ibid. 91.

34. Ibid. 92.

35. Terris, Ben. "Mitch McConnell Doesn't Care What You Think. He Just Wants to Win." *Washington Post.* January 24, 2020.

36. MacGillis, Alec. *The Cynic.* New York: Simon & Schuster, 2014. 64.

37. Tumulty, Karen. "GOP Filibuster Forces Byrd to Abandon Effort This Year: Campaign Finance Bill Stalled in Senate." *Los Angeles Times.* September 16, 1987.

38. McConnell, *The Long Game.* 95.

39. Ibid. 94.

40. McCain, John; and Salter, Mark. *The Restless Wave: Good Times, Just Causes, Great Fights, and Other Appreciations.* New York: Simon & Schuster, 2018. 203.

41. Bacon, Perry, Jr. "GOP Outnumbered in Senate, but McConnell Tries to Ensure It Is Not Outflanked." *Washington Post.* June 22, 2009.

42. Thompson, Dennis F. *Ethics in Congress: From Individual to Institutional Corruption.* Washington, DC: Brookings Institution Press, 2000. 39–40.

43. Nowicki, Dan; and Muller, Bill. "John McCain Gets into 'a Hell of a Mess' with the Keating Five Scandal." *Arizona Republic.* April 2, 2018.

44. Lewis, Michael. "The Subversive." *New York Times Magazine.* May 25, 1997.

45. Cannon, Lou. "Mike Curb Will Replace Richard DeVos at RNC." *Washington Post.* August 14, 1982.

46. Mayer, *Dark Money.* 288–89.

47. "Excerpts from McCain's Speech Declaring Candidacy." *New York Times.* September 28, 1999. A22.

48. Balz, Dan. "McCain Stuns Bush in N.H. Primary." *Washington Post.* February 2, 2000.

49. Sen. McConnell (KY). "Bipartisan Campaign Reform Act of 1999." *Congressional Record* 145, Pt. 18 (October 14, 1999). 25417.

50. McGrory, Mary. "Back-Lott Bullies." *Washington Post.* October 21, 1999.

51. Teachout, Zephyr. *Corruption in America.* Cambridge, MA: Harvard University Press, 2014. 3.

52. Ibid. 9.

53. Roll Call Vote 54, 107th Congress, 2nd Session, United States Senate, March 20, 2002. Accessed June 16, 2020.

54. United States Supreme Court. *McConnell, United States Senator, et al. v. Federal Election Commission, et al.* December 10, 2003.

55. McConnell, *The Long Game.* 151–52.

56. Kennedy, Anthony. "Opinion of Kennedy, J." *McConnell v. Federal Election Commission.* 540 U.S. 93 (2003).

57. Gold, Martin B.; and Gupta, Dimple. "The Constitutional Option to Change Senate Rules and Procedures: A Majoritarian Means to Overcome the Filibuster." *Harvard Journal of Law & Public Policy* 28, no. 1 (Winter 2005).

58. Toobin, Jeffrey. "Blowing Up the Senate: Will Bush's Judicial Nominees Win with the 'Nuclear Option'?" *New Yorker.* February 28, 2005.

59. Ibid.

60. Toner, Robin. "Man in the News; a Political Partisan with a Zeal for Focus—Addison Mitchell McConnell Jr." *New York Times.* November 14, 2002.

61. "Trent Lott Announces His Resignation." NBC News. November 26, 2007.

62. Sen. McConnell (KY). "Nomination of Priscilla Richman Owen to Be United States Circuit Judge for the Fifth Circuit." *Congressional Record* 151, Pt. 8 (May 19, 2005). 10421.

63. Kirkpatrick, David. "Cheney Backs End of Filibustering." *New York Times.* April 23, 2005. A1.

64. Ibid.

65. Hulse, Carl. "Many Republicans Are Already Eager to Challenge Agreement on Filibusters." *New York Times.* May 25, 2005. A18.

66. Roll Call Vote 245, 109th Congress, 1st Session, United States Senate, September 29, 2005. Accessed June 16, 2020; Kirkpatrick, David. "Debate in Senate on Alito Heats Up over '85 Memo." *New York Times.* November 17, 2005. A26.

67. Roll Call Vote 2, 109th Congress, 2nd Session, United States Senate, January 31, 2006.

68. Lewis, Neil. "Senators Renew Jousting over Court Pick." *New York Times.* May 10, 2006.

69. Roll Call Vote 159, 109th Congress, 2nd Session, United States Senate, May 26, 2006.

Chapter Nine: THE UNITER

1. Broder, John. "Democrats Gain Senate and New Influence." *New York Times*. November 10, 2006. A1.
2. McConnell, Mitch. *The Long Game: A Memoir*. New York: Penguin Random House, 2016. 157.
3. Ibid. 158.
4. Alberta, Tim. *American Carnage: On the Front Lines of the Republican Civil War and the Rise of President Trump*. New York: Harper-Collins, 2019. 43.
5. Grunwald, Michael. "The Victory of No." *Politico*. December 4, 2016.
6. Hulse, Carl. "Senator, after Scandal, Won't Run Again." *New York Times*. March 7, 2011. A18.
7. Draper, Robert. *Do Not Ask What Good We Do: Inside the U.S. House of Representatives*. New York: Free Press, 2012. xvi.
8. Member's Room. Library of Congress. Accessed July 20, 2020. https://www.loc.gov/visit/online-tours/thomas-jefferson-building/members-room/.
9. Grunwald, Michael. *The New New Deal: The Hidden Story of Change in the Obama Era*. New York: Simon & Schuster, 2012. 147–49.
10. Ibid.
11. Ibid.
12. "GOP's McConnell Sees Hope for a Stimulus Plan." *Morning Edition*, National Public Radio. January 9, 2009.
13. Saad, Lydia. "Trump Sets New Low Point for Inaugural Approval Rating." Gallup. January 23, 2017.
14. Hamilton, Alexander; Madison, James; and Jay, John. *The Federalist Papers*. Mineola, NY: Dover Publications, 2014. 368, 103.
15. "Barack Obama's Remarks to the Democratic National Convention." *New York Times*. July 27, 2004.
16. *Newsweek*. January 3, 2005.
17. Gillin, Joshua. "Inaugural Crowd Sizes Ranked." PolitiFact. January 20, 2017.
18. Naylor, Brian. "Obama's Acceptance Pledge: Fix 'Broken Politics.'" National Public Radio. August 29, 2008.
19. Garrett, Major. "Top GOP Priority: Make Obama a One-Term President." *National Journal*. October 29, 2010.
20. Reid was in line with the norm in his two years as minority leader under Bush, leading fifty-four filibusters.

21.   "Senate Action on Cloture Motions." United States Senate. Accessed June 16, 2020. https://www.senate.gov/legislative/cloture/clotureCounts .htm.

22.   Mudd, Roger. *The Place to Be: Washington, CBS, and the Glory Days of Television News*. New York: PublicAffairs, 2008. 157.

23.   Koger, Gregory. *Filibustering*. Chicago: University of Chicago Press, 2010. 97.

24.   Chafetz, Josh. "The Unconstitutionality of the Filibuster." *Connecticut Law Review* 43, no. 4 (May 2011): 1003–40.

25.   Smith, Steven. *The Senate Syndrome*. Norman: University of Oklahoma Press, 2014. 99.

26.   Gold, Martin B. *Senate Procedure and Practice*. 3rd ed. New York: Rowman & Littlefield, 2013. 54–64.

27.   U.S. Senate. Cloture Motions. Senate.gov, accessed July 21, 2020. https://www.senate.gov/legislative/cloture/clotureCounts.htm.

28.   Binder, Sarah; and Smith, Steven. *Politics or Principle? Filibustering in the United States Senate*. Washington, DC: Brookings Institution Press, 1997. 14.

29.   U.S. Senate. Cloture Motions.

30.   Green, Joshua. "Strict Obstructionist." *Atlantic*. January 2011.

31.   Nagourney, Adam; and Hulse, Carl. "Senate G.O.P. Leader Finds Weapon in Unity." *New York Times*. March 16, 2010. A13.

32.   McConnell, *The Long Game*. 191.

33.   Grunwald, *The New New Deal*. 19.

34.   Alberta, *American Carnage*. 43.

35.   Acosta, Jim. "Romney Once Touted Parts of 'Romneycare' as a National Model." CNN. March 7, 2011.

36.   Lane, Thomas. "Obamacare & Romneycare Are 'the Same Fucking Bill' Says Former Romney Adviser." Talking Points Memo. November 16, 2011.

37.   Butler, Stuart. "Assuring Affordable Health Care for All Americans." Heritage Foundation. 6.

38.   Ornstein, Norm. "The Real Story of Obamacare's Birth." *Atlantic*. July 6, 2015.

39.   Brill, Steven. *America's Bitter Pill*. New York: Random House, 2015. 93.

40.   Alberta, *American Carnage*. 69.

41.   Nagourney; and Hulse. "Senate G.O.P. Leader Finds Weapon in Unity."

42.   *C-SPAN Newsmakers*. June 12, 2009. Accessed May 22, 2020. https://www.c-span.org/video/?286998-1/republican-senate-agenda.

43.   Levey, Noam. "Baucus and Grassley Team Up on Bipartisan Healthcare Compromises." *Los Angeles Times*. July 9, 2009.

44. Calmes, Jackie. "G.O.P. Senator Draws Critics in Both Parties." *New York Times*. September 22, 2009.

45. Alter, Jonathan. *The Promise: President Obama*. New York: Simon & Schuster, 2010. 257.

46. Montopoli, Brian. "Grassley Warns of Government Pulling Plug 'on Grandma.'" *CBS News*. August 12, 2009.

47. Mullins, Anne Schroeder. "Twitter Fight between Grassley and Specter!" *Politico*. August 14, 2009.

48. Halloran, Liz. "Is Grassley Abandoning Bipartisan Health Bill?" National Public Radio. August 20, 2009.

49. Brill, *America's Bitter Pill*. 149.

50. *Fox News Sunday*. June 14, 2009.

51. Gallup. Presidential Approval Ratings, Barak Obama. Accessed July 21, 2020. https://news.gallup.com/poll/116479/barack-obama-presidential -job-approval.aspx.

52. Bolton, Alexander. "Sens: Snowe's Healthcare Vote Puts Her Top Commerce Perch at Risk." *The Hill*. October 13, 2009.

53. Newton-Small, Jay. "Let's Make a Deal." *Time*. June 4, 2011.

54. McConnell, *The Long Game*, 193.

55. Evers-Hillstrom, Karl. "More Money, Less Transparency: A Decade under Citizens United." Open Secrets. Center for Responsive Politics. January 14, 2020.

56. Rutenberg, Jim; and Zeleny, Jeff. "Democrats Outrun by a 2-Year G.O.P. Comeback Plan." *New York Times*. November 3, 2010. A1.

57. Debenedetti, Gabe. "New Crossroads Ad Reminds GOP: Clinton Is the Target." *Politico*. March 29, 2016.

58. Farnam, T. W. "Head of Crossroads GPS Once a McConnell Aide, Now His Political Ally." *Washington Post*. October 30, 2012.

59. Kirkpatrick, David. "A Quest to End Spending Rules for Campaigns." *New York Times*. January 24, 2010. A11.

60. Childress, Sarah. "James Bopp: What Citizens United Means for Campaign Finance." *Frontline*, Public Broadcasting Service. October 30, 2012.

61. Kirkpatrick, David. "A Quest to End Spending Rules for Campaigns." *New York Times*. January 24, 2010. A11.

62. Zengerle, Jason. "Did Somebody Say 'Fringe'?" *GQ*. September 22, 2010. "Everyone in Kentucky also knew that Grayson—who in 2003, at the age of 31, had been elected secretary of state—was McConnell's choice to replace Bunning. In a Republican state party that is extraordinarily hierarchical, even by Republican state-party standards, it was Grayson's turn."

63. Kraushaar, Josh; and Raju, Manu. "GOP Pressures Bunning to Quit." *Politico*. January 22, 2009.

64. Jacobs, Jeremy. "Bunning: McConnell Is a 'Control Freak.'" *Hill*. May 9, 2009; Abdullah, Hamilah. "Bunning Slams McConnell's Leadership, Specter's Switch." McClatchy Newspapers. May 5, 2009.

65. Keck, Kristi. "Ron Paul's Son Following in Father's Footsteps." *CNN Politics*. August 6, 2009.

66. McArdle, John. "Kentucky: Paul Event Hardly Bombs with $170,000." *Roll Call*. December 16, 2009.

67. Kraushaar, Josh. "McConnell Bats for Grayson." *Politico*. May 4, 2010.

68. Welna, David. "Losing Bet in Ky. Primary Puts McConnell in a Bind." *Weekend Edition*, National Public Radio. May 22, 2010.

69. Zengerle, "Did Somebody Say 'Fringe'?"

70. Ibid.

71. Hamby, Peter. "How Mitch McConnell Crushed the Tea Party." CNN. Accessed June 16, 2020. https://www.cnn.com/interactive/2014/politics/hamby-midterms/.

72. Raju, Manu. "McConnell Hires Campaign Aide to Ron and Rand Paul." *Politico*. September 13, 2012.

73. Titus, Elizabeth. "McConnell Aide: 'Holding My Nose.'" *Politico*. August 8, 2013.

74. Grier, Peter. "Will 'Nosegate' Really Hurt Mitch McConnell at the Polls?" *Christian Science Monitor*. August 9, 2013.

75. Hamby, "How Mitch McConnell Crushed the Tea Party."

76. Bacon, Perry, Jr. "GOP Outnumbered in Senate, but McConnell Tries to Ensure It Is Not Outflanked." *Washington Post*. June 22, 2009; McGrory, Mary. "Back-Lott Bullies." *Washington Post*. October 21, 1999.

77. Raju, Manu. "McConnell Employs Reid's Hardball Tactic." *Politico*. July 30, 2015.

78. Wallner, James. "McConnell Maintains Firm Grip despite Pledging to Restore the Senate." *Washington Examiner*. February 11, 2019.

79. "GOP's Favorability Rating Takes a Negative Turn." Pew Research Center. July 23, 2015.

80. "Mitch McConnell Favorable Rating." HuffPost Pollster. Accessed May 17, 2020. https://elections.huffingtonpost.com/pollster/mitch-mcconnell-favorable-rating#!mindate=2014-11-01&estimate=custom.

81. Kane, Paul. "New Senate Majority Leader's Main Goal for GOP: Don't Be Scary." *Washington Post*. January 4, 2015.

82. "2016 Republican Presidential Nomination." Real Clear Politics. Accessed May 17, 2020. https://www.realclearpolitics.com/epolls/2016/president/us/2016_republican_presidential_nomination-3823.html.

83. DeBonis, Mike. "Ted Cruz Calls Mitch McConnell a Liar on the Senate Floor." *Washington Post*. July 24, 2015.

84. Everett, Burgess; and Kim, Seung Min. "With Boehner Out, McCon-

nell Could Become Right's Main Bogeyman." *Politico.* September 25, 2015.

85. Ibid.

86. Burns, Alexander; Haberman, Maggie; and Martin, Jonathan. "Inside the Republican Party's Desperate Mission to Stop Donald Trump." *New York Times.* February 27, 2016. A1.

87. McConnell, *The Long Game,* 259–61.

88. Hulse, Carl. *Confirmation Bias: Inside Washington's War over the Supreme Court, from Scalia's Death to Justice Kavanaugh.* New York: HarperCollins, 2019. 12.

89. Everett, Burgess; and Thrush, Glenn. "McConnell Throws Down the Gauntlet: No Scalia Replacement under Obama." *Politico.* February 13, 2016.

90. Bresnahan, John. "McConnell, Grassley Rally Conservative Groups for Supreme Court Fight." *Politico.* March 3, 2016.

91. Tweet by @ron_fournier, verified account. March 16, 2016. Accessed June 15, 2020. https://twitter.com/ron_fournier/status/710127031623745537.

92. Ferraro, Thomas. "Republican Would Back Garland for Supreme Court." *Reuters.* May 6, 2010. Accessed June 16, 2020. https://www.reuters .com/article/us-usa-court-hatch/republican-would-back-garland -for-supreme-court-idUSTRE6456QY20100506.

93. Hulse, *Confirmation Bias.* 22.

94. Gass, Nick; and Kim, Seung Min. "Conservatives Hammer GOP Senator over Supreme Court Dissent." *Politico.* March 25, 2016.

95. Everett, Burgess; and Kim, Seung Min. "Moran Threatened with Primary after Supreme Court Remarks." *Politico.* April 5, 2016.

96. Katz, Josh. "Democrats Have a 60 Percent Chance to Retake the Senate." *New York Times.* August 24, 2016.

97. Levy, Gabrielle. "Mitch McConnell: I Didn't See Trump's Win Coming." *U.S. News & World Report.* December 20, 2016.

98. Klein, Ezra. "Democrats Won the Most Votes in the Election. They Should Act Like It." *Vox.* November 22, 2016. Percentages of population represented by Senate seats are author's calculations.

99. McConnell, *The Long Game,* 270.

100. Flegenheimer, Matt. "Senate Republicans Deploy 'Nuclear Option' to Clear Path for Gorsuch." *New York Times.* April 6, 2017.

101. Roll Call Vote 111, 115th Congress, 1st Session, United States Senate, April 7, 2017. Accessed June 16, 2020. https://www.senate.gov/legislative/ LIS/roll_call_lists/roll_call_vote_cfm.cfm?congress=115&session=1 &vote=00111.

102. "Supreme Court Nominations (1789–Present)." United States Senate. Accessed June 16, 2020. https://www.senate.gov/legislative/ nominations/SupremeCourtNominations1789present.htm.

103. Kosoff, Maya. "Trump Thanks McConnell for 'All That He Did' to Ruin Merrick Garland." *Vanity Fair.* April 10, 2017.

104. Marcus, Ruth. *Supreme Ambition: Brett Kavanaugh and the Conservative Takeover.* New York: Simon & Schuster, 2019. 1–3.

105. Pogrebin, Robin; and Kelly, Kate. "Brett Kavanaugh Fit In with the Privileged Kids. She Did Not." *New York Times.* September 14, 2019.

106. "'We're Going to Plow Right Through It,' McConnell Says on Kavanaugh Nomination." *Washington Post.* September 21, 2018.

107. Everett, Burgess; and Bresnahan, John. "McConnell Works Feverishly behind the Scenes to Save Kavanaugh." *Politico.* September 17, 2010.

108. Cummings, William. "'Unfazed and Determined': Top Grassley Aide Vows to Confirm Kavanaugh despite Allegations." *USA Today.* September 20, 2018.

109. Mascaro, Lisa. "Kavanaugh's 'Revenge' Theory Spotlights Past with Clintons." Associated Press. October 3, 2018.

110. Bump, Philip. "How the Republican Tax Bill Benefits the Rich, according to Government Analysis." *Washington Post.* November 30, 2017.

111. "Healthy Congress Index." Bipartisan Policy Center. Accessed August 15, 2020. https://bipartisanpolicy.org/congress/.

112. Mejdrich, Kellie. "GOP Leaps on Congressional Review Act to Kill Obama Rules." *Roll Call.* February 23, 2017.

113. Golshan, Tara. "The Republican Tax Reform Bill Will Live and Die by This Obscure Senate Rule." *Vox.* November 14, 2017.

114. Prokop, Andrew. "Trump Wants 'Mitch' to Use the 'Nuclear Option.' Here's What That Means." *Vox.* December 21, 2018.

115. Maier, Lilly. "On Changing the Rules for Filibusters on Presidential Nominees." PolitiFact. November 22, 2013. (PolitiFact rated McConnell a "flip-flopper" for opposing Democrats' push to go nuclear after supporting Bush's push in 2005; see earlier section on Gorsuch for McConnell's decision to go nuclear on his nomination.)

116. Kane, Paul. "Why Senate Republicans Aren't Listening to Trump's Pleas to 'Go Nuclear.'" *Washington Post.* April 3, 2018.

117. Memoli, Michael; and Mascaro, Lisa. "GOP Ready to Make 'Pledge to America.'" *Los Angeles Times.* September 23, 2010.

118. Werner, Erica; and Fram, Alan. "No Repeal for 'Obamacare' in Humiliating Defeat for Trump." Associated Press. March 24, 2017.

119. Rovner, Julie. "Timeline: Despite GOP's Failure to Repeal Obamacare, the ACA Has Changed." *Kaiser Health News.* April 5, 2018.

120. Scott, Dylan; and Kliff, Sarah. "Why Obamacare Repeal Failed." *Vox.* July 31, 2017.

121. Pear, Robert; and Kaplan, Thomas. "Senate Rejects Slimmed-Down Obamacare Repeal as McCain Votes No." *New York Times.* July 27, 2017. A1.

122. Cummings, William. "Senate Republicans Resist 'Knee-Jerk' Drive to Name Building after McCain." *USA Today.* August 28, 2018.

123. "Trump Team's Conflicts and Scandals: An Interactive Guide." Bloomberg News. March 14, 2019.

124. Miroff, Nick. "Trump's Use of Military Funds for Border Wall Construction Is Illegal, 9th Circuit Court Rules." *Washington Post.* June 26, 2020.

125. Thrush, Glenn. "Mitch McConnell, Never a Grandstander, Learns to Play by Trump's Rules." *New York Times.* April 14, 2019. A12.

126. Liptak, Kevin; and LeBlanc, Paul. "Whistleblower Timeline: Team Trump Contacts and Ukraine." CNN. November 13, 2019.

127. Gregorian, Dareh. "Trump Impeached by the House for Abuse of Power, Obstruction of Congress." NBC News. December 18, 2019.

128. Garcia, Victor. "Hannity Exclusive: McConnell Says 'Zero Chance' Trump Is Removed, 'One or Two Democrats' Could Vote to Acquit." Fox News. December 12, 2019.

129. Leibovich, Mark. "Romney, Defying the Party He Once Personified, Votes to Convict Trump." *New York Times.* February 5, 2020.

130. Guskin, Emily; and Clement, Scott. "Republicans' Obamacare Repeal Was Never Really That Popular." *Washington Post.* July 28, 2017; Easley, Cameron. "Poll: Voters Aren't Happy with GOP Oversight of Trump Administration." *Morning Consult.* June 21, 2017; Enten, Harry. "The GOP Tax Cuts Are Even More Unpopular Than Past Tax Hikes." FiveThirtyEight. November 29, 2017.

131. "U.S. Senate Election Results 2018." *New York Times.* May 15, 2019. Some argue that citing the national popular vote in Senate elections is misleading because when there is a Senate election in California, as there was in 2018, it dramatically increases the total number of votes cast for Democrats. But in 2018, there was also a Senate election in Texas, the second-most populous state, where Democrat Beto O'Rourke ran a close race against Republican Ted Cruz. The fact that Democrats are competitive in Texas but Republicans are no longer competitive in California—or New York, the third-most populous state, which also held a Senate election in 2018—is an illustration of Republicans' ever-narrowing appeal and should not be excused. The skewing effect in Democrats' direction was especially strong in 2018, because California's primary system sends the top two vote-getters to the general election, and in 2018 the top two were both Democrats. But again, the fact that Republicans could not finish better than third in the nation's most populous state—which produced Ronald Reagan and Richard Nixon, and where Republicans held the governor's mansion as recently as 2011—is an illustration of their problem, not an aberration that should be dismissed.

132. "U.S. Senate Election Results 2018." *Politico*. Accessed August 20, 2020. https://www.politico.com/election-results/2018/senate/.

133. Garrett, Major. "Top GOP Priority: Make Obama a One-Term President." *National Journal*. October 29, 2010.

Conclusion: HOW TO SAVE THE SENATE

1. Wegman, Jesse. *Let the People Pick the President*. New York: St. Martin's Press, 2020. 148–52.

2. Kilgore, Ed. "The Ghosts of the '68 Election Still Haunt Our Politics." *New York*. October 16, 2018.

3. Lee, Kurtis. "In 1969, Democrats and Republicans United to Get Rid of the Electoral College. Here's What Happened." *Los Angeles Times*. December 16, 2016.

4. Rothman, Lily. "The Electoral College Votes Today. But Politicians Have Been Trying to Reform It for Decades." *Time*. December 19, 2016.

5. "States' Sentiment on Election Proposal." *New York Times*. October 8, 1969.

6. United States Congress. House. *Congressional Record*. September 18, 1969. 26008.

7. Kilpatrick, Carroll. "Nixon Asks Senate to Pass Direct Vote." *Washington Post*. October 1, 1969. A1.

8. Kristol, Irving; and Weaver, Paul. "A Bad Idea Whose Time Has Come." *New York Times Magazine*. November 23, 1969. 43.

9. United States Congress. Senate. *Congressional Record*. September 29, 1970. 34025.

10. United States Congress. Senate. *Congressional Record*. August 14, 1970. 28999.

11. Wegman, *Let the People Pick the President*. 154–55.

12. Hurt, Bob. "Election Bill Showdown Due." *Atlanta Constitution*. September 16, 1970. 13A.

13. "Bayh Foresees Passage of Direct Amendment Vote." Associated Press. September 6, 1970; Weaver, Warren, Jr. "Direct Election Plan Is Facing Key Test in the Senate This Week." *New York Times*. September 7, 1970. 10.

14. Hurt, "Election Bill Showdown Due."

15. Weaver, "Direct Election Plan Is Facing Key Test."

16. Wegman, *Let the People Pick the President*. 157–59.

17. Rothman, "The Electoral College Votes Today."

18. Wegman, *Let the People Pick the President*. 157–59.

19. Everett, Burgess; and Levine, Marianne. "'Everything Stays on the Table': 2020 Dems Weigh Killing the Filibuster." *Politico*. January 31, 2019.

20. Rosenbaum, David E. "Bill to Bar Busing Killed in Senate as Closure Fails." *New York Times*. October 13, 1972. A1.

21. Author's analysis based on Congressional Research Service. "Senate Cloture Rule: Limitation of Debate in the Congress of the United States." United States Congress. Senate. Report prepared for the Committee on Rules and Administration. 112th Congress. 1st Session. December 2011.

22. Motion to Invoke Cloture on S. Amdt. 1958 to H.R. 2579. Senate Vote No. 35. February 15, 2018.

23. Tausanovitch, Alex; and Berger, Sam. "The Impact of the Filibuster on Federal Policymaking." Center for American Progress. December 15, 2019.

24. The health care bill Senate Democrats unveiled in November 2009 included a public option. It was removed after Senator Joseph Lieberman, who by then was an independent, came out against it, denying Democrats the sixty votes they needed. See, e.g., Pear, Robert; and Herszenhorn, David. "Senate Says Health Plan Will Cover Another 31 Million." *New York Times*. November 18, 2009. A1; "On Sunday, Mr. Lieberman told the Senate majority leader, Harry Reid, to scrap the idea of expanding Medicare and abandon any new government insurance plan or lose his vote." Pear, Robert; and Herszenhorn, David. "Lieberman Rules Out Voting for Health Bill." *New York Times*. December 13, 2009.

25. Roberts, David. "If You Want to Pass Climate Legislation, Fix U.S. Politics." *Grist*. January 17, 2013.

26. McGann, Anthony. *The Logic of Democracy*. Ann Arbor: University of Michigan Press, 2006. 174.

27. Hamilton, Alexander; Madison, James; and Jay, John. *The Federalist Papers*. Mineola, NY: Dover Publications, 2014. 102–3.

28. See, e.g., Lee, Frances E. *Insecure Majorities*. Chicago: University of Chicago Press, 2016.

29. "Vote Tallies for Passage of Medicare in 1965." Social Security Administration. Accessed August 20, 2020. https://www.ssa.gov/history/tally65.html; Arenberg, Richard. "Unintended Consequences of Killing the Filibuster." *The Hill*. August 18, 2020.

30. Zelizer, Julian. "How Medicare Was Made." *New Yorker*. February 15, 2015.

31. Walsh, Kenneth T. "The Politics of Medicare and Medicaid, 50 Years Later." *U.S. News & World Report*. July 30, 2015.

32. Zelizer, "How Medicare Was Made."

33. "State Population Totals: 2010–2019." U.S. Census Bureau. Accessed August 20, 2020. https://www.census.gov/data/datasets/time-series/ demo/popest/2010s-state-total.html.

34. "Households/Income Data for City: District of Columbia." DC Health Matters. Accessed August 20, 2020. https://www.dchealthmatters.org/ demographicdata?id=130951&sectionId=936.

35. "State Population Totals: 2010–2019."

36. "Block the Vote: Voter Suppression in 2020." American Civil Liberties Union. February 3, 2020.

INDEX

Page numbers after 260 refer to endnotes.